THE WORLD OF SPIRITS

AND ANCESTORS

IN THE ART OF WESTERN

SUB-SAHARAN AFRICA

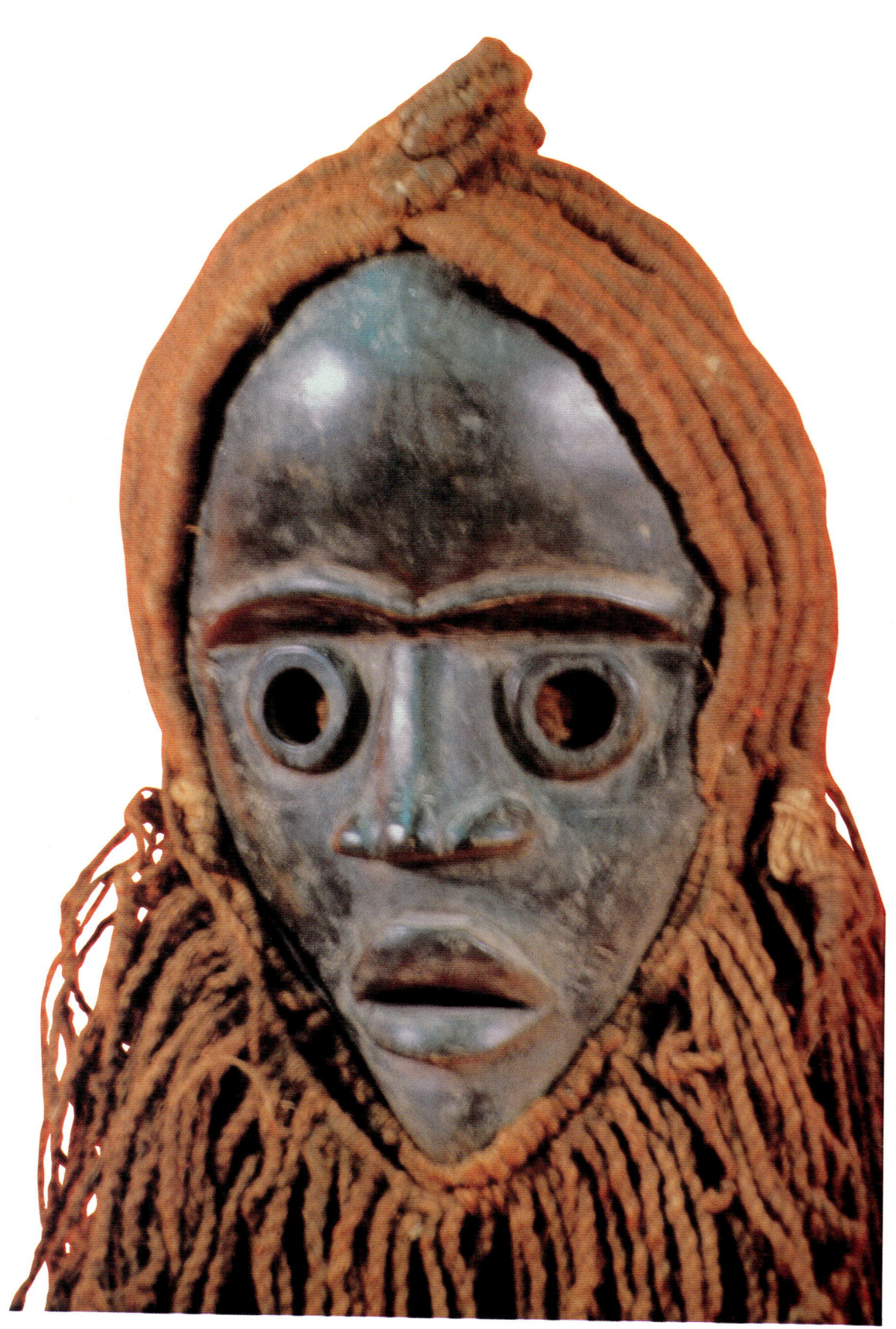

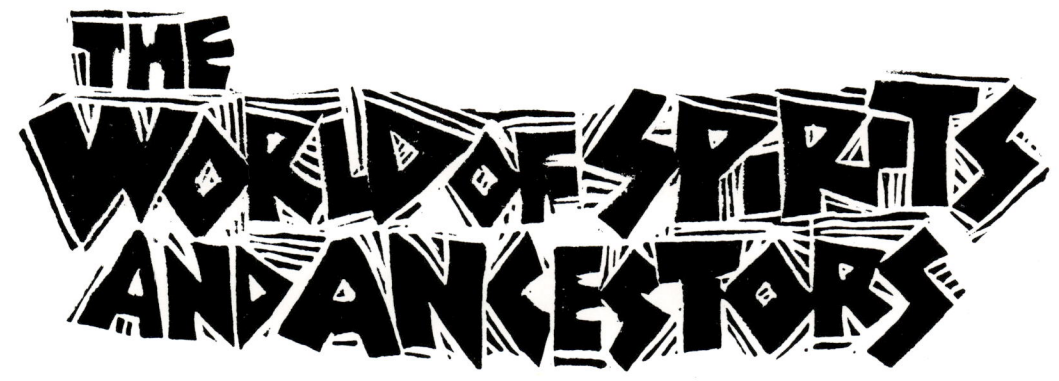

THE WORLD OF SPIRITS AND ANCESTORS

In the Art of Western

Sub-Saharan Africa

Elizabeth Skidmore Sasser

Photographs by Thomas Judson Sasser

and

Elizabeth Skidmore Sasser

Texas Tech University Press

This book was set in Galliard and printed on acid-free
paper that meets the guidelines for permanence and
durability of the Committee on Production Guidelines
for Book Longevity of the Council on Library
Resources.

Design by Barbara Whitehead
Printed and manufactured in Hong Kong

Library of Congress Cataloging-in-Publication Data
Sasser, Elizabeth Skidmore, 1919-
    The world of spirits and ancestors in the art of
western sub-Saharan Africa / Elizabeth Skidmore
Sasser ; photographs by Thomas Judson Sasser and
Elizabeth Skidmore Sasser.
        p.   cm.
    Includes bibliographical references and index.
    ISBN 0-89672-346-1 (cloth)
    1. Art, Black–Africa, Sub-Saharan. 2. Art,
Modern–20th century–Africa, Sub-Saharan.
3. Howard, Elliot–Art collections. 4. Art–Texas–
Lubbock. 5. Texas Tech University.
Museum. I. Sasser, Thomas Judson. II. Title.
N7391.65.S26 1995
730'. 0966'074764847–dc20   94-36381
                                                 CIP

95 96 97 98 99 00 01 02 03 / 9 8 7 6 5 4 3 2 1

Texas Tech University Press
Lubbock, Texas 79409-1037 USA
800-832-4042

To the memory of my mother, Maria Louise Trabue Skidmore and to my uncle, Dr. Louis W. Carl, whose love of books is the richest inheritance a child could receive.

As always to my husband, Tom and our daughter, Lisa.

To the memory of two African-American women: Mrs. Jessie Childs, daughter of a slave, who greatly enriched my childhood and Mrs. Louise Baker, who gave Lisa love and care for the first eight years of her life.

To Ethelene Bucy, former student and friend and without whom there would be no Elliot Howard Collection at the Museum of Texas Tech University and no book.

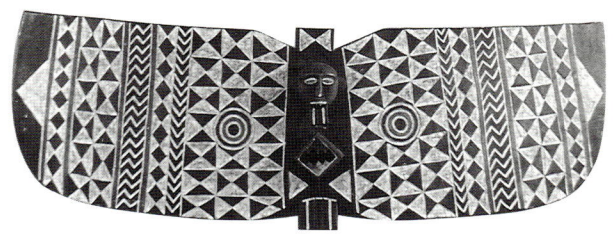

This theme put quite simply is that African peoples did not hear of culture for the first time from Europeans; that their societies were not mindless but frequently had a philosophy of great depth and value and beauty, that they had poetry and, above all, they had dignity.

CHINUA ACHEBE in
"The Role of the Writer in a New Nation,"
from *Nigeria Magazine* (June 1964)

CONTENTS

LIST OF ILLUSTRATIONS

Photographs of sculpture from the Museum of Texas Tech University by Thomas and Elizabeth Sasser. All sculptures, i.e., figures with numerical designations, unless otherwise indicated, are from the African Collection of the Museum of Texas Tech University. Photographic permission was granted by Museum Director Gary Edson and in the case of the Julius Walker Collection jointly given by Gary Edson and Idris Traylor, Deputy Director of the International Center for Arid and Semiarid Lands Studies (ICASALS).

FOREWORD

The acceptance of private collections, or bequests, has been a significant factor in the enlargement and enrichment of some museums and in the very emergence of others. Although some museum directors have been troubled by what has been called "the private lives of public museums," a number of others have been inspired by the philosophies and convictions of the benefactors, even though the bequests of the latter may reflect very personal and individual tastes. Thus, while the late Elliot Howard, whose collection forms the basis of *The World of Spirits and Ancestors in the Art of Western Sub-Saharan Africa,* selected his sculptures for their variety and aesthetic appeal, his hope was that his collection would one day provide an opportunity for instruction and discovery for students and university museum patrons young and old.

By accepting and exhibiting such collections from other cultures, museums face a critical choice. They may elect to represent said cultures from a western perspective—by classifying and presenting their art as "primitive" or "tribal"—or they may accept the responsibility of deepening understanding and enhancing mutual respect among peoples. The latter they can accomplish by treating such art on its own merits and terms, by showing how it exemplifies basic, universal responses to environmental and other challenges.

As a student of history and a museologist who is fairly familiar with some of the cultures from which the sculptures in this work derive, I applaud *The World of Spirits and Ancestors in the Art of Western Sub-Saharan Africa* as an introduction to sub-Saharan art for both a student and popular audience interested in developing an appreciation of the art and cultures from which it derives, this work facilitates a rich educational opportunity.

As represented and symbolized in the sculptures of the Howard collection, the world of spirits in sub-Saharan African art unfolds within these pages. Sasser reveals that the creative genius, which is more cultural than artistic, is a response to the environmental challenge, autochthonous to the land and its people, rather than the result of outside "civilizing" Semitic or Caucasian influences. This, coupled with the author's sensitivity to and avoidance of certain previously held and still prevailing stereotypes about Africa, will make this work appeal to and enlighten audiences of all cultures. This sensitivity and her ability to provide a global context reflect an ardent embracing of multiculturism.

One hopes that this work and the sub-Saharan African collection of the Museum of Texas Tech University will broaden understanding of the African manifestation of some universal human themes, especially the general personification of natural phenomena, as in ancient Egyptian, Greek, and Roman mythologies. I do not hesitate, therefore, to endorse *The World of the Spirits and Ancestors in the Art of Western Sub-Saharan Africa* as an introduction to sub-Saharan art and culture alike, enriching to both lay and specialist audiences well beyond those with immediate access to the Texas Tech Museum.

SILAS OKITA
President, Museums Association of Nigeria

EXECUTIVE DIRECTOR'S FOREWORD

The African Art collection came to the Museum of Texas Tech University to meet a perceived need rather than growing out of the research activities of an academic unit. Although the history of much of Africa is taught with reference to material culture including masks, musical instruments, societal paraphernalia, and socio-religious imagery, courses on the Tech Campus had no tangible evidence of that achievement. Similarly, the African-American citizenry of Lubbock and the surrounding area had no examples of their cultural legacy. Both conditions stimulated a desire for a collection of African objects, and when this material became available, a decision was made to acquire as many pieces as possible. From the very beginning, the collection was viewed as a means for providing information to the University for student educational enhancement and to the community for informal education and enjoyment.

Individual objects for the collection were chosen for three primary reasons: 1) they are aesthetically pleasing, 2) they exemplify a variety of cultural interests, and 3) they provide a meaningful group of objects for study and research. Together, they form a representative collection related to a specific area of the world and to a definable group of cultural entities. These objects from western sub-Saharan Africa are viewed as part of the greater community of global art. Within their own context, they are as viable and aesthetically profound as the more familiar works recognized and appreciated by Western audiences.

In addition to serving the focus groups mentioned above, the African Art collection is important for popular viewing. It adds a dimension not available in many other art forms. Given a choice, most people favor the familiar. However, a regular diet of common fare, regardless of its content, soon lulls the viewer into a stupor of complacency that arrests intellectual growth and retards cultural awareness. What is important about studying the material culture of another land and another people is that it provides the viewer with a look at the universe as perceived by others. This insight allows each person to reexamine his or her own beliefs in comparison and contrast with those of a different people.

When looking at art, the viewer normally is inclined to make primary selections based on personal preference. Often the more sophisticated the "eye," the more simple, direct, and unassuming the choice. Each person has a concept of beauty. For some it is a colorful work by a modern master; for others, a sculpture from the Renaissance Period. Art objects that evade categorization are at times described as "primitive" or "exotic" art. The diverse traditions of sub-Saharan Africa offer a complex artistic heritage that is, at least at first view, mysterious to the Western mind.

The first general encounter with African sculpture by Western Europeans occurred during the fifteenth century. At that time, it was viewed as the curious production of an exotic people. The viewer inexperienced with African, Oceanic, or some forms of Native American art may not immediately appreciate the universal nature of these objects. Nor may they understand the creativity and "life force" that inspired such works. The onlooker may consider the objects an isolated example of interesting but obscure art. Others will try to see the pieces in the context of their environment and in association with the culture that inspired their creation. Both viewing experiences are important as each adds to the onlooker's knowledge and understanding. The process fosters deeper appreciation for all objects, which in turn heightens sensitivity and transforms observation into emotional response. However, when the art comes from areas distant in miles and remote in cultural complexity, the context is unfamiliar and guidance is necessary to assure viewer appreciation.

The objects from sub-Saharan West Africa are a form of social communication with a message that may be simple or complex. It may vary according to the receptivity of each viewer. It is an art form that depicts and reflects the society from which it originates unrestricted by political or geographic boundaries.

Agricultural people living south of the Sahara Desert in West and West-Central Africa made the objects in this collection. They produced wood sculptures rooted in tradition, however, some pieces are of relatively recent origin. Most date from the late nineteenth to the mid-twentieth century. Owing to the environment and the perishable nature of the materials, few truly old wood sculptures remain. The gradual restructuring of the social order in all parts of Africa has changed traditional sculpture production, and some pieces in the collection reflect more than one cultural influence. A number of the pieces were made for popular distribution, as well as for use within the immediate community. The objects were made to be used, repaired, and replaced. New objects took the place of the old ones not as a substitute but as a continuation of the original. Each of these elements adds to the special nature of the collection and enhances its importance for study and research.

The African objects in the Museum have been removed from the cultural continuum of the region that produced them. The pieces are shown in an artificial environment and out of the social order in which they were used. However, each object is much more than it appears at first view. The complexity of the cultural information embodied in the art presents an interesting and exciting challenge. The art of West Africa is a whole art that combines religious, social, and esthetic elements. It is unlike the secular, often fragmented art of Europe and the United States. Owing, in part, to this fact, it is difficult to consider the aesthetics of African art in isolation without distorting the meaning of the pieces.

The Museum is an integral part of the educational mission of Texas Tech University. It is a primary strength of the Museum to function as a conduit of information from the University outward and from the public inward. Owing to the nature of its service role, the Museum's collections are varied to compliment related academic units either directly or indirectly and to reflect public interests and needs. As the Executive Director of the Museum, I view this collection as extremely important to the educational mission of this institution and its service to current and future generations of visitors. The collection is valuable as a reference for artistic and ethno-cultural study. It also furthers the Museum's mission to address the needs of the immediate constituency as well as those of the international museum community. Most of all, it is enjoyable to view and to reflect upon.

The African pieces, as with the other objects in the Museum, call attention to the cultural and scientific heritage of our world and its people. Such collections allow us to trace the various contributions of different races and regions to our present culture. They verify that the heritage that surrounds us today was developed by a cross-fertilization of ideas from other times and continents. The African collection is one of the threads of influence that tie together and finally connect the remote corners of the universe.

This collection is part of the Museum because a number of generous supporters share a vision of a better tomorrow for all people.

GARY EDSON
Executive Director
Museum of Texas Tech University
June 1994

PREFACE

In a book about a collection of African masks and sculptures, titled *The World of Spirits and Ancestors in the Art of Western Sub-Saharan Africa,* it would be strange if a numinous sense of inevitability did not exist. The destiny that brought the western sub-Saharan carvings to the Museum of Texas Tech University on the flatlands of West Texas is described by Ethelene Bucy in "About the Elliot Howard Collection." It is a remarkable story about artist and collector Elliot Howard, who wished his collection of African sculpture, assembled over many years, to be placed where it would add to the appreciation of the art of African people. The reader might ask, why the Texas High Plains, where cotton fields are quilted on the land and cattle ranches reach to the horizons? If a page of West Texas history is turned back just a century and a half, an uninhabited, semiarid, grassy prairie is revealed, a land not unlike the dry savannas and grasslands of portions of western sub-Saharan Africa. As late as the 1870s, the Texas Panhandle was the grazing ground for pronghorn and millions of buffalo. To the thousands of miles of uninhabited pasture, parties of nomadic Indians came periodically to hunt. These Indians of the American plains and many of the ethnic peoples of western sub-Saharan Africa who live on the grasslands and savannas, supplementing their diet by hunting, have much in common. Both peoples continue to place an emphasis on costumes and ceremonial paraphernalia. They celebrate the forces of nature and their ancestors with dances accompanied by drumming and chants.

As in Africa, the Plains Indians applied rich textures to functional objects. Bead work, fur, fringed hides, and quills decorated woven bags, tobacco pouches, saddle blankets, clothing, and moccasins. Function was the first requirement for people on the move, but beauty frequently resulted. Following the buffalo did not permit the transport of heavy objects; therefore, large sculptures and masks were not made.

In the sedentary society of the Pueblo Indians of New Mexico, masks and headdresses of great complexity played and continue to play an important role in rituals. Like the African ethnic groups, the pueblo inhabitants honor the supernaturals and the "old ones" through offerings, dances, and chants. They pray for rain on the dryland fields and blessings for their villages.

Surrounded by the strong heritage of vernacular arts and building traditions of Native Americans of the Southwest, West Texas is a remarkably suitable environment for an appreciation of African masks and sculptures that touch the roots of African-Americans and appeal to people of all cultures.

The first purpose of this book is to introduce unpublished pieces of twentieth-century western sub-Saharan African art that were assembled by Elliot Howard and are now part of the collection of the Museum of Texas Tech University. The African carvings at the Museum also include pieces presented to the International Center for Arid and Semiarid Lands Studies (ICASALS) by former Ambassador to Burkina Faso, the Honorable Julius Walker, and Mrs. Walker. ICASALS has placed the Walkers' gifts on permanent loan to the Museum.

The World of Spirits and Ancestors in the Art of Western Sub-Saharan Africa is not, however, a catalog–that task remains to be done. The illustrations in the book were chosen as examples of the arts, usually ceremonial, of western sub-Saharan African ethnic groups represented in the Museum's collection.

The subject of the book's first chapter is western sub-Saharan African countries, some with recently drawn boundaries and unfamiliar names, for example, the Republic of Benin, formerly Dahomey. Environments that range from the arid stretches of Mali to the tropical mangrove swamps along the coast of Nigeria are considered. In the next chapter, the relationships among climate, resources, shelter, and the arts are examined. Contrasting conditions are based upon a comparison of the Dogon, living in semiarid portions of Mali, and the Senufo agriculturists, some of whom inhabit the moist savannas and grasslands of Ivory Coast. A third chapter is devoted to craftsmanship, apprenticeship, and what constitutes a fine piece in the eyes of the artists themselves. The last chapters are devoted to figurative carvings and masks.

To become acquainted with African art, one must take certain hurdles in stride. The maker of an African carving or mask does not intend to create a beautiful masterpiece that will last for centuries in the security of a museum or private collection. The finished product is not "art for art's sake." It is made for a purpose. The figure may honor an ancestor or petition for help in times of need. A mask is worn at masquerades that are held to bring about success in planting or harvesting or on the occasion of great funerals for important elders. The term *masquerade* itself is confusing. To Americans a masquerade is a costume party held at Halloween or dances associated with the *Ecole des Beaux Arts* celebrations, Mardi Gras, and Venetian carnivals. To an African villager, the masquerade is an important event in which costumes and masks play a ceremonial role combined with music, chant, and dance. Together, the arts participate in a traditional multimedia celebration of great importance in the ritual life of a people. After a mask is worn once, it may be destroyed, or placed in a special house and later refurbished for another occasion. If a carved figure does not fulfill its function in securing the goodwill of the ancestors or spirits, protecting against illness, or securing safety in the hunt, it is discarded, and a new more efficacious figure will be made. African art is essentially functional. Its purpose is to make life less dangerous. The forces in the universe may be considered either guardians or menacing elements bent on mischief. To keep the supernatural forces at bay, a powerful priesthood is necessary. With the aid of a shaman, the carver fashions a "power object" to ward off evil. A supernatural being takes over the mask when it is put on. The masked dancer, during the time the mask is worn, *becomes* the spirit the mask personifies.

Even without recognizing the reasons, the strong life-force in African sculpture is felt by most observers. And yet, in the museum, visitors need to remember that the carvings they confront in display cases are quiescent and removed from their original purposes. Masked and costumed dancers are at the center of dynamic action united with the surge of the drums, with songs, color, and frenzied activity that reinvigorate traditional rituals handed down for generations.

One of the privileges of writing *The World of Spirits and Ancestors in the Art of Western Sub-Saharan Africa* is the opportunity to help in the realization of Elliot Howard's dream of introducing students and visitors to a new world of art experience or reinforcing the fascination of an art that has already captured the imagination of the observer. It is hoped that these pages will assist in facilitating Mr. Howard's goal.

And so in the tradition of the Asanti storytellers, who so capably distinguish the end of one episode from the beginning of another, *Kungurus kan kusu,* "Off with the rat's head!"

ACKNOWLEDGMENTS

At the beginning there was Ethelene Bucy, who initiated the placement of the Elliot Howard collection at the Museum of Texas Tech University. A debt of special gratitude must go to Howard who wished the Africa sculpture that he loved to be used for teaching and informing students and others about a splendid art. Gratitude extends to Howard's friend and benefactor, Bayard Herr, who helped to make the acquisition possible. Dr. Herr died in September, 1994. Gary Edson, Executive Director, the Museum of Texas Tech University and Collette Murray, former Vice President for Development at Texas Tech University, visited Howard in Houston. Both recognized the importance of acquiring the collection. At Howard's death, the acquisition was made possible by a grant from the Helen Jones Foundation and by gifts of friends of the Museum.

Further grants from the Helen Jones Foundation made possible a gallery designed especially to display the African sculpture and the writing and publication of *The World of Spirits and Ancestors in the Art of Western Sub-Saharan Africa*. Special appreciation for her support and belief in this project belongs to Louise Willson Arnold.

Without the enduring assistance of my co-photographer and husband Thomas Sasser, who read countless versions of the manuscript and offered helpful suggestions, while retaining a cheerful disposition, this book might not exist.

For permission to photograph the African sculpture used as illustrations in this book, our gratitude is extended to: Museum Executive Director Gary Edson, not only for making the sculptures from the Elliot Howard Collection available but also for assigning museum space in which to work and the assistance of the museum staff, Denise Newcomb and Jim Sanders; to Idris R. Traylor, Director of ICASALS, for joint permission with Director Edson to photograph African sculpture given to ICASALS by Ambassador Julius Walker and Mrs. Walker, and now on permanent loan to the Museum.

Many friends have made valuable contributions to the visual information contained in this book. I wish to express my thanks to Gary Elbow, Chairman, Department of Geography, Texas Tech University, for the map of western sub-Saharan Africa; to Virginia Mahaley Thompson, Associate Professor, School of Architecture, Texas Tech University, for her ink and wash drawings; and to S. Elizabeth Sasser, AIA, Assistant Chief Architectural Historian, National Park Service, Washington, D.C., for pen and ink drawings. John O. Evans III gave permission to photograph several sculptures in his personal collection and to reproduce photographs he took in Liberia. Evans was kind enough to read the manuscript and provide helpful suggestions. I am deeply grateful to Saralyn R. Daly, retired professor of Linguistics, for her insightful comments on the text, her careful editing, and her encouragement.

Silas Okita, President of the Museums Association of Nigeria, was recommended as a reader by Museum Director Gary Edson. Okita graciously accepted. His review reinforced my belief in the approach I had chosen. His understanding of what I had hoped to do was one of the most heartening occurrences in the writing process. The foreword he has written is something for which I shall always be grateful.

Last but by no means least, I wish to thank Editor Judith Keeling of the Texas Tech University Press for her ability to endure the writer's quibbling over detail, ups and downs. Her talent and friendship are appreciated. So is the help given by Carole Young, Fran Kennedy, and Marilyn Steinborn of the Press and their steadfastness through the long process of producing the book.

THE WORLD OF SPIRITS

AND ANCESTORS

IN THE ART OF WESTERN

SUB-SAHARAN AFRICA

Introduction

It seems to me that people in the West, including some
African art scholars and experts, refuse to acknowledge
[the] drastic changes in Africa, particularly in the sculpture.
As a result, they have completely ignored the contemporary
traditional sculpture. Contemporary traditional sculpture,
in many cases, is of a very high aesthetic quality
and it is about time that we accept that not every
"ancient" sculpture is a masterpiece and not every
recent traditional sculpture is a fake.

ESTHER A. DAGAN
from *Tradition in Transition*

T

he term contemporary traditional, used by Esther Dagan in the quotation, is an apt description of the sculpture that is illustrated and discussed in this book. The carvings and masks do not belong to the early generation of African art that during the late nineteenth century first attracted the attention of anthropologists and European dealers in antiquities—those pieces that in the early 1900s, inspired the French painters and influenced the development of Cubism. The exact ages of the carvings reproduced in *The World of Spirits and Ancestors in the Art of Western Sub-Saharan Africa* are not known, but they are considered to be twentieth century; many were probably done after 1950. Unless the sculptor is known and the provenance established, very few examples of African art can be assigned a precise date, and virtually no work in wood is old by historical standards. The hot, damp climate in equatorial sub-Saharan Africa is not conducive to a long life-span. Wood rots and termites take their toll. In many cases, longevity is not an aim. Some masks are kept and refurbished; others are destroyed after use in a single ritual performance or masquerade. Figurative sculptures may also be replaced if they are not successful in producing the results for which they were intended.

In the last seventy-five years, conditions of change—political, economic, and those influencing long held beliefs and customs—have had a profound effect upon western sub-Saharan Africa. The growth of urban populations has reduced the number of villages based upon extended family units. Ethnic religious beliefs have been replaced by conversions to Islamic and Christian faiths. Carvings intended to foster a harmonious existence in the midst of harsh natural forces, or to honor the ancestors and appease the supernaturals are less frequently commissioned. The wood-carvers may supplement their livelihood with orders from collectors, art galleries, dealers, and the tourist trade. Traditional techniques, however, continue to be taught in some workshops by master craftsmen who are growing old and wish to hand down their knowledge and skills to a new generation. The carvers, however, make use of tools and paints manufactured commercially. Despite changes, the pieces sold to collectors and to a market outside of Africa continue to perpetuate the subjects and styles that come from a familiarity with the carvings placed in shrines and with the ceremonial masks remembered from childhood.

On behalf of the African artists who face a different world but maintain a respect for their heritage, Ms. Dagan writes, "'old' does not necessarily guarantee artistic excellence." She states that in her opinion "the quality of some recent sculptures . . . clearly carved to be sold" deserves respect and attention.[1]

In the last decades, the materialistic aspect of the arts is present in all countries. It is generally accepted that painters and craftsmen, gallery owners and museum directors to survive must be aware of business and marketing practices. Can contemporary African artists be blamed for trying to sell their work where there is a market? Does this necessarily impact the quality of the artist's work? The answer is an ambivalent one. John C. Messenger has investigated local communities known as "carving villages" among the Anang in southeastern Nigeria. He explains that people once came from distant settlements to buy the pieces that were exhibited in front of the compounds of craftsmen who were known for the excellence of their work. Some independent artisans continue to supply the need for ritual figures and masks while filling commissions from collectors and dealers. These men are often critical of the results produced by the young members of the woodcarving guilds, initiated in the 1940s. Instead of setting high standards as a goal, guild members received only a brief training period of about three months. Each was encouraged to specialize in performing an "assembly line" function, that is, making a special part or painting particular details. The money from sales was divided among the participants in this process of mass production.[2] Needless to add, the carvings were poorly done and sold to middle men who resold the work in distant markets and to the increasing number of tourists eager for something made in Africa by Africans. Ms. Dagan believes that the change in African art goes beyond the guild system or the use of manufactured tools and commercial paints. She suggests:

> the erosion now represents the change from spiritualistic art [to translate *l'art spirituel* as spiritual art seems more expressive] to materialistic art. The only way to preserve even a minimal amount of the sculptural heritage is for the African carvers to persist in doing what they do best—to carve in the tradition handed down by their predecessors. In the process

of transition, the changes in African sculpture will be evolutionary. While previous changes were limited to style, shape, and form, the traditional purpose remained intact. Now the purpose is also changing. The question we should ask ourselves is: Should the African artist abandon carving because of this essential change?[3]

A similar dilemma occurred in New Mexico and Arizona during the early twentieth century. The marketing of Pueblo Indian crafts to families, who swarmed west on the new Santa Fe Railroad and in touring cars, was in the hands of clever salesmen, selling cheap imitations of Indian bracelets, "conch" belts, or shoddy pots to buyers who wished to take home a memento that was "made by Indians" or "made on the reservation." Thin silver, cheap beads, and tooling equipment designed to stamp "Indian motifs"—thunderbirds, bows and arrows, swastikas—on metal or leather were distributed by entrepreneurs who paid low wages for "art" to unload on uninformed travelers This can be equated with the era of poorly carved animals, wooden spoons, and woven baskets turned out by African villagers for souvenir-hunting visitors. In the period following the Second World War, a revitalization of the pueblo arts was encouraged by tribal organizations that were eager to keep the traditional heritage from perishing and to acquaint a new generation with the beliefs of their ancestors. Arts and crafts centers and Indian art associations sponsored exhibits and provided an outlet for selling new "traditional art" to a better informed public willing to pay fair prices for well-crafted objects. With fewer and fewer "old" pieces by anonymous pueblo artists available, the work of the no longer nameless contemporary potters, jewelry makers, painters, and sculptors is attracting a new generation of appreciative buyers. Like early pueblo artists, African carvers were never anonymous among their own people, and they were frequently known and their work recognized by other ethnic groups. Today, names and personal styles of African artists and their students are beginning to be identified thanks to the efforts of scholars of African art and culture. William Bascom notes:

> the works of individual artists, Maria Martinez and Nampeyo as potters, Tom Burnside as a silversmith, Dot-so-la-lee as a basketmaker, and other distinguished American Indian artists had received attention as individuals before there was any study of individual African artists. Few African museum pieces are identified by the name of the carver, but in recent years William Fagg has been identifying and comparing the works

of Yoruba carvers such as Agbonbiofe and Ologunde of Efon-Alaiye, Olowe of Ise, Bamgboye and Arowogun from near Osi, Kobadoku of Igbesa, and Adugbologe and Ayo of Abeokuta. Father Kevin Carroll has added the study of the works of other Yoruba carvers. . . .[4]

Modern traditional Indian art in the Southwest acts as a catalyst for bringing a younger generation back to their roots. African contemporary traditional art may also be a powerful factor in keeping alive the customs and values of the people. At a time when there is a constant bombardment of visual messages on the television screen, computers, illustrated journals, movies, videos, and video games, it is the pictures and the accompanying sounds that capture and transmit meaning. African sculpture communicates eloquently by visual means. It is a part of a multimedia expression, which draws together oral literature, music, dance, theater, and art. To write it off because its purposes are changing, or because it has become commercially profitable, would cut African people off from one of the splendors of their past and an inspiration for the future. This would result in a severe loss for people of all races.

Tradition is never static, whether in Africa or the Four Corners region of the southwestern United States. Among the kachina dancers new figures appear, including a Mickey Mouse kachina. Some of the dancers and an occasional kachina doll wear blue jeans as a parody of Anglo visitors to the pueblos. On the African scene, an illustration in Herbert Cole's *Icons* shows an Ewe carving of a soldier dressed in a European uniform, blowing a bugle and carrying imported weapons. Figures of this kind, the reader is told, are purchased as guards for shrines.[5]

When traditions fail to remain flexible and to absorb the impulses signaled by a new time, they die and their visible remains are shown in museums as artifacts, aesthetic experiences, or historical notations. Africa's contemporary traditional carvings are alive and well; they are an important link between today and the past. They are also the antiques of tomorrow that will preserve indispensable information for the future.

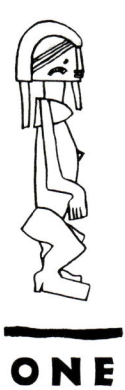

ONE

Lands and Peoples
of Western Sub-Saharan
Africa

Thou hast a lap full of seed,
And this is a fine country.

from "In a Myrtle Grove" by
WILLIAM BLAKE

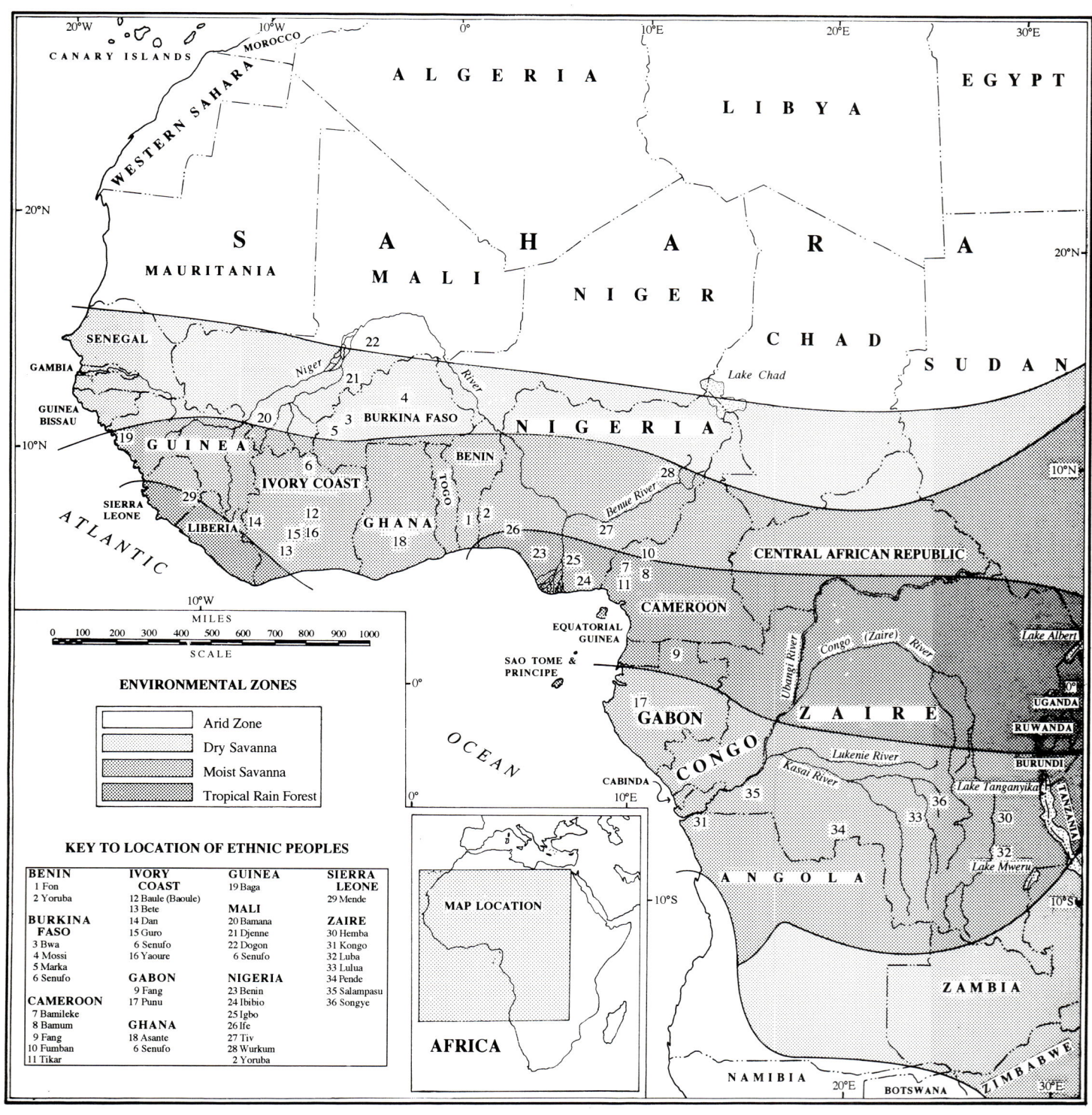

ENVIRONMENTAL ZONES

	Arid Zone
	Dry Savanna
	Moist Savanna
	Tropical Rain Forest

KEY TO LOCATION OF ETHNIC PEOPLES

BENIN
1 Fon
2 Yoruba

BURKINA FASO
3 Bwa
4 Mossi
5 Marka
6 Senufo

CAMEROON
7 Bamileke
8 Bamum
9 Fang
10 Fumban
11 Tikar

IVORY COAST
12 Baule (Baoule)
13 Bete
14 Dan
15 Guro
6 Senufo
16 Yaoure

GABON
9 Fang
17 Punu

GHANA
18 Asante
6 Senufo

GUINEA
19 Baga

MALI
20 Bamana
21 Djenne
22 Dogon
6 Senufo

NIGERIA
23 Benin
24 Ibibio
25 Igbo
26 Ife
27 Tiv
28 Wurkum
2 Yoruba

SIERRA LEONE
29 Mende

ZAIRE
30 Hemba
31 Kongo
32 Luba
33 Lulua
34 Pende
35 Salampasu
36 Songye

MAP LOCATION

AFRICA

Western sub-Saharan Africa. Drawn by Gary Elbow.

In western sub-Saharan Africa and the western part of central Africa, there are broad environmental bands that follow an east-west pattern. The land is separated into four zones based on rainfall and vegetation: the arid zone, the dry savannah or grassland, the moist savannah, the tropical rain forest. A knowledge of the homelands and the conditions shaping the lives and beliefs of the inheritors of long traditions of sub-Saharan African arts and crafts is important for an appreciation of an art that was largely unknown to the world community until the twentieth century. For the purpose of this book, from among hundreds of distinct ethnic groups, those chosen for the readers' special attention are the makers of selected carvings, masks, and metal pieces at the Museum of Texas Tech University.

The choice of western sub-Saharan Africa as a starting point leads immediately to an encounter with the arid and semiarid regions. Encroached upon by the Sahara, Mali exists in baking heat and a rainfall of less than twelve inches a year. To this poorly endowed land, the Dogon migrated during the fifteenth century. Some settlements were located on the flat lands that stretch along the top of walls of rock; other groups built homes and granaries that cling to the steep slopes southwest of the great bend in the Niger River. There are hundreds of villages along the ninety-mile escarpment formed by the cliffs of Bandiagara. The mud and rock structures cling like brown crystals to a cave-pocked vertical matrix of stone. A vivid impression from the air has been recorded by Marcel Griaule, director of the French ethnographic field studies in Africa for a quarter of a century; he observed, "the village is like . . . the great pall for the dead with its black and white squares. The buildings are the filled-in areas of the facade of the house, while the courtyards and approaches are holes. The flat roofs shining in the sunlight and the shadows thrown on the ground reproduce the black and white colors of the pall. The streets . . . are the seams joining the strips together."[1]

Just as the houses and courtyards of the Dogon create a repetition of contrasting mass and space, the seasonal contrasts are sharply divided between periods of wet and dry. The year falls into three divisions. It is dry and cooler beginning in November through February; hot and dry from March until June. In June, the humidity increases, and days are marked by temperatures that begin their upward rise from one hundred degrees Fahrenheit early in the morning. The heat is interspersed with rains that fall from June to September. The gnarled trees lose their leaves during the dry months, then flower just before the rains descend. The first downpours indicate that the time has come for planting millet and other grains in the square fields marked off by mud ridges that form an abstract pattern at the bottom of the cliffs.

In an arid country, the absence of trees exerts an influence on the work of the craftsman; this is apparent among the Dogon. Forested regions provide wood for practice and experimentation while skills in carving are developed. Choices of timber are offered—lightweight wood for masks, hard and finely grained wood that is useful for detailing complex designs. The absence of an abundance of wood may be a factor in the austere and abstract carvings of the Dogon. The simplicity and dignity of Dogon masks and figures also are related to the blacksmiths' work at the forge. The iron pieces produced by the smiths are of necessity linear and reduced to forceful calligraphic statements. The abstractness and essentiality of Dogon art have attracted scholars and critics who find in it a relation to cubism.

Farther to the south in Mali in the upper reaches of the Niger River, the Bamana (called by Francoise Stoullig-Marin "the Bambara") make their home.[2] Stoullig-Marin, noted that ninth-century Arabic texts recorded the histories of such cities as Djenne, famous today for its magnificent mud brick mosque, and Timbuktu. Like the elusive antelopes that are carved on the headdresses worn by the *tyi wara* society, the Bamana—farmers whose principal crop is millet—live in wary concern for their livelihood, which suffers equally in times of drought and during periodic flooding. Despite hardships caused by the aridity and undependable rains, the Bamana maintain a traditional ceremonial life and produce an abundance of art. Bamana carvings are admired by twentieth-century Europeans and others for their naturalism, careful detail, a sweetness of expression, and especially for representations of women with children that began to make an appearance on the market in the 1950s.[3]

East of Mali, in Niger, the arid zone continues. Two thirds of the land is covered by the Sahara Desert. It is the domain of the Tuareg and Fulani, Islamic nomads who subsist on herding camels, cattle, and goats. The Hausa, a group who refused to accept the Moslem faith, make up nearly a half of Niger's population. The southern part of the country is a dry savanna, or grassland. A subsistence agriculture endures frequent plagues of locusts and long periods of drought. During a fortunate year, twelve inches of rain may be expected. The approach of the storms is poetically expressed by Chinua Achebe in his novel *Things Fall Apart*. "At last the rain came," the modern Nigerian novelist writes, "it was sudden and tremendous. For two or three moons the sun had been gathering strength till it seemed to breathe a breath of fire on the earth. All the grass had been scorched brown, and the sands felt like live coals to the feet. . . . And then came the clap of thunder. It was an angry, metallic, and thirsty clap . . . A mighty wind arose and filled the air with dust. Palm trees swayed as the wind combed their leaves into flying crests like strange and fantastic coiffure."[4]

Palm trees grow along the sprawling course of the Niger River as it moves closer to the eastern border of Burkina Faso, or "the land of upright and honest people."[5] A part of the semiarid belt south of the Sahara known as the Sahel, Burkina Faso, formerly was called Upper Volta. This is the home of the Mossi and of the Bobo and Bwa. Although the Bobo and Bwa share many characteristics—the worship of the god, Dwo, and the absence of a centralized system of government—they are not, however, descendants of common ancestors.[6] Both ethnic groups are agriculturists whose primary crops are millet, sorghum, and cotton. The Bwa dye and weave cotton, whereas much of the cotton grown by the Bobo is sent to weaving establishments in the cities.

It is the Bwa who make extraordinary plank masks, six or seven feet in height. These are used at purification ceremonies that take place at the end of the dry season and at funeral rituals and initiation rites. Other masks represent supernatural flying creatures believed to inhabit the bush. To live in harmony with these spirits brings blessings to the homes and families. In the south and northwest where the Bwa and Bobo live in close proximity, the masks of the two groups are almost identical. This similarity is present among a number of ethnic groups in Burkina Faso; it is sometimes the result of borrowings and in other cases, thefts take place.[7]

The Mossi represent a third of the population of Burkina Faso. They spread over three zones. In the north the land is a desert steppe;

farther south the landscape changes to savannas dotted with trees; then, the savannas give way to agricultural land used for cattle breeding and the cultivation of cotton, which was introduced by the French during the colonial period.[8]

Burkina Faso is one of four countries in which more than a million Senufo live. The other lands inhabited by this ethnic group are southern Mali, northern Ivory Coast, and Ghana. The distribution of the Senufo, which overlaps present boundaries, is common to many ethnic people in modern Africa. Colonial empire builders were concerned with control of land that would extend their power along the coast from a trade center or into the interior if natural resources supplied a motive. The interests of indigenous people and their allegiance to tribal units were ignored. With the granting of independence, the arbitrary colonial boundaries often remained unchanged. In some cases, when ethnic societies were divided between countries, it worked to the advantage of smaller populations no longer forced to compete with more populous groups, however, internal conflicts were inevitable if peoples with a long history of hostility were combined within the same borders.

In the lands inhabited by the Senufo, the villagers farm and hunt. Farmers cultivate their crops in the savannas that are broken by bush and woodlands. Trained wood-carvers live in the company of blacksmiths and potters in a district apart from the agriculturists. The training of a worker in wood is taken seriously and may include an apprenticeship of seven or eight years. Many carved pieces are produced at the workshops and are in considerable demand outside of Africa.

The Sahelian countries just discussed create a northern demarcation for the land lying between the savannas and the coast. This includes Guinea, Sierra Leone, Liberia, Ivory Coast, Ghana, Togo, the Republic of Benin (formerly Dahomey), Nigeria, and Cameroon. In the inland portion of these countries, the rainfall measures between twenty to forty inches a year. Along the coast, as much as sixty to eighty inches of rain may fall, causing the vegetation to shift from tall grasses and bush to tropical forests.

Guinea is the home of the Baga who live along the ocean in the southern part of the country. Rice is the principal crop grown in the marsh lands. Tending the rice fields is the responsibility of the women; the men fish and raise kola nuts. For six months of the year, when rains bring flooding, the means of transportation is the pirogue or dugout canoe. Not surprisingly in a wet environment, some of the supernaturals are represented as snakes. Birds are also associated with supernatural powers; the elek, a composite of a bird and human, is a common subject found in family shrines. The *nimba* is one of the most easily recognized of Baga masks. The carved head of a woman is connected to elongated breasts by an extended neck. The dancer who balances the mask upon strong shoulders is concealed by a fiber skirt. The *nimba* and the accompanying rituals are intended to invoke human fertility and the fertility of the fields.

Guinea surrounds Sierra Leone in an arc, except for the southeastern border shared with Liberia. In the fields of Sierra Leone and across the border in Liberian territory, soapstone sculptures have been found in fields. These remain a mysterious phenomenon, attributed to the prehistoric past. The Mende, living in the district, believe the stone carvings possess supernatural powers. Whatever the case, it is generally agreed that the stones bear no relation to the art of the present day Mende people, who attribute their prosperity to the mediation of nature spirits and to the ancestors who are believed to inhabit the rivers. The Mende, as well as related ethnic groups living nearby, are farmers who raise rice, peanuts, yams, cocoa beans, and collect palm oil.

Defined by Sierra Leone on the northwest, Guinea in the north, and Ivory Coast on the east, Liberia's longest boundary is the ocean. Beyond the coastal plains, there are plateaux covered by rain forests where sixty to eighty inches of rain descend between June and September. Overlooking the woodlands, mountain ranges send peaks three thousand feet into the steamy air. Many of the Dan live in northeastern Liberia; their villages spread into the northwestern part of Ivory Coast. Hunters and fishermen, they also practice agriculture. In the southern region, forests are periodically cleared to create new fields to replace those that have been exhausted by years of planting. In the north there are savannas and bush. The bush plays an important role among the powerful societies who retreat into these mysterious and tangled thickets to give initiatory education to young men.[9] Masks represent the bush spirits and the wearer of a powerfully charged carving is believed to become the spirit while the mask is worn.

The Dan divide the world into two parts which represent the environment in which the people live. On the one hand there is the village, a realm of humans and of manmade utensils and objects. The forest that lies outside of the village, with its animal life and supernatural beings, forms the second portion of the Dan's concept of place.[10] Many masks, required at all important functions, are necessary to accommodate the spirit forces and to ensure their benevolence.

Ivory Coast lies east of Guinea and Liberia. As the name suggests, ivory, a commodity prized by early Portuguese traders and by later merchants, gave its name to the coastal area where it was sold. Nearly half of Ivory Coast is occupied by tropical rain forests. The remaining country is rolling terrain carpeted with wooded savannas. Long rivers empty into the ocean. The Bandama River divides the two types of coastal topography: to the west there are rocky cliffs; to the east of the river, sandy islands and long lagoons spread out in a textured pattern.

The Baule, or Baoule, inhabit the partly wooded savannas on the east side of the Bandama. The social organization of the Baule has at its center the extended family. Political structures and the rigidity that a highly organized society implies are disliked. The individualism of the Baule is reflected in the variety of the sculpture that is produced. Some figures are characterized by realistic tendencies. Elegant hair styles are designed with numerous braids; men's beards also are often braided in strands. The patina is smooth and polished. Sculptors may be trained in studios away from the family village, and styles that have been observed while traveling are often adapted. Baule carvings are pleasant in appearance, in contrast to the frightening aspect of power figures intended to frighten away evil spirits. Clients who are impressed with a particular artist may come from a distance to commission a piece of the carver's work.[11]

Traveling from the west, Ivory Coast gives way to the "gold coast" of Ghana. Ghana's eastern border is parallel to Togo. The fertile soil of the coastal plain receives heavy tropical rains, bringing heat and humidity in their wake. Further inland, the rich coastal soil becomes moist savanna. In the eastern part of the country, Lake Volta sprawls like a giant crocodile.

Once a part of the Asante, or Ashanti, Empire, Ghana, during the sixteenth century, was a mecca for Portuguese seamen. The Ashanti Court monopolized gold, thus contributing the European title "gold coast." As in pre-Columbian Peru, the shining metal symbolized the sun, and the king considered himself the representative of the sun on earth. Goldsmiths were highly regarded professionals who received special privileges. Although most of the early work in gold has disappeared—recast, reused, lost—many gold weights of cast brass remain. As the name suggests, these brasses were used to weigh gold dust. They were decorated with miniature scenes from fables and folklore, as well as with the various professions and ordinary people carrying out daily tasks.

Participating in the long history of trade, Togo lies between Ghana and the Republic of Benin that stretches north and south like an elephant's head dipping its trunk in the ocean.

The very name Benin conjures up the Kingdom of this name and the reports by early travelers of palaces covered by remarkable bronze reliefs. A courtly lifestyle was carried on in the midst of awesome splendor. It is confusing, but today the Republic of Benin does not embrace the site of the fabulous city whose name it has been given. The Kingdom of Benin was actually situated in the forests of what is modern Nigeria. Here, the great fortified palace of smoothly polished adobe with bronze castings encasing the wooden pillars dazzled European visitors. Unfortunately, and with little reason, in 1897, the British conducted a punitive expedition against the city that was already sinking into oblivion. The remains of Benin's former grandeur were ground into the earth and two thousand bronzes became a prize for European collectors.

The present-day Republic of Benin was formerly Dahomey. According to legend, Dahomey was created by the daughter of a Yoruba king. When the young girl went into the forest to look for water, she encountered the leopard spirit. From their union, Agasu, ancestor of the Fon was born.[12] The leopard continues to be a symbol of royalty among many African societies.

At the beginning of the eighteenth century, the French established on the coast of what is now the Benin Republic a base for a profitable slave trade. Slaves, thousands of them taken from the neighboring Yoruba, were sent to Brazil, Cuba, and Haiti; they carried with them *vodun* (voodoo), an affirmation of the supernatural spirits and the practices that were used to contact the other world. *Vodun* is closely related to the *orisha* of the Yoruba.[13]

Nine or ten million Yoruba live in the Republic of Benin and in the southwestern part of Nigeria. Talented and vigorous, the Yoruba are proud of an ancestry that is traced back to ancient court life at Ife. Their sculptures include figures from a pantheon of more than six hundred deities and other personages. Masks honor the ancestors, dead heroes, and shamen. Carvings include *ibeji* figures representing the much sought for twins, trays used for divination, figurative pillars that support porch roofs of palaces, drums, and vessels used in everyday life.

Two thirds of the Yoruba are farmers; even those who live and work in the city maintain a hut close to the fields to which they return to cultivate corn, cocoa beans, and yams.[14] The Yoruba artisans include blacksmiths, copper workers, wood-carvers, and other arts handed down from father to son. Well-established merchants help to market craft objects as well as food products.

The variety of occupations suggests that Nigeria, unlike some of its neighbors, enjoys abundant resources. There are formidable reserves of petroleum and natural gas and rich coal deposits. The country produces cotton, palm oil, rubber, and timber. The Niger River, flowing across Nigeria and fanning out into a delta on the Gulf of Guinea, offers transportation for the valuable raw materials.

The products contributing to Nigeria's well-being indicate that the country is not limited to a single climatic zone. In the north, the semiaridity marked by tall grass and thickets becomes moist savannas where each year sixty inches of rain drench the landscape. As the woodlands are transformed from light tropical vegetation to inland rain forests and mangrove swamps along the coast, the rainfall increases to eighty inches per year and temperatures average above eighty-six degrees Fahrenheit throughout the hot season. Peter Matthiessen's verbal picture describes the changes that occurs along the Niger River. He writes,

> At noon, the dust is bright and the hot wind of the harmatta[n] blows unimpeded through the naked branches of the flame trees . . . a track goes north . . . while the main road . . . turns south among citrus groves, guava, and cashew trees. From hilly terrains of thickening vegetation flow thick streams, and farther south the savanna gives way to tropical forest. In the distance, tall pale boles of teak appear at the edge of the green wall, and at the forest edge are birds—big, dark forest hornbills, red-eyed doves, . . . pygmy kingfishers, elegant shikras and a Gabar goshawk, cattle egrets in multitudes, a tawny eagle.[15]

The Igbo and the Ibibio whose livelihoods depend upon agriculture live close to the Atlantic on either side of the Niger River. Eight million Igbo create a densely populated region. Yams are grown in the semifertile marshlands. Fishing supplies another food to supplement the diet. In the nineteenth century, the Igbo and the Ibibio acted as providers of palm oil and almonds for trade.[16] Both ethnic groups construct masks that symbolize the spirits of the dead. The carvers are also responsible for ornamenting the community houses and providing decorations for festivals honoring the guardian beings who watch over the welfare of the people.

Across Nigeria's southeastern boundary is Cameroon, which occupies a volcanic region forming a natural division between west and central Africa. Like Nigeria, Cameroon crosses three of the four, broad western sub-Saharan climatic-vegetative zones. These combined with volcanic eruptions give the country a diverse topography. This land of extremes is marked by a dramatic rise from lowlands and swamps along the ocean to an elevation of thirteen thousand feet above sea level at the summit of Mt. Cameroon. In the southwest, not far from the mountains, grasslands and fertile soil abound.

The grasslands also provide a home for the Bamileke, the Bamun, and the Tikar, three ethnic groups with ancestors in common. The so-called Grassfields were governed by the *fon*, or king. In legend the ruler possessed supernatural powers that allowed him to change into an animal—the favorites were the elephant, leopard, or buffalo.[17] With such an ability, the *fon* was responsible for opening the collective royal hunt. Other duties included carrying out the rituals for planting and harvesting, for leading expeditions to war, and for celebrating the annual festival of the dry season.[18]

The purpose of art objects created by royal artisans was to serve and to enhance the *fon's* prestige and that of his chieftains. Competition among sculptors and craftsmen was important because they did not inherit their rank in society. The goal of the artist's work involved increasing his own status by celebrating the ancestors of the ruler.

Masks among the societies of the Grassfields are similar. They are lavishly decorated with beads, cowrie shells, and copper. Buffalo and elephant masks represent strength, the spider masks, intelligence. Also, stag and bird masks and those with human heads are present.[19] For the masquerades (a term that in African use refers to a ceremony in which masks are worn), the head pieces are decorated with mythical creatures whose faces are distinguished by toothy smiles that seem to be frozen in place. Even the animal masks display amused grins.

The inhabitants of Cameroon practiced the widest range of crafts: beadwork of a remarkable complexity and exuberance; ceramics; wood carving; textile dyeing and embroidery; metal work, including gold-smithing and castings in brass using the lost wax method. Curious brass castings of human subjects, overflowing with a tremendous energy and intensity, are made by the Fumban. Some of these are quite large and represent multiple figures in complicated and animated poses. In the western part of Cameroon, the Ekoi have developed a strong personal and riveting sculptural style associated in some instances with a double-faced "Janus head" from which twisting horns emerge.

Cameroon shares borders with the Central African Republic on the east, and touches three countries on the south: Congo, Gabon, and tiny Equatorial Guinea. The equator passes through both Congo and Gabon. Tropical rain forests are wrapped in sultry heat. The long southwestern demarcation of Congo is shaped by the course of the Congo-Zaire River as it moves to the Gulf of Guinea. Until the twentieth century, the dense, trackless jungle and strength-sapping heat discouraged penetration by even the hardiest adventurers bent on making fortunes through slaving and the acquisition of ivory. Lines from a chant of the Gabon Pygmies called "Tracking Father Elephant" capture the mystery and unease of night in the forest blackness:

> In the weeping forest, under the wing of the evening
> the night all black has gone to rest happy:
> in the sky the stars have fled trembling,
> fireflies shine vaguely and put out their lights:
> above us the moon is dark, its white light is put out.
> The spirits are wandering.[20]

The wooded lands covering most of Gabon rest on a poor stratum of clay, which makes it impossible to carry on more than subsistence farming. This negative condition is balanced by a network of rivers that carry timber and rubber to ports on the ocean where slaves and elephant tusks were once loaded into the holds of sailing vessels. The region along the coast and the valley of the Ogooue attracted the Fang people, who moved from Cameroon to resettle in Gabon.

The Kota also migrated to the lands occupied by modern Gabon and the Republic of Congo. Kota carvings and those of the Mahongwe clan share similar characteristics. Both make stylized heads that are placed on top of baskets containing relics of the deceased; the Europeans called them *naja* because of their resemblance to the head of an erect snake. Covered with brass or copper worked in relief, the heads are held on a tall slender column usually wrapped in copper wire. This neck branches downward into a lozenge shape, the sides of which serve as a handle by which the basket can be lifted.[21]

Another of Gabon's more than forty ethnic peoples, the Punu, are known for their white masks, a mask type that became widespread among other societies. Sharing a tropical climate with Gabon and other equatorial lands, present-day Congo is the site of diverse art expressions. The Kongo, or Bakongo, who live south of Brazzaville, extend their base into southeastern Zaire and northern Angola. Carvers are frequently called upon to make "power figures," sculptures popularly known as "nail fetishes," because of the spikes and slivers of metal driven into the wood by a shaman to protect a person or an extended family against witches and the evil spirits. Not all Kongo carvings are associated with turning danger against the would-be perpetrator. Artists are responsible for making ceremonial paraphernalia—staffs, fly whisks, musical instruments, fans, and swords—for members of the royal court.[22] Subjects for sculpture include hunters, royal wives, mothers holding children, and musicians. Postures indicate particular classes or meanings, for example, a hunter kneels to pay homage to a king; a hand touches the cheek as a sign of mourning.

East of the Congo River, Zaire is represented on the map as a land laced with the tributaries of the great river. In the north, there are dense forests; farther south, these give way to wooded savannas that spread over rolling terrain. Like other equatorial countries, Zaire's population is made up of many societies. These include the Luba, who have exerted a powerful influence on their neighbors. For a time the Hemba of southeastern Zaire, who inhabit the plains bordered by streams and marshland fringed with high hills, were subjects of the Luba empire. The similarities of the wood carvings of the Hemba and the Luba are indicated by the hyphenated title, Hemba-Luba frequently appearing as identification. Given a polished and handsome patina, the figures of the Luba and the Hemba-Luba have protruding navels; the arms are brought forward and rest on the belly. The hair arrangements are elaborate, with a cross-shaped pattern at the back of the head. The coiffures and elaborate scarification are indicators of rank.

The Lulua are a subgroup of the Luba. Like Luba figurative sculpture, the Lulua carvings are distinguished by complex cicatrices. Multiple migrations, providing exposure to many patterns, are given as a reason for this.[23] The heads are exaggerated in scale and rest on long necks. The hair usually rises to a curving point on the top of the head, while some strands are drawn into a small knot at the back. The arms attached to the projecting navel resemble a similar convention adopted by the Hemba-Luba. This is interpreted as a sign of strength. The navel may be surrounded by concentric circles symbolizing life.[24] Wood-carvers rarely make masks.

The Dengese developed an intensely personal style of sculpture, emphasizing the head and torso and ending a male figure at the hips. Like the Lulua, scarification is important and covers the surface with symmetrical patterns; the designs are not carved but painted on the wood. A cone-shaped headdress emerges from a boat-shaped brim that crowns the head. This is described as a wooden cylinder covered with fiber that tops a finely braided bonnet.[25] Masks do not play a role in Dengese rituals.

The history of the Songye, or Songhay, is also closely tied to that of the Luba, with whom they share ancestors. Threatened by the Arabs, a group of the Songye moved to Lulua territory in 1887; there they created a curious and original style of sculpture. Possibly because of the dangers to which they had been exposed, power figures were favored. Such carvings frequently have a horn on top of the head that is a repository for magical materials necessary to ward off sorcery.[26]

Still another ethnic group living in Zaire is the Kuba, which means "people of lightning."[27] Settling in a region where river valleys are bordered by forests and hills overgrown with brush, fields had to be cleared before planting could be done. This was men's work. Once space was provided, however, the Kuba depended upon their women to do the farming. The crops—manioc (cassava), bananas, and pineapple—provided a varied diet. Furnishing a supply of meat and fish was a cooperative activity of male hunting parties. Growing tobacco was also men's work. Trades were specialized and supervised by guilds. There were generally no more than one or two carvers in a settlement and they were regarded with high esteem.[28]

Even the briefest survey of the geography and climate that divide western sub-Saharan Africa into treeless deserts on one hand, and moist savannas, woodlands, and equatorial forests on the other, suggests the wide range of problems facing the inhabitants. A meagerness of materials offers a particular challenge to craftsmen; vastly different possibilities present themselves when a wealth of natural resources are ready and waiting. The sculptures of the arid and semiarid regions where wood is in short supply tend to be severe and abstract; nothing is wasted. When sun and aridity are constant companions, line and mass are visible over long distances, thus encouraging a clarity of form. If the solid is penetrated by openings or concavities, the importance of light and shadow are dramatized. In the tropical forests, the eyes are barraged by dense foliage and a camouflage of birds and animals that lurk, appearing in a flash and then slipping from sight. In such an environment, there are many kinds of wood from which to choose as well as vines and bark, pelts of beasts, tusks, and feathers that permit the artist to indulge in a "baroque" outpouring of detail. Carvings may be inspired by the grotesque terrors that hide in the "bush," where some spirits confront humans with their malicious intentions. In the equatorial jungles of the Congo, fear of vengeful supernaturals requires the creation of "power figures" bristling with nails and blades. Masks designed to frighten away evil forces, or to appease them, take the form of dangerous creatures intertwined with horns, fangs, and ferocious teeth. Such carvings are rare in the arid regions, where vision is not obstructed and danger does not remain hidden.

Natural resources, topography, and climate exert a strong impact on the nature and diversity of the arts of the western sub-Saharan societies of Africa. Shelters also are the result of problem solving and discovering solutions to varied environments and the requirements of divergent ethnic groups. Constructing dwellings involves protection from climatic hardships; living areas for shared experiences and responsibilities within a family or village; sacred spaces to contact the ancestors and the gods. The accomplishment of these ends depends upon the ingenious use of available materials coupled with an ability to find inventive and intelligent solutions to challenging conditions.

The next chapter will contrast housing constructed by the Dogon, inhabiting an arid land, with that built by the Senufo, who live in the savannas where rainfall is more plentiful. The solutions arising from contrasting conditions and resources sharpen the focus upon forms that achieve functionality and answer the needs of the people. Although the results differ, the dwellings of the Dogon and the Senufo are not only functional but are aesthetically pleasing.

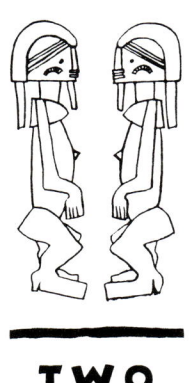

TWO

Shelter in Western Sub-Saharan Africa: the Dogon and the Senufo

Western sub-Saharan Africa, as a map indicates, is like a puzzle made up of intricately cut pieces, countries that vary in topography, climate, and rainfall. Each is inhabited by a number of ethnic groups that spill across the arbitrarily fixed borders from one land into another. Each society has its own customs, costumes, ceremonies, housing, and arts and crafts. Common denominators were once the practice of agriculture and hunting, but with the growth of cities this is changing. Nevertheless, the differences in life-style are in many cases rooted in the abundance or frugality of nature that dictates crops grown, the rituals necessary for success, and the materials from which the ceremonial arts are crafted. In areas removed from easy access to machine-made products, the types of shelter built are determined by the raw materials at hand and traditional responses to a way of building and living. The mass-produced universal appearance of cities growing like children's stacked Legos over the face of the globe, has not yet exerted an all-encompassing persuasion in rural western sub-Saharan Africa. It is still impossible to consider the art of wood carving, metal casting or the making of domestic and ceremonial objects without placing function first. Architecture is the shelter for everyday living; therefore, it is also the background for the craftsman and his work, the shaman and his magic, as well as the housewife and mother pursuing her daily tasks, the farmer returning from the fields, and the hunter from encounters in the bush or forest.

Building comfortable shelters when faced with difficult climatic conditions, the need to rely on the raw materials available, and a lack of modern technology, does not imply an absence of skill or a lack of sensitivity to site, proportion, and space. Of necessity, living arrangements may be required to function at several levels: protection in the performance of everyday chores and from extremes in weather; storage

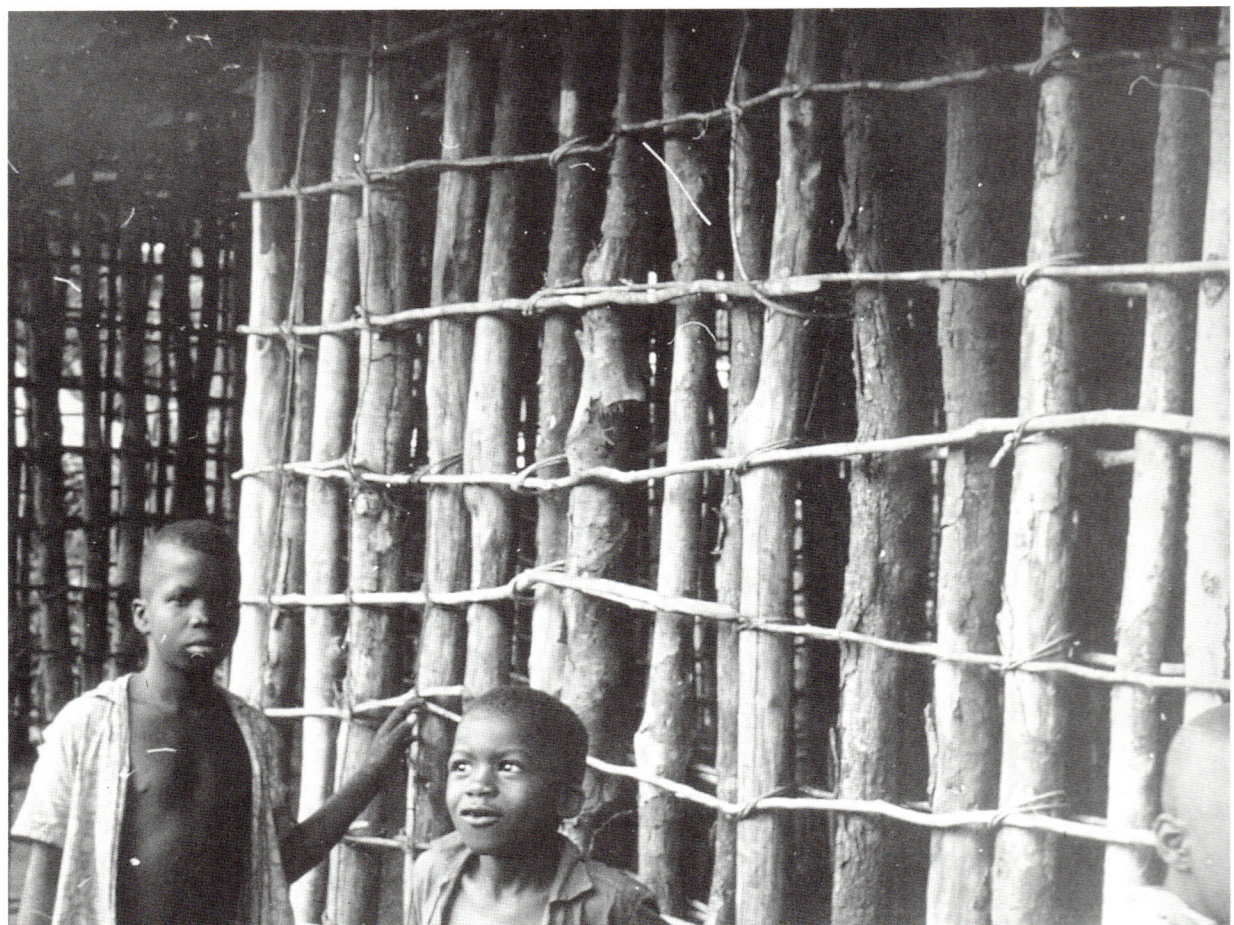

*Fig. A
Framing for a Liberian
village house (1968).
(Photo by John O. Evans
III)*

for possessions and food; ceremonial purposes that through design and orientation express views of the cosmos. Because there is little distinction between builders and craftsmen, a link is forged uniting methods of construction for living and similar techniques and patterns used in the traditional crafts. For example, there is a striking relation between the underlying construction (figure A) of a Liberian village house (used with variations in many regions of sub-Saharan Africa) and the emphasis upon the strong verticals and horizontal bands of a Senufo ceremonial shirt (figure B). Even the X pattern may be considered in the context of the cords binding the horizontal and vertical house-framing members.

The materials and tools employed by the villagers who work together to build a family compound or a shrine are similar to those employed by the craftsmen. This similarity is apparent in both technical skills required in construction and in ornamentation: columns and doors for a chieftain's quarters, the carved shutters for granaries, painted house walls or applied mud reliefs that add symbols for

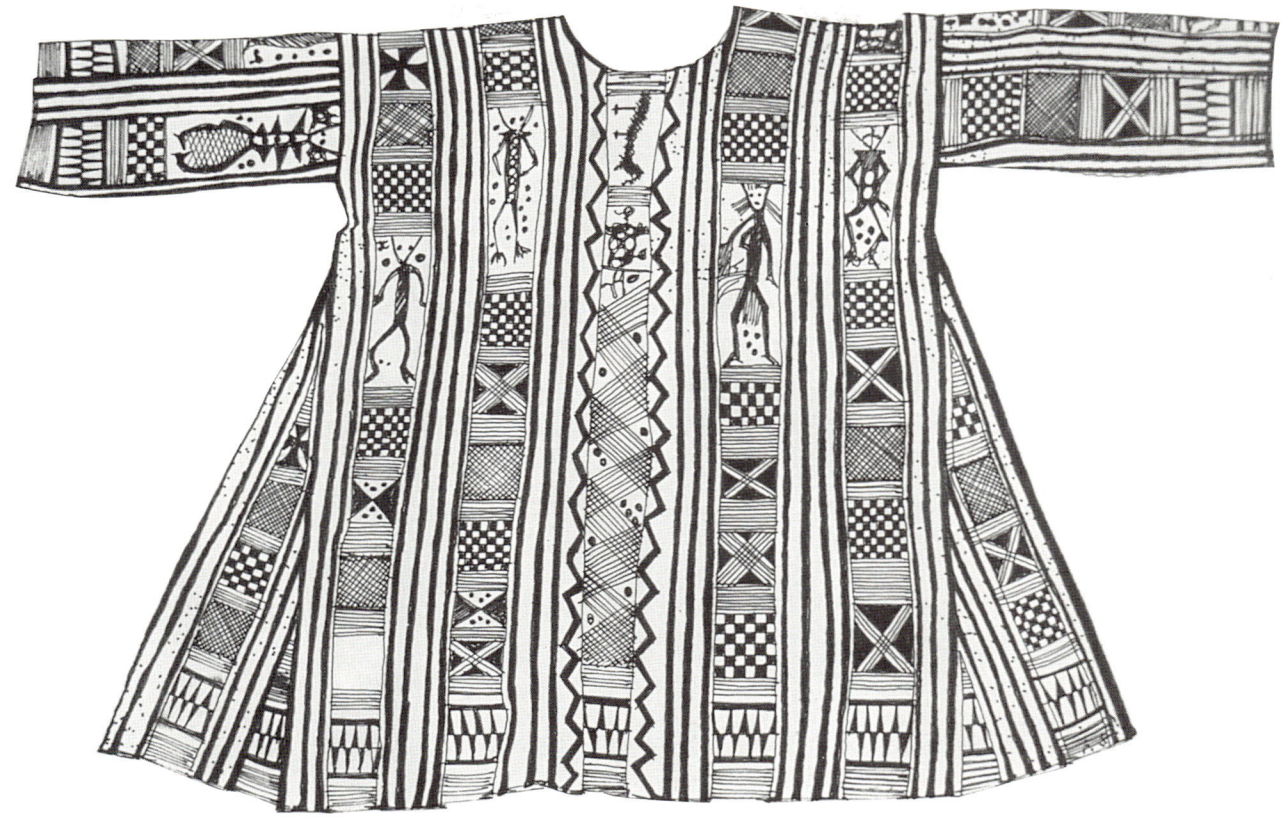

protection against supernatural forces. Figure C shows a decorated house in Kpelle, Liberia.

If African builders have a primary concern for utility, usefulness is also a responsibility of the wood-carver and his collaborator, the shaman. Should a figure of an ancestor or a deity fail to respond favorably to the requests directed to it, the carving is usually destroyed and a new and more efficacious sculpture substituted.

Shelters, like figurative sculptures and the masks, are products of techniques and forms handed down from the past. They are not reinvented for each generation. This respect for traditional methods is popularly known in architecture as the "vernacular" style. *Vernacular* is neither an adjective to be confused with crudity or ineptness, nor is it a synonym for *primitive* (a term misapplied by an earlier generation to African art). In an architectural context, "vernacular" refers to structures whose form is dictated by function, by climatic conditions, by the utilization of materials at the site, and by traditional methods of construction passed from father to son. Vernacular architecture is built without benefit of a trained architect or modern technology, and it is usually the result of a cooperative effort.

Fig. B
A fila shirt (Senufo) painted by Siityenyime Tuo of Karafine. Source: Anita Glaze, Art and Death in a Senufo Village. *Drawing by S. Elizabeth Sasser.*

The qualities of "vernacular" building were reduced to their essence by an American architect, the late Louis Kahn. Upon returning from a trip to Africa, Kahn said, "I saw many huts that the natives made. They were all alike, and they all worked. There were no architects there. I came back with the impression of how clever was the man who solved the problems of sun, rain, wind."[1]

The vernacular architecture and the accompanying ceremonial art of the Dogon of Mali and the Senufo of Ivory Coast discussed in this chapter, represent solutions based upon differing geographic locations, climatic factors, and materials. Both groups have arrived at satisfactory and, yes, even aesthetic solutions despite conditions that appear adverse and even insurmountable to anyone living in air-conditioned comfort and within easy reach of supermarkets and lumberyards.

I

The Dogon of Mali
Inhabitants of the Hot and Arid Zone

*The blacksmith descended from the sky to the earth.
The blacksmith put all kinds of seeds into the hand of man.
The man took the seed and put it into the hand of woman.
The woman put the seed into a calabash.*

from "Dogon Narrative" in *The Art of Metal in Africa*

In arid sub-Saharan Mali where the rainfall may be less than twelve inches during the course of a year, the Dogon people appeared between the tenth and fourteenth centuries A.D. Some settled the flat land on cliff tops; others found a home along the sheer walls of the Bandiagara Escarpment. The site is situated over a ninety-mile stretch of cave-pocked and wind-eroded rock, six hundred miles east of the Atlantic coastline and one hundred and fifty miles south of Timbuktu. Like swallows cementing their nests to the matrix of a rock wall, here the Dogon live in small villages, taking advantage of the protection offered by a sheer vertical ascent. Access is by means of stairs, with steps as high as chair seats cut into fissures of the cliff. The houses and granaries

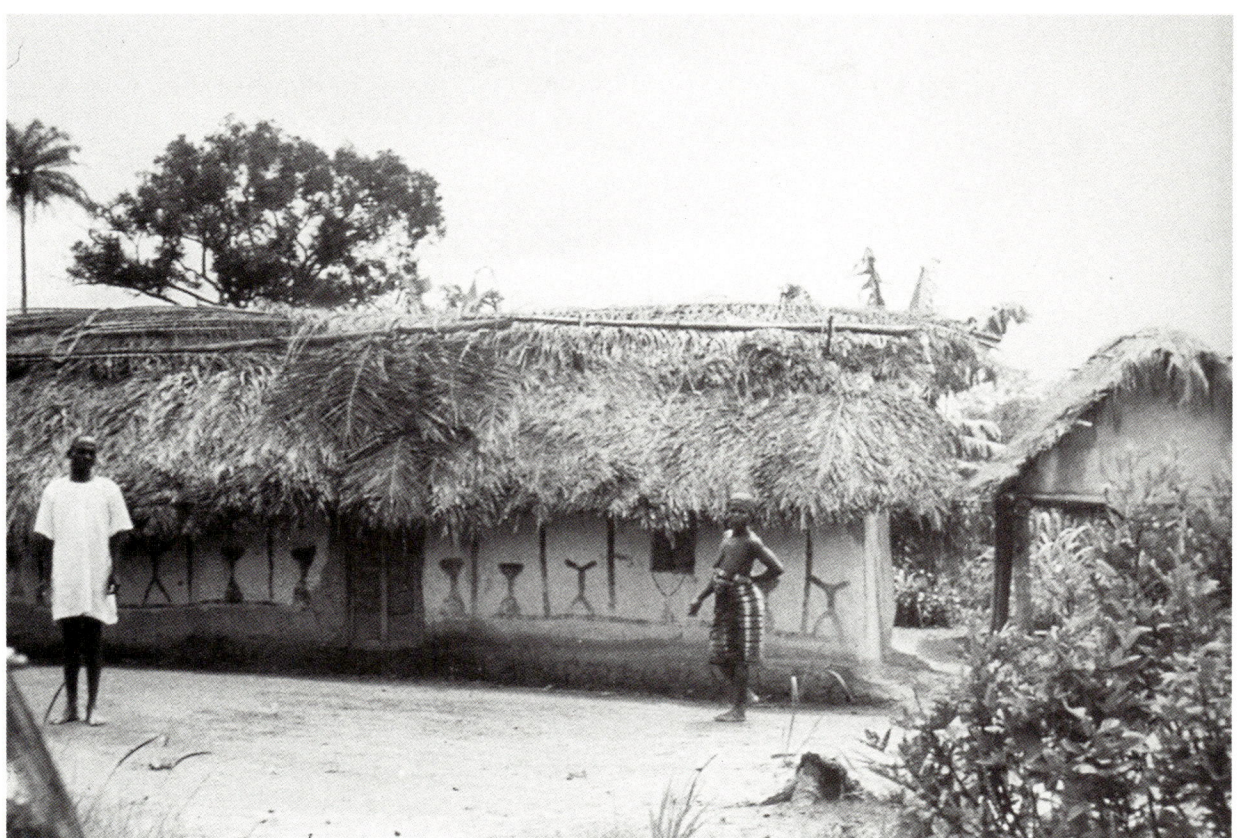

nestling wherever a flat shelf permits are built on foundations of rough stone, with walls of mud—the primary building materials in a dry land where wood is scarce. Gnarled branches of the baobab trees growing at the foot of the escarpment are available as supports for the roofs. Round or square granaries with rakish "hats of peaked straw" provide a contrast to the rectilinear austerity of the honeycomb of buildings.

If the climb to a village is precarious, it is a small price to pay to preserve the flat fields at the bottom of the rock for farming. Even on the cliff tops, the patches for cultivation and the settlements are scattered over a landscape wrinkled like folds in fabric. Marcel Griaule has given this description of such a site:

> Ogol, like all Dogon villages, was a collection of houses and granaries crowded together, flat roofs of clay alternating with cone-shaped roofs of straw. Picking one's way along its narrow streets of light and shade, between the truncated pyramids, prisms, cubes or cylinders of the granaries and houses, the rectangular porticoes, the red or white altars . . . one felt like a dwarf lost in a maze. Everything was mottled by the rains and the

heat; the mud walls were fissured like the skins of pachyderms. Over the walls of the tiny courtyards might be seen, under the floors of the granaries, fowls, yellow dogs, and sometimes great tortoises, symbols of the patriarchs.[2]

Along the cliff walls, where villages fit into the rock like pieces of a puzzle and where flat geometry is almost nonexistent, a small public square is given priority with a *toguna,* or meeting place for the men, skillfully wedged into the rocky terrain.[3] The spaces for living are divided into quarters, each occupied by several family compounds, or *ginna,* presided over by an elder member of an extended family and addressed as the *Ginna Bana.* The land allotted for agriculture is the possession of the *ginna* and is worked communally. Some fields are parceled out to individuals to be used for growing vegetables or the only important cash crop, onions. The land can be neither owned nor sold, because the fields in the distant past were the property of the ancestors who play an important role in all earthly activities.[4] Families living today are considered custodians of this ancient heritage, which is passed from one generation to the next.

Within a compound the *Ginna Bana* occupies the largest house. Typically, it rises from a stone foundation; the walls are mud brick carefully stacked and then plastered. In plan the house is usually square or rectangular, two stories in height covered by a flat roof (figure D). The roof terrace is the gathering place for the family on the hottest nights and a place where produce—"red pepper, purple fruited sorrel, yellow millet that makes a clear sound in falling and is called 'tinkling gold'"—is spread to dry beneath the scorching sun.[5] The facade possesses a simple dignity, rhythmical and ordered, but never rigid—the plasticity of clay prohibits this. A central door (although there may be two doors in some instances) at ground level is flanked by recessed niches between round columnar dividers. At the second level, a rectangular niche placed above the entry repeats the shape of the door at a slightly smaller scale. On either side, the upper rectangular spaces are divided in a grid pattern of recessed squares. Beneath the slightly overhanging roof, there is often a horizontal line of so-called swallow holes. Marcel Griaule's informant told him that the niches were considered the homes of the ancestors and "should never be closed for the ancestors need to breathe the outdoor air." The circular holes close to the roof occupied by nesting swallows are considered "the poultry yard of the ancestors."[6]

At first glance the niches suggest the presence of windows, but this is not the case. There are no windows in Dogon houses, neither in the great house occupied by the family elder nor the shelters elbowing it and filling available nooks and crannies with accommodations for the women and older children. When asked why the houses were window-less, a native replied, "White people put windows in their houses. We Dogon don't do that . . . Anybody who wants light can go outside. In the house it should be dark. It's better that way." This is reminiscent of the pueblo dwellers of the American Southwest. In the terraced pueblo apartments, very few windows occur, because these would weaken the adobe walls and allow blowing dust and cold night air to infiltrate the interior. During the day, life is lived in the sunny plazas and on the rooftops where the women gather to gossip and do household tasks. Here, red peppers and vegetables are dried through-out the summer months. After the heat and brilliant sunlight, the cool shade of the dusky interiors provides a pleasant relief. Thus, the adobe rooftops in New Mexico as well as those along the cliffs of Bandiagara provide "out-of-door rooms" for living.

From pre-Columbian times to the present, the plazas of the New Mexican pueblos have been the stage for dances and ceremonies. The people continue to sit and stand on the upper terraces of the pueblo dwellings to observe the rituals handed down from ancient times. Among the Dogon, where space is compacted by a difficult terrain, the flat roofs are themselves, in some instances, the staging area for ritual performances. The most important part of the ceremony for the dead is a masked dance that takes place on the small rectangular roof covering the house of the deceased. The earthen space "symbolizes the heavenly places. . . . The masks representing the world of animals and men . . . draw the soul of the dead man into the pattern of . . . action and lead it away beyond the domain of the earth" to join the realm of the ancestors.[7]

African ethnic architecture is often interrelated with the other arts and crafts practiced by the group. Frank Willett noted this and focused attention on a Dogon house in the town of Sanga, pointing out its similarity to a Dogon mask representing *walu* the antelope.[8] The mask has a rectangular enclosure for the head of the wearer, not unlike the basic house form (figure D). There are openings for the eyes similar to the double entries found in many typical dwellings. Decorative bands appear at the upper level of the mask; they resemble the grid of niches on the second story of the Dogon headman's house. Willet observed, "The Dogon of the Niger Bend have rectilinear houses and tall tubular granaries of great elegance, and the flat surfaces of the house walls are often relieved with vertical rectangular recesses which are also found on the faces of their masks."[9] The Dogon mask in figure E suggests the

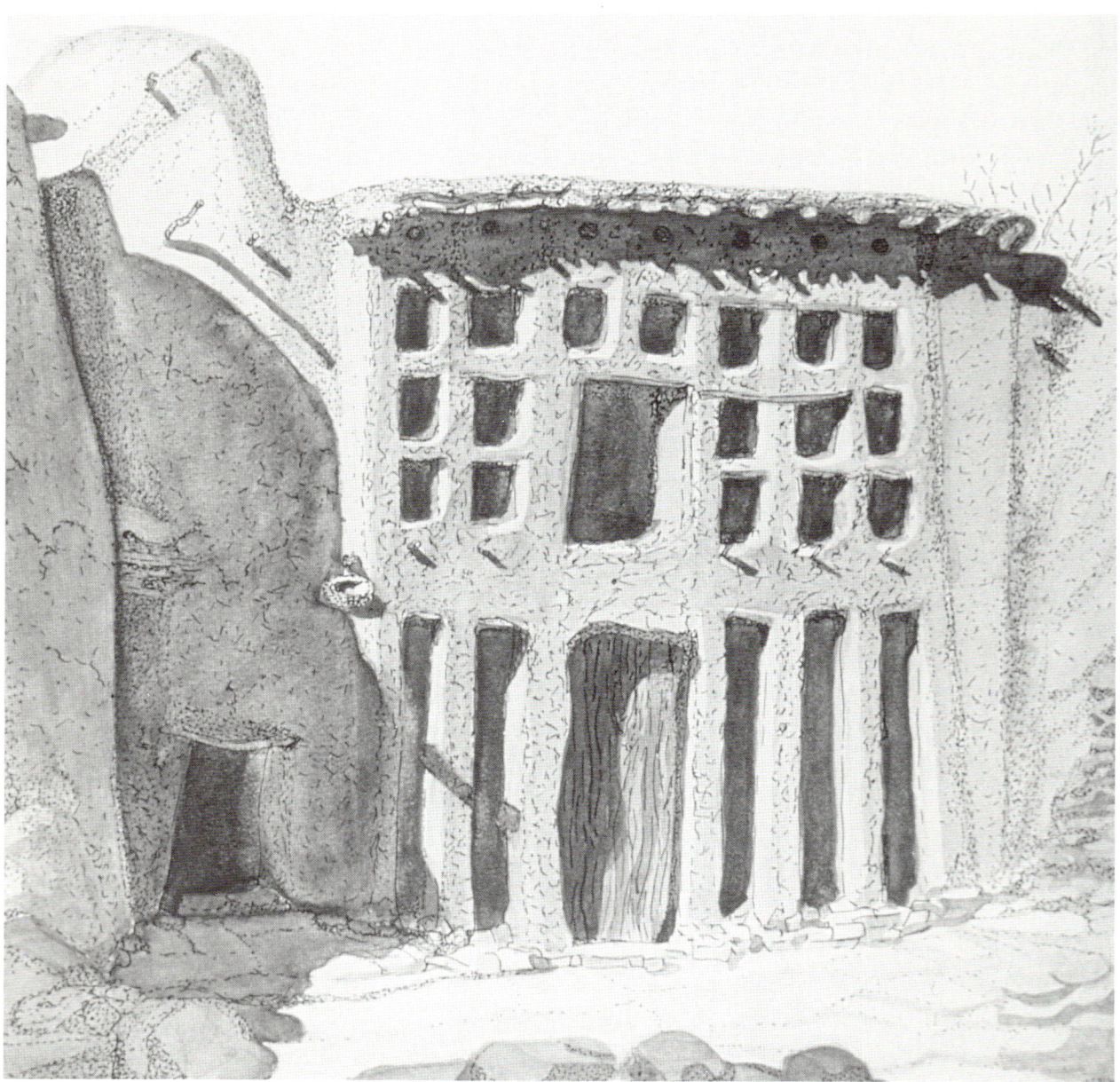

*Fig. D
Dogon house, Mali.
Drawing by Virginia
Mahaley Thompson.*

house design. It repeats the tall recesses that are separated by the narrow ridge of the nose; the square eye holes relate to the niches at the upper story of the facade; the textured and rounded surface of the mask is a reminder of the granary walls with their rough plastering of mud.

It is the granary that best illustrates the relation of architecture to Dogon cosmology (figure F). The importance of providing protection for the grain cannot be exaggerated. The innumerable granaries, both round and square, are insurance against the precarious livelihood yielded by a poor soil and lack of sufficient rain. Within the *ginna,* the largest granaries belong to the *Ginna Bana.* Here, food is reserved

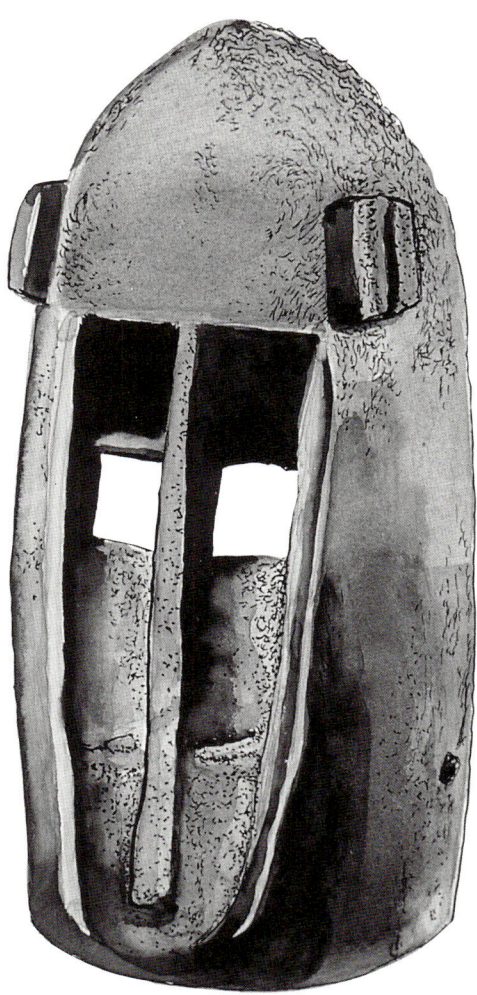

Fig. E
Dogon mask (19th cen-
tury), Mali, wood.
Sketch by E. S. Sasser.

for that time when crops fail and there is danger of famine. Within the extended family, every man gives a portion of the millet, sorghum, rice, and beans harvested to each of his wives. This grain feeds the family members between the growing seasons.

The granary that is life fulfilling and life preserving is at the center of Dogon myth. The First Granary is intertwined with the mythic beginnings of the people, but the origins of the earth and the heavens precede even the granary's appearance. According to the wise man, Ogotemmeli, who was Griaule's source in these matters, the world was put in motion by the god Amma. Clay was present at the beginning. The stars originated as pellets of mud tossed into space, but Ogotemmeli admitted it was quite true that after humans began to inhabit the earth, the women pulled the stars down and gave them to their children as toys. The youngsters put spindles through the bright objects and began to spin the stars like luminous, whirling tops. This game was used to illustrate how the earth rotated.[10]

Fashioning the sun and moon was a more serious matter. It led to Amma's first invention, pottery. Amma took a ball of clay and shaped a pot that he heated to a white hot state; he then put a spiral of glowing red copper around the pot and threw it into the sky, where it began to radiate heat and brilliant light. It was from this time that copper was identified as the metal of the sun.[11] The moon has been described as an unfired pottery vessel, but Ogotemmeli, himself, said it was actually fired a quarter at a time. He added that Africans were creatures "of light emanating from the fullness of the sun; Europeans were creatures of the moonlight, hence their immature appearance."[12]

Amma's next action was to squeeze out a lump of the ever present mud, which he threw from him. As it slipped from his hands, it spread out and became Earth. Earth was chosen by Amma to be his wife and their first offspring was Yurugu, the fox (sometimes referred to as the jackal).[13] Yurugu with great zest and untamed spirits danced for joy on the roof of the house of heaven. It is said that the prints left by his dancing feet were the first communications from god to be received by the people. The steps of the dance continue to be a powerful message sent by the Dogon to the ancestors and supernaturals.

Amma and his mate were not altogether happy with their difficult and foxy offspring. Yurugu was a shifty loner and a thief; he stole from Amma the knowledge of the future and became for all time associated with divination, the mysteries of the night, and the dark world of death. So Amma and Earth tried again; this time they produced a strange being called Nummo (an English translation of Nommo, preferred by the French). Nummo represented a duality bound together into both feminine and masculine elements, like the Chinese yin and yang. Similar also to the Indian Nagas, serpent deities associated with water, Nummo was a creature of moisture and fertility. Each portion of this united pair had two arms and two legs, so eight became a sacred number. The arms and legs writhed like the bodies of snakes and had no firm skeletal substance. Nummo looked at Earth. Seeing her without protective covering, fibers were brought from the heavenly region and green bundles were dropped on the Mother Deity. Some of the fibers twisted and coiled as they fell, forming tornadoes and torrential rivers.

Having clothed Earth, Nummo next disclosed a second gift from Amma. This was speech that rises from the moisture of the mouth and flows into the ear of the one who listens. Speech was joined by the invention of weaving. To accomplish this, it is said, Nummo spit out eighty cotton threads that were crossed and uncrossed by the forked tongues of the united pair. During the process, words were spoken that "filled all of the interstices of the [woven] stuff" making the cloth whole. This, Ogotemmeli said, was why woven material is called *soy* which means, "It is the spoken word."[14] Today, Dogon weavers continue to accompany their weaving with incantations that have been passed

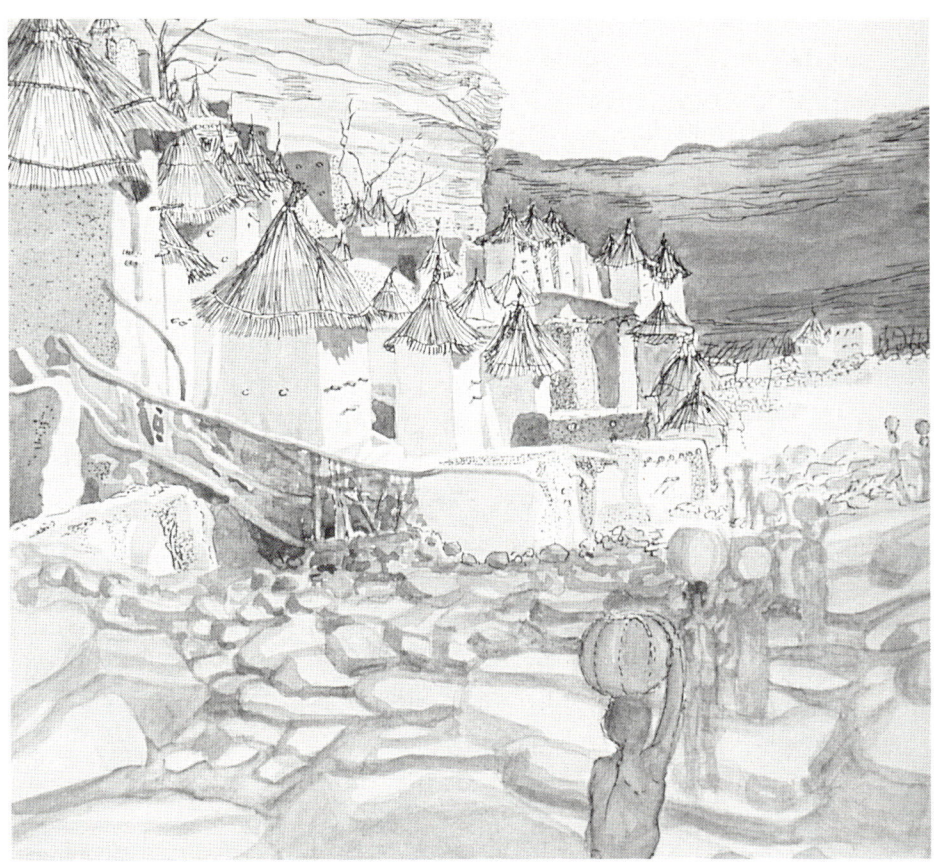

Fig. F
Dogon granaries, Mali.
Drawing by Virginia
Mahaley Thompson.

from generation to generation. The clacking of the shuttle as it is pushed back and forth is called "the creaking of the word."[15]

Amma, apparently pleased with the success of the first Nummo, decided to mold eight more from clay. In time their number was increased to eighty; these Nummos became the earliest generation of mankind. They continue to be honored as the immortal ancestors by later descendants. But to return to the eight Nummos, Amma gave each of them a different kind of grain–little millet, white millet, dark millet, female millet, beans, sorrel, rice, and *Digitaria*.[16] Naturally, this brought about the need for storage containers, and Amma searched for a satisfactory solution. The result was the First Granary, known also as the Granary of Pure Earth. This, so it is said, is the model for the granaries so prominently placed throughout modern Dogon villages.

Amma's invention was closely related to the craft of basketry, for which the contemporary Dogon people continue to be well known. Contemplating a solution for grain storage, Amma, it is related, took a basket with a circular opening and gave it a square base. Immediately seeing that the basket needed to be enlarged, Amma increased the size of the circle at the top and turned the container upside down. (Today a basket woven in this manner is sometimes reversed to serve as a seat.) The square was now above and the much larger circle became the base.

This differs, of course, from the straw "hats" used to cover the circular and square granaries in modern villages. To return, however, to that first mythical construction, Amma must have discovered the weakness of the woven fibers of the basket, so he replaced these with a framework of branches covered with puddled mud from the clay of heaven.[17]

As in so many cosmologies throughout the world, each geometric figure of the granary was given a symbolic interpretation. The circular base represented the sun; the roof covering the granary was the sky and a small circle left at the top of the roof was identified with the moon.[18] In Amma's prototype, there were four stairways facing the cardinal points of the compass, like some of the pyramids in Mesoamerica. On the north side, at the sixth step there was an entry door.[19] Such a door, handsomely carved and equipped with a lock, was once a common feature of Dogon granaries, but now those that survive are usually preserved in museums. The door of the First Granary was viewed as the mouth, and the interior as the belly of the world.[20] Griaule sums up the creative process by explaining:

> A whole constellation of symbols . . . appeared. In the first place there was the miraculous granary itself symbolizing the world system . . . the plaited basket [from which the granary was devised] was to serve men as a unit of volume. The unit of measure was the tread or rise of the steps of [the] stairways. The unit of area was provided by the flat roof, whose sides were eight cubits. [The square became the unit into which fields were divided, as well as the black and white squares making up the Dogon funeral pall.] The two primary geometrical figures were shown in the square of the roof and the circular base, which in the basket, was in fact the opening. This was the model granary in which men were to store their crops.[21]

Having constructed a model granary, one thing was missing—the proper tools for agriculture. These were quickly hammered out at the forge of the first blacksmith and placed on the granary roof. Amma needed only to arrange for the safe transportation of his inventions to earth. The task was assigned to the seventh of the eight Nummos, because seven was considered the most perfect of all numbers. The reason for this stems from the belief that seven is the sum of three—the masculine number—plus four—the feminine number. Amma saw to it that the granary was loaded with all of the creatures that would inhabit the earth and everything necessary to maintain a good life. The seventh Nummo then placed the anvil in a sling around its neck; the granary together with the blacksmith's iron hammer were held in its wavy arms.

Amma directed the Nummo to descend to earth over the rainbow bridge. When the journey was almost completed, the unthinkable happened—Nummo tripped. The granary tumbled over and over at the foot of the rainbow; its contents were scattered in clouds of dust, sending animals and vegetables and tools rolling in all directions. The shock of the Nummo's landing, made more precipitous by the weight of the anvil and hammer, broke the fragile arms and legs at those points where humans have elbows and knees. From that time on, Nummo's flowing appendages were replaced by joints that made it easier to work at the forge and in the fields.[22] After this climactic happening, the seventh Nummo was followed down the rainbow by the leather-working Nummo and others according to their expertise until all eight were assembled on earth, taking their places as the ancestors of the people who were to come. These old ones continue to be honored by the Dogon at their village shrines and altars.

Even before houses were begun, according to tradition, it was the shrine that was the first structure built. In the villages along the Bandiagara cliffs, a shrine might be no more than a wall covering the entrance to a cave, or the plan might be a square with rounded corners forming small towers topped with flat projecting stones to protect the mud plaster from erosion when the rains splashed down (figure G).

Such towers are associated symbolically with altars.[23] A small open space leads to the shrine door above which, customarily, there are two square niches. Between the towers, the facade with parapets of molded adobe is silhouetted against the sky. An iron hook may appear on this cresting. It is to remind the people of the first blacksmith and the importance associated with his occupation. According to Griaule's information, the hook is accepted as a symbol of the anvil carried to earth by the seventh Nummo, whereas the sanctuary itself represents the place where the first smithy was located in a square field as a remembrance of the square roof of Amma's granary.[24]

Like a magnet the iron hook has attracted layered meanings that increase with each generation. Branches seem to expand from the vertical shaft. The ends of these are tightly curled like the horns of the celestial ram. The spiraling horns are associated with rain clouds swirling across the sky and bringing in their wake the long-awaited rainy season. The horns are also equated with cupped hands that carry the moisture and, therefore, ensure a rich harvest.[25] "Because of the beneficent properties of these iron hooks," Griaule was told, "and in memory of the eight ancestors, eight ears of corn gathered at the harvesting of the field belonging to the sanctuary are hung at the top of the facade . . . when sowing is to begin, the ears which are to provide

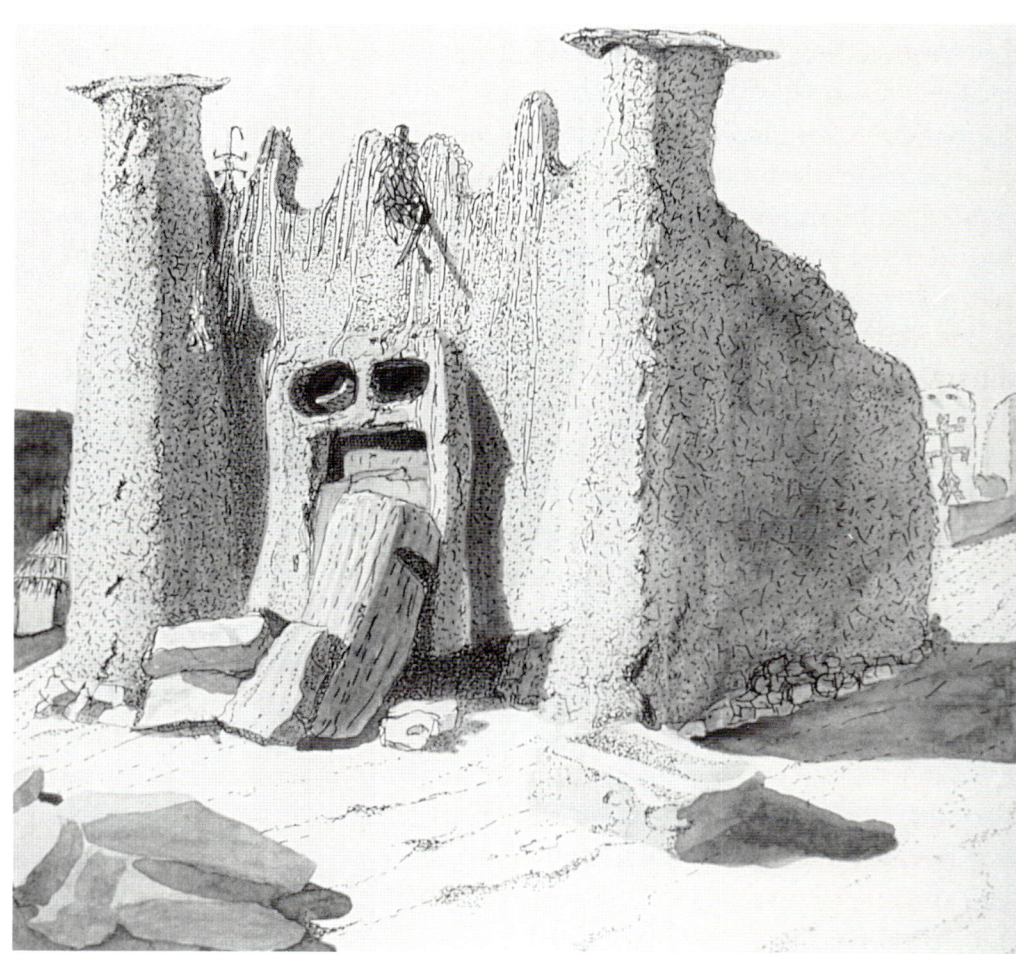

*Fig. G
Dogon shrine, Mali.
Drawing by Virginia
Mahaley Thompson.*

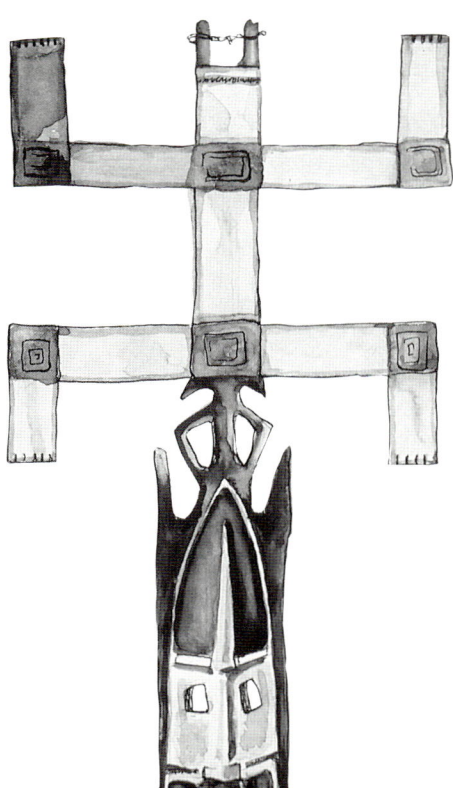

*Fig. H
Dogon* Kanaga *mask,
Mali. Sketch by E. S.
Sasser.*

the seed are spread on the roof. There they absorb . . . the forces of renewal" present in the symbolic horns.[26]

In the midst of stark aridity during the season when no rain comes, water is a precious commodity that is obtained only with perseverance and effort. Because of this, creatures associated with wet places are considered benevolent and essential to the well-being of the Dogon. One of these is the crocodile. The belief that is passed from father to son is that the first human inhabitant of the escarpment became very thirsty. He saw a crocodile and followed it, hoping that it would lead him to a place where water could be found. Suddenly he was standing at the edge of a large pool guided there by the reptile. From that day until the present, crocodiles are viewed as friends. No Dogon would ever wound a crocodile, and the crocodiles in their turn have returned the favor of nonviolence.

Kjermeier believes it is the crocodile that is intended by the abstraction appearing on the Dogon *kanaga* mask.[27] The tall wood carving, resembling the Cross of Lorraine, is reduced to a bare essentiality befitting the leanness that is a part of existence in an arid land (figure H). The double cruciform is viewed by some scholars as the *komondo,* mythical bird. Seen in this way, the superstructure becomes outstretched wings, whereas the triangular shape of the mask that descends on the wearer's head is equated with a beak.[28]

The Dogon masks, moving through rituals whose origins are lost in time, activate the dark shadows caught in the striations of the cliffs and seem to draw breath from the flames that pierce the blackness. The imagery of height and the extension of the vertical seams in the rock face are present in the most spectacular of all Dogon masks, the Great Mask. More than thirty feet high, it is worn every sixty years at a ritual called the *sigi.* Over the angular face, there is a geometric design connected to wide-open jaws that are a reminder of the crocodile who befriended the first Dogon.[29] Kept in a shrine where offerings are brought to honor it, this "Mother Mask" is regarded as the abode of the primeval human soul and the immortal life force.[30]

The rich ceremonial heritage has been maintained over the centuries by the Dogon despite life in a difficult climate, where heat and aridity are broken by infrequent rains. Building materials are largely earth and rocks. Densely structured villages cling to footholds in the cliffs. The tan earthen walls are clustered like honeycombs receiving the full impact of sunlight and dramatic shadows. The simple architectural masses are present in the abstract boldness of the masks and sculpture.

The Dogon way of life offers a stark contrast to that of the Senufo, agriculturists, who inhabit the fertile and rainy hinterlands of Ivory

Coast. In a landscape of tall grass and tangled bush, the vegetation is reflected in the roofs of natural fibers that overhang the clay walls. The masks of the Senufo possess the complexity and grotesqueness associated with the fearful creatures, real and imaginary, that wait in the underbrush. The results of contrasting environments and the effects exerted on art and architecture are vividly illustrated by the Senufo farmers of the savannas and the Dogon who inhabit a semiarid land.

II

The Senufo
Inhabitants of the Savannas and Woodlands of Ivory Coast

"Do not call the forest that shelters you a jungle."

an African Proverb

The Africans living away from modern cities frequently follow the ways of their ancestors when shelters are built. The materials used are those found in nature; they are free and rarely need to be transported over long distances. In short, building a shelter requires diligence and hard work but little capital. The Dogon, as has been pointed out, cope with arid conditions and little arable land by creating villages of mud and stone that adhere to the cliffs like wasps' nest in order to preserve the flat fields at the cliff base for subsistence farming. In the moist savannas, grasslands are interspersed with dense patches of bush. The Senufo of Ivory Coast are inheritors of a productive agriculture, thanks to adequate rain and good soil. The abundance of grass provides building material, particularly for making roofs; clay is available for adobe walls, and wood is obtained from nearby groves.

The rainfall that makes farming a profitable occupation for the Senufo amounts to more than forty inches a year with a dry season from December to January. The moisture is coupled with temperatures ranging from sixty-eight degrees Fahrenheit in the winter to eighty-six degrees Fahrenheit or above in the summer. Thus the growing season is extended throughout most of the year. René Gardi describes the rotation of the seasonal labors in this way:

> . . . the dry season . . . is the time for clearing and hoeing, then the first yams are planted. February and March mark the last weeding and loosening of the soil. . . . [When] the first

rains have come in April, the corn is planted, then manioc
and sweet potatoes, and finally peanuts. . . . During the long
rainy season, in June until July, come the first harvests of
yams. These fields are then lightly hoed, and beans are planted
(millet in the north). At the end of July, the corn planted in
April is harvested, and after a superficial hoeing, a second crop
is planted. August through September is a strenuous period.
Rice is planted—with an ingenious irrigation system that
requires maintenance—the second corn crop is harvested,
then manioc, peanuts, sweet potatoes. The rice is weeded and
the beds improved. October through November is the season
for harvesting the rice and picking cotton. [Cotton has
recently become a profitable crop for the Senufo.] . . . But
that is not all. Bananas, tobacco, pepper, and all sorts of
vegetables are planted near the villages. Calabashes are made
from the woody shells of enormous gourds. The women and
children gather the fruits of the karite tree that grows wild,
and from which they produce butter [an ingredient particularly sought after for use in cooking].[31]

After such a recital of productivity from the intensive cultivation of the land, it would be surprising if the Senufo did not place a
high value on the skills of the farmer. For a young man to be recognized
as "a disciplined and skilled cultivator" is at the center of the Senufo
sense of identity.[32] One of the most sought-after honors is to be chosen
as "a champion cultivator." Hoeing competitions are taken as seriously
as the challenge offered to the world's best athletes by the Olympic
Games. Contests in wielding the hoe are multimedia events involving
songs, dances, the display of sculpture, and other traditional observances. The winner of such a competition is awarded the "champion-
cultivator staff" as a trophy. This is passed from one generation to the
next and is prominently displayed at the funeral rites held for important
elders.[33]

Certain compounds in a village are designated as the quarters of
the farmers, known as *Fodonon*. A family unit is the *katiolo*, based on a
matrilineal clan.[34] This arrangement includes several households that
work together in the fields and share produce that is communally
harvested. A number of interrelated *katiolos*, including those allotted
to artisans, form a settlement that may have a population of eight
hundred people or as many as twelve hundred.

Each of the *katiolos* is self-contained and physically marked off
from neighboring enclaves. If the compound is located on the village
outskirts, a semicircular boundary defining one side of the settlement

will be oriented to the fields beyond the village. Mud walls between structures and the open landscape ensure protection and privacy (figure I). The most prominently positioned house is that of the head man. Each of his wives with her children occupies her own quarters. If there is a former chief or elder statesman, he, too, has a place. Recently completed buildings tend toward rectangular plans with walls of mud brick covered by corrugated tin roofs. The older buildings and granaries are usually circular. Granaries are built so they act as buttresses for the houses or to reinforce family courtyard barriers. A guardian of life and the continuity of the family group, the granary is a place for the storage of yams and rice, the primary foods until the following harvest. Because the Senufo have less to fear from drought and famine than the Dogon, the largest granary in a *katiolo* is selected for storing the food supply necessary at important funeral celebrations.[35]

A large open space on which the courtyards face is used as an out-of-door work area (figure J). It is particularly auspicious to have a mango or other shade tree spreading cool shadows over the communal activities of cooking and gossiping. There are hearths for preparing food, a roofed kitchen for boiling *karite* butter, as well as a grass thatched "shade," lifted on four forked wooden posts to provide protection for the animals—an assortment of goats, fowl, and an occasional cow. In this shared area, several huts containing fetish figures and sacred objects are located.

As in the Dogon villages along the Bandiagara Escarpment, clay and rocks are serviceable for house construction. Because the grassland people have little access to stone, mud is the primary material for building walls. Working with adobe is much the same throughout sub-Saharan Africa, even though the finished wall treatment may vary in appearance and texture. Pits are dug in the earth to contain the clay and sandy laterite; to these ingredients water is added and the mixture is kneaded with bare feet. Chopped straw or cow dung thrown into the mud paste acts as a binder. Gardi points out that the latter additions release microorganisms that encourage "chemical and biological processes that promote hardening."[36] The addition of ground rubble from buildings that have crumbled with age, or soil from termite mounds containing sticky slime are believed by some to be beneficial to the concoction. After the first trampling of the mud, the clay is aged, that is, allowed "to ripen" before more water is added and another kneading occurs. Once the mixture has been seasoned properly, the workers exchange their feet for hands, the best possible tool for laying up walls. A technique used in some Senufo villages is that of shaping the clay into balls. These may be pressed into rolls or simply added in ball shape to the wall under construction. The clay units are pressed together and

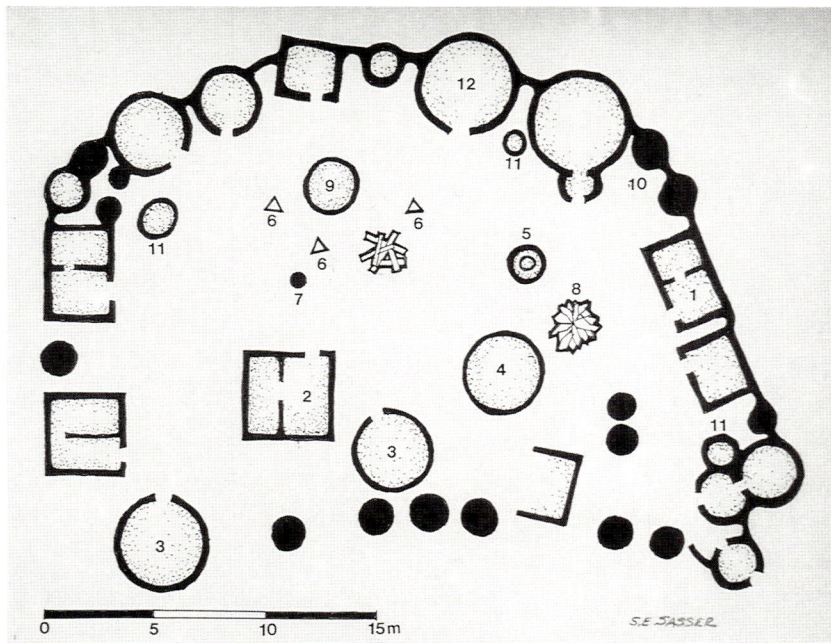

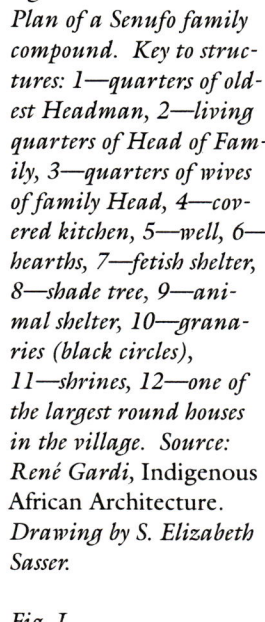

Fig. I
Plan of a Senufo family compound. Key to structures: 1—quarters of oldest Headman, 2—living quarters of Head of Family, 3—quarters of wives of family Head, 4—covered kitchen, 5—well, 6—hearths, 7—fetish shelter, 8—shade tree, 9—animal shelter, 10—granaries (black circles), 11—shrines, 12—one of the largest round houses in the village. Source: René Gardi, Indigenous African Architecture. *Drawing by S. Elizabeth Sasser.*

Fig. J
Senufo compound courtyard. Drawing by Virginia Mahaley Thompson.

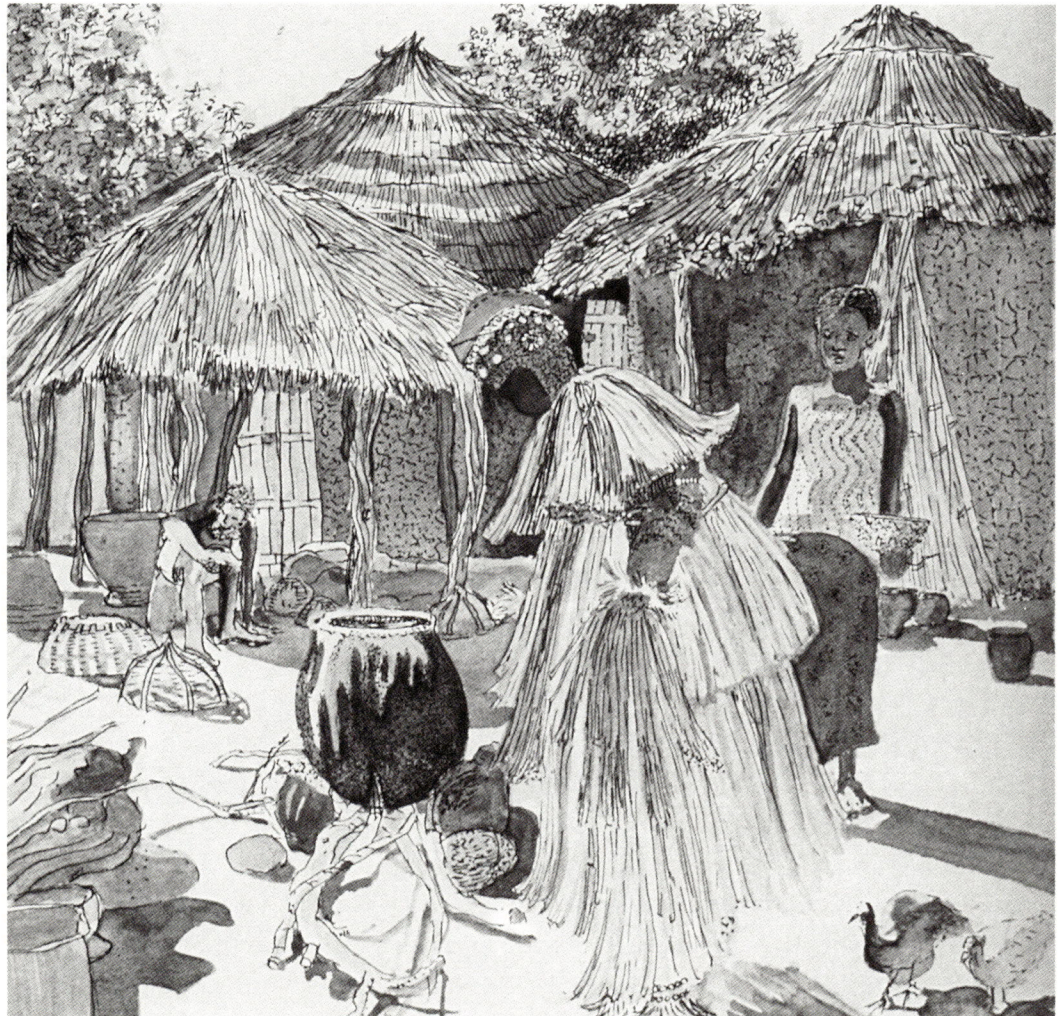

smoothed to eliminate cracks that develop as the clay dries. The Senufo men are the builders, whereas the women's work is carrying water to moisten the clay and mixing the paste to smooth over the wall surface. The heat of the African sun is the drying agent. Like Dogon dwellings, the Senufo adobe walls are not punctuated by windows. The mud walls would be weakened by openings, and the shade provided by the dark interiors gives welcome relief from the brightness outside in the court-yards or fields where daily tasks are performed.

The rains that allow a long growing season, also provide the Senufo with some wood for building and carving. Trees clustered near the *katiolo* and the dense growth in the nearby "bush" supply forked tree trunks and sizable branches to drive into the ground to reinforce the adobe walls and to support grass roofs.

In the savannas, grasses are woven into baskets and by extension used for thatching. Grass or straw is gathered, bundled and bound to thatch the framework of the peaked roofs. In some areas, roofs are made at a time when work in the fields is forced to wait upon the weather and well in advance of a structure's completion. It is reported that upon occasion eight or ten legs may be seen walking a roof to the site where it will be placed on top of a granary or other building. Unlike the beautifully woven roofs seen in the Mandara Mountains of Cameroon, Senufo roofs are shaggy like the raffia that is used as costuming for masquerades, a term applied throughout western sub-Saharan Africa to the masked dances and ceremonies.

It is not only farmers that contribute to the self-sufficiency and well-being of a village, but the various craftsmen who are respected members of the community and have their own living areas. The blacksmiths, or *Fono,* occupy a place of special importance in the farm community. Just as the blacksmith Nummo of the Dogon forged the tools placed on top of the granary that was carried to earth, Senufo smiths hammer into shape the scooped-out blades of the short-handled hoes. They also carve and attach the wooden hoe handles that make it easier for the farmer to cultivate his fields efficiently.[37] Anita Glaze describes the *tiya* or arched hoe as "a tool that exhibits an impressive sculptural quality in its balanced design and purity of form."[38] One of the first skills taught an apprentice blacksmith before he approaches the forge is working with wood. The techniques learned are sometimes put to use in carving figures.

The Senufo believe that the creator deity distributed all of the social orders when people were first placed on earth. Each group was assigned a special occupation—farmers, wood-carvers, blacksmiths, and another class of metal workers, the brass casters. The brass casting industry has died out in recent times, but according to Anita Glaze, from 1969 to 1970, there were two Senufo master workers in brass in the kufuolo region. The unusual mask shown in figure K represents the skill of a brass caster known as Songi of Dikodougou.[39]

Among some African ethnic groups, the wives of blacksmiths are the potters. This is logical because fire is used both at the forge and for firing clay vessels to make them strong and waterproof. The women, however, married to Senufo smiths practice the craft of basketmaking. This is also related to the nature of the smithy, which in Senufo villages is a large subterranean pit located on the outskirts of the quarter inhabited by the blacksmiths. The pit, entered by means of a log ladder, is kept covered at night and in rainy weather to protect the interior from downpours and to keep the secrets of the craft from prying eyes. During the heat of the day, the underground space is cooler for the smith's work with molten metal, and it provides the smith's wife an ideal place to keep a supply of moist and supple fibers for plaiting baskets and mats.[40]

With land on which to spread out, the Senufo are able to allot generous spaces for farming and for personal and ceremonial needs. Huts, called *sinzanga,* are hidden in the dense groves that hem the edges of a settled area. These are the retreats associated with Poro organizations for men. The *sinzanga* are used for teaching, holding political meetings, and for religious observances. Some mud structures are for boys passing through the stages of initiation that end when they are qualified to become "finished men", thus attaining full membership in Poro.[41] The huts also provide storage space for elaborate masks and ceremonial regalia and as staging areas where initiates prepare for ritual performances.[42]

Each *katiolo* has its own Poro society. The function of Poro in Glaze's words is "to tame and civilize, to inculcate values and standards of behavior in each generation."[43] Other duties are to protect members and their families from evil forces through the knowledge of secret magic and power-filled ceremonies and to participate in elaborate funerals for village elders.

Sandogo is the organization for women. To gain acceptance by the village, it is necessary for a man to be a member of Poro; this is not the case with Sandogo. Not all women are required to join, but every family must be represented by a Sandogo member.[44] If Poro has the responsibility for supervising the social, political, and economic health of the community and honoring the dead with great funerals; the women of Sandogo are the intermediaries between the people and the gods, the ancestors, and the bush spirits.[45] It is towards these three classes of spiritual beings that religious worship, prayers, and sacrifices are directed. The responsibility of maintaining the goodwill and blessings of the supernatural ones is the particular province of Sandogo. Bush spirits can be unruly and dangerous. These entities inhabit the streams and fields, where farmers may accidentally act at cross-purposes with them when the crops are sown or harvested. The Sando diviners are skilled at gestures of appeasement and diplomacy to restore the spirits' goodwill.[46]

The women have round shrine houses, topped by grass roofs, similar to the houses found in the *katiolos*. The grasses used for roofing among the Senufo, form a unity with the masks and dance costumes that employ the same textured tendrils, just as the austere massiveness and abstraction of Dogon masks are related to the solid geometry of the houses and shrines built against the cliffs. In the savanna, where the flowing grasses sweep over the countryside and rotund granaries nap under a fringe of straw in the noonday sun, the masqueraders wear voluminous skirts of grass or raffia. Raffia cuffs are tied around the ankles and on the wrists. A high raffia polychrome collar hides the base of a helmet mask. Layers of raffia wrapped about the body create a shape like a moving mound or anthill covered with tiers of cream and crimson grasses. The Senufo farmer who puts on the *Gbongara* mask (Big Raffia Mask) is jokingly compared to "a haystack in motion."[47] The Senufo say that this costume is "wide like a house."[48] A special enclosure surrounds a dressing room and storehouse built from long bunches of grass thatch where the *Gbongara* mask and costume are kept and the masquerades are practiced. To indicate the relation to the farmers, tall poles with carved hoe handles fastened to their tops enclose the site.[49]

The fiber masquerades of the Senufo introduce a fascinating dimension to African art, an art that is customarily thought of in terms of wood carving or metal. Anita Glaze calls the *Yalimidyo* masquerade, in which fiber costuming is introduced, a "striking example of soft sculpture, created by a mixed-media assemblage incorporating stuffed fibers, textiles, metal, and cloth appliqué [and] braiding."[50]

If the variety of fibers used in the costumes for the masquerades is synonymous with the grasslands of the savannas, there are other types of masks influenced by the threatening "bush." One of these constructions is the Senufo zoomorphic helmet mask carved from wood (figure L). It thrusts out fierce tusks and horns, and double lines of teeth. Hyena and wildcat skins are added to the costuming. Grass and raffia are ignored, although green leaves from the sacred grove are joined by porcupine quills representing the lethal arrows, tipped with herbal poisons, used against an enemy. The mask is the embodiment of the knowledge and sorcery necessary to turn aside dangerous animals or humans; it speaks of blood and danger. It is an anti-evil device, intended to thwart aggression, either earthly or that sent by malevolent spirits bent on disrupting the harmoniousness of life.

In contrast, the animal masks of the Dogon are Apollonian in their calm abstraction (see figures E and H). On the arid plateaux, little is hidden from sight. The contrast is clearly drawn between the imagery of the inhabitants of a land where the sun shines in the clear air, where the eyes can travel to distant horizons, and those who live close to thick wooded growth and impenetrable brush that turn the day into perpetual gloom and night into a frightening blackness that conceals unimaginable and terrifying creatures.

It could be said with some truth, "We are where we live."

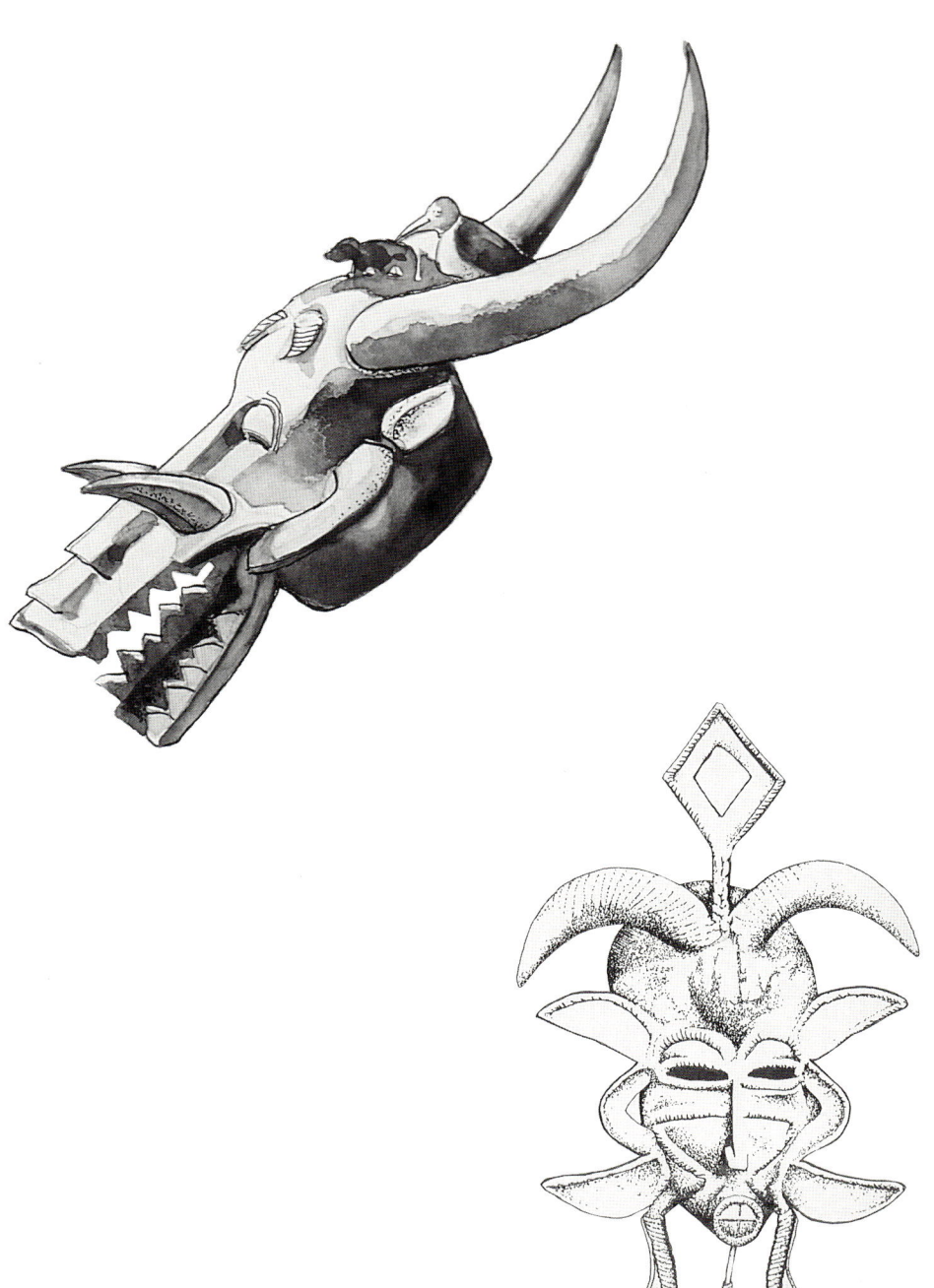

Fig. L
Senufo Kponyugo *mask.*
Sketch by
E. S. Sasser.

Fig. K
Brass mask by Songi of Dikodougou (Senufo). Source: Anita Glaze, Art and Death in a Senufo Village. *Sketch by S. Elizabeth Sasser.*

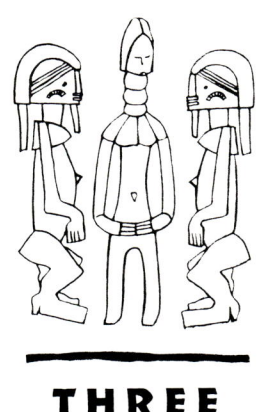

THREE

Craftsmen:
Their Materials, Techniques,
and Aesthetic Values

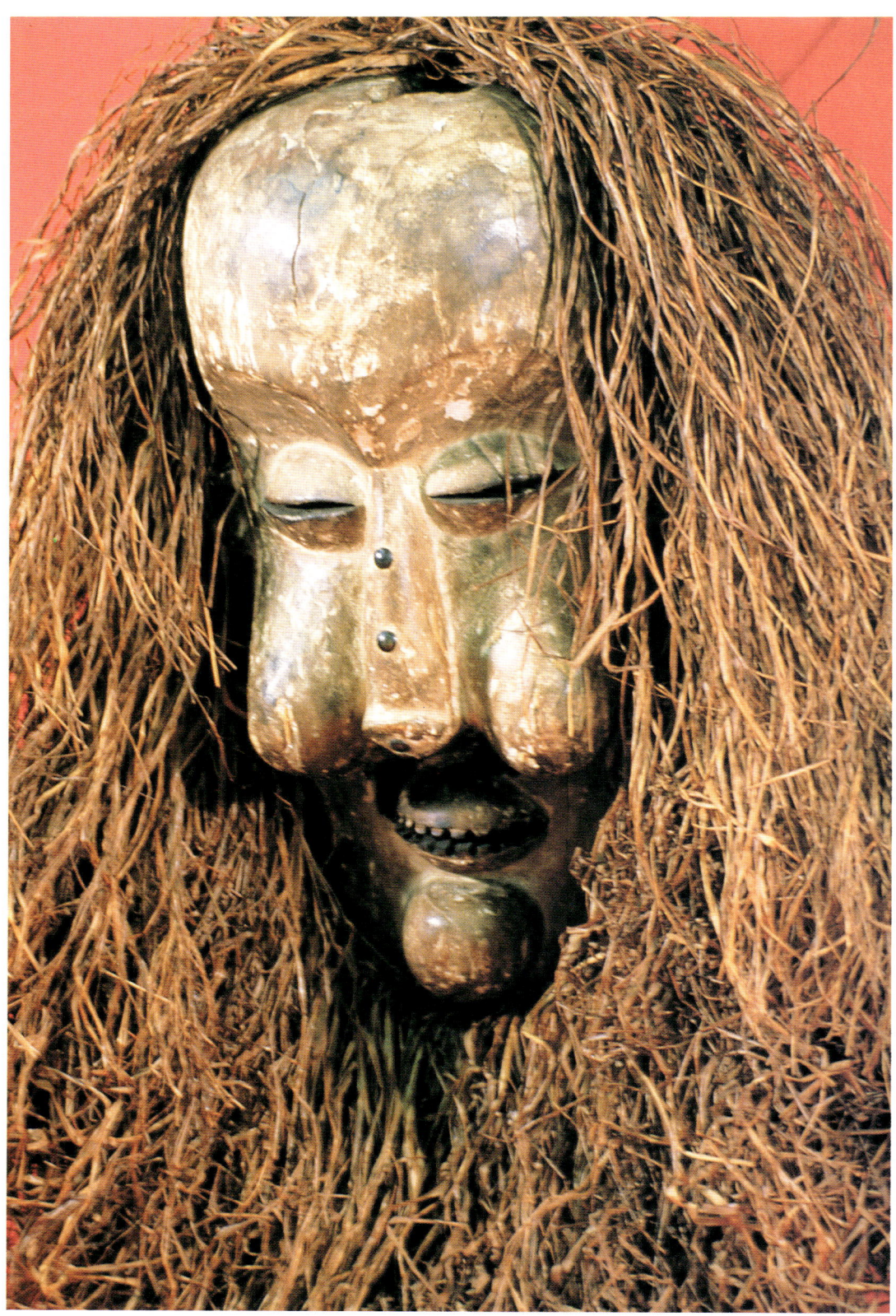

Fig. 7
Kakungu *mask, Suku, Zaire, wood, raffia, H. 29 in.*

I
Working with Wood

I shall always praise you, Olowe!

Olowe, who carves the iroko tree,

The master carver,

❧

Who carves the iroko tree with the ease

of carving a calabash.

quoted by JOHN PEMBERTON in

The Traditional Artist in African Society

Undoubtedly, many small boys (in ethnic African societies, boys, and rarely girls, were taught the crafts of wood carving and working metal at the forge), watching their elders shape branches and tree trunks into figures of hunters, mothers and infants, ancestors or supernaturals, coaxed fathers and uncles to let them try their hand at making wooden people and animals. Such experiments in childhood helped to establish a community of adults who from their own experiences are able to understand and appreciate the work of the specialist carver. When an adolescent displayed an unusual talent at carving wood, further training was given by a family member or an apprenticeship was arranged with a well-known craftsman in another village.[1] The Yoruba believed that a boy whose work exhibited a skill above the ordinary received his ability at birth from the sky god Olorum. This concept provided youngsters of lesser talent an excuse for their ineptness, after all they were not the lucky ones upon whom the god smiled.[2]

The art of carving flourished with special vigor in the moist savannas and tropical forests of western sub-Saharan Africa where wood was easy to acquire. Wood carving developed among agriculturists whose sedentary lifestyle was bound to the fields. During the rainy seasons, those gifted at the craft had the leisure to work on ceremonial objects that would benefit the crops and make the rituals of planting and harvesting more effective. A settled way of life also permitted care and storage of the objects produced.

The wood-carver's work was not intended for museum display or for the building of personal collections. The purposes served were to remind the ancestors and deities that they were not forgotten, to request the benevolence and goodwill of the ancient ones, to ask for aid in averting disaster, to seek a cure for illness, and to turn the ill wishes of malevolent supernaturals and witches against those initiating the intended evil. A carving was expected to fulfill a specific purpose; therefore, the craftsman carried the heavy burden of producing a piece that satisfied the expectations of a family or group and was also pleasing to the gods and ancestors.

To become adept at working with wood, apprenticeship customarily began when a boy was between the ages of twelve and eighteen. When a master carver accepted a pupil, the amount to be paid for his training was determined. This might include a goat and a large calabash of palm wine plus a sum of money. John C. Messenger writes that at mid-twentieth century among the Anang there was a fee of six pounds and five shillings (about $9.88 today) for a year's training.[3] In return, the pupil received from the teacher food, materials, and often shelter. It was not unusual, in the years after the apprenticeship was successfully concluded, for a former student to continue to pay the master a part of each commission that he completed.

At first the apprentice acted as hands and feet for the instructor; he picked up scraps, cleaned the work area, and ran errands. While doing the menial jobs, he learned by watching the work in progress. The first work allotted to him would be peeling the bark from a part of a branch or tree trunk and cutting away the outer portions, readying it for the master. The next step might involve carving simple objects to which the teacher would add the finishing touches. As technical proficiency grew, the assignments became more difficult. When a carving was finished by the apprentice, it belonged to the instructor as did any payment that might be received for it.

For the master craftsman, a commission began with the thoughtful selection of a tree from which the carving would be made. The African approach to working with wood parallels the respect and veneration for nature's materials that is held by the Japanese. In Japan the term *kami* is associated with Shinto and the belief that all things animate and inanimate—rocks, trees, streams, minerals, animals—possess spirit. Traditionally, a tree chosen by the African carver is regarded as a living entity. Because spirits are believed to inhabit trees, before work can be undertaken, the artist must propitiate the forces that his ax and knives will release. Appropriate rituals are necessary. This ensures that any pain caused the tree by cutting and shaping its wood will win the forgiveness of the spirit force. Throughout the process of carving, the craftsman prays, makes sacrifices, and fasts to bring about the success of his work. Acquiring the right tree frequently involves lengthy negotiations with the tree's owner. An Anang craftsman, who met the terms asked by the owner of an anukot tree, paid a pound sterling, made a gift of a cock, and was expected to cut down the tree.[4]

A characteristic of the anukot tree, preferred by Anang carvers, is a thick sap that seeps out when it is first cut; in time the sap dries and the wood becomes lighter, making it an agreeable material especially for carving masks, whose weight is important.

The techniques used in carving are dictated to some extent by the type of wood that is available. In the Sudan, where hard wood is found, surfaces of the finished object tend to be angular and somewhat rough in texture. Softer woods receive a smoother and more polished finish. If the dense and finely grained ebony or mahogany are at hand, rubbing results in a handsome sheen. To be useful, a tree should be at least five years old or older. A craftsman might expect a large tree to give sufficient wood to last for a year.

The first step, following the rituals addressed to the spirit of the tree by the carver, is to remove the bark from a selected portion of the log. This process is carried out with an ax; the wood is then smoothed and scraped with an adz, a tool that has an arched blade set at right angles to the handle.[5] A chisel or knife is selected for the finest details. When an opening is required as a part of the design, for example, a separation of the legs or of elbows bent at right angles to the body, if a drill is not available, a hole penetrating the wood is begun by applying a piece of red hot iron to the surface. If tradition is observed, the final polish is brought about by rubbing the carving with splinters of stone or abrasives.

The carved figures are often left unpainted, but the green wood preferred by the craftsmen requires protection from termites and weathering. Naturally light in color, the wood receives a finish, both protective and admired, by immersing the carving in a mud bath for several days. When the immersion is completed, the figure is blackened with smoke and dust is rubbed into the surface. A further treatment may be given by the addition of palm oil and resins mixed with soot. The handsome bronze-colored patina that is sometimes seen is a result of age and of many hands rubbing and touching the piece, as well as from blood offerings and beer. A dark patina and polished surface are apparent in figure 1 (All figures with numerical designations unless otherwise indicated are from the African Collection of the Museum of Texas Tech University), whereas in figure 2 the natural wood is partially revealed.

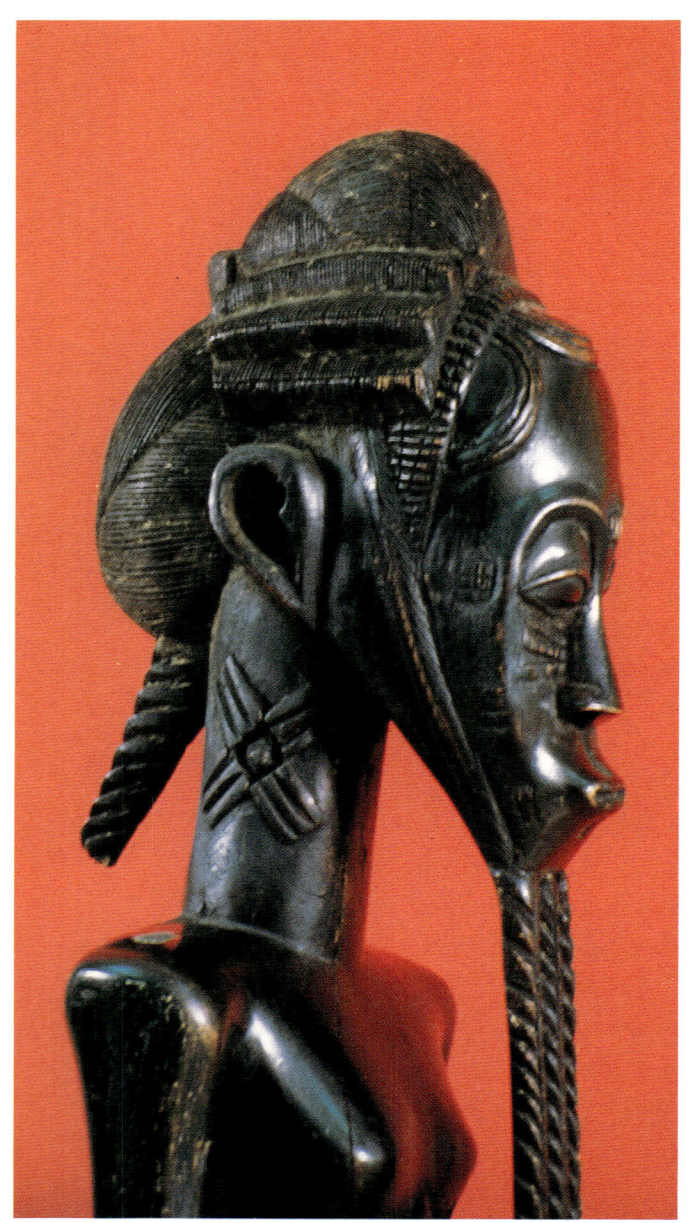

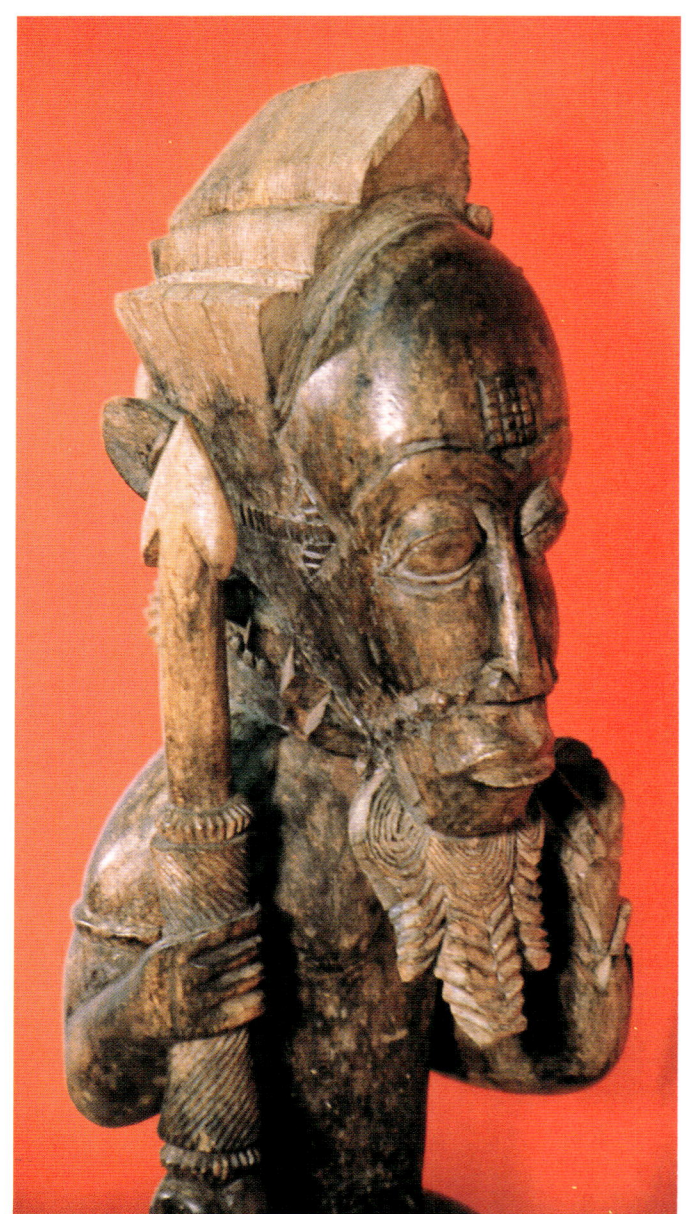

Fig. 1
Detail of seated male
figure (side view),
Baule, Ivory Coast,
wood, H. 32 in.

Fig. 2
Detail of seated male
figure, Baule, Ivory
Coast, wood,
H. 22 ½ in.

The African carver does not work from sketches but approaches the roundness of the tree trunk directly, though he may notch the wood to indicate the placement of head and neck, torso, legs, and other anatomical parts. Realism in the western sense is not an aim. The cylindrical tree trunks and branches dictate both the size and the shape of a figure. Separately carved parts are rarely added. In freeing the carving from the wood, the quality of solidity is a constant reminder of the monolithic nature of the wooden block.

The differences in figurative carving and crafting a mask result from the functions of each. A mask, which will be worn, is carved from light wood, while figurative sculpture is solid and heaviness may be equated with a firm balance. Wood selected for its fine grain is preferred (figure 3). A figurative sculpture is expected to have greater longevity than a mask. A figure is usually passive; although some carvings are carried in masquerades by the dancers. The primary purpose of masks is participation in the intense drama of multimedia events. Performance-oriented, the mask is a dramatic device that quivers and moves with the motion of the dancer, but balance and stability must be maintained while the wearer is engaged in vigorous actions (figure 4). Color and texture as well as form are necessary for an easy identification of the masqueraders, who are frequently seen at night in the light from darting flames of a bonfire. Mask designs are associated with specific societies and with particular ceremonies; some masks are intended to be kept from year to year and refurbished; others are discarded after a single appearance and new ones made.

Despite hundreds of mask types that differ according to ethnic groups and geographic areas, in the first stages of construction, masks of wood are begun in much the same way. (Wood is the usual material, but some masks are made from combinations of wood, metal, cloth, animal hides, fur, feathers, fibers, or vegetation. See figures 5, 6, 7, 8.) The mask size determines the part of the tree trunk selected. Once the proper diameter of the log is decided upon, a segment is cut away and the bark stripped. If the mask is to be helmet shaped, the entire wooden cylinder is hollowed to slip over the head of the performer (figures 9, 10); a variation in construction is to fasten wood segments together with hide thongs. If a mask is to fit only the face, the log is split in half, permitting two masks to be made. The straight plane of a half cylinder is scooped out to fit the face of the wearer, and the features are carved on the outer curve of the wood from which the bark has been removed. Pronounced features like beaks or snouts may be carved separately and added (figure 11).

The placement of the features, colors, and decorative accessories are stored in the mind of the carver who has watched masquerades and ceremonies from childhood. In Senufo villages, young children have their own masquerade, which is known by the name *Kamuru,* associated with

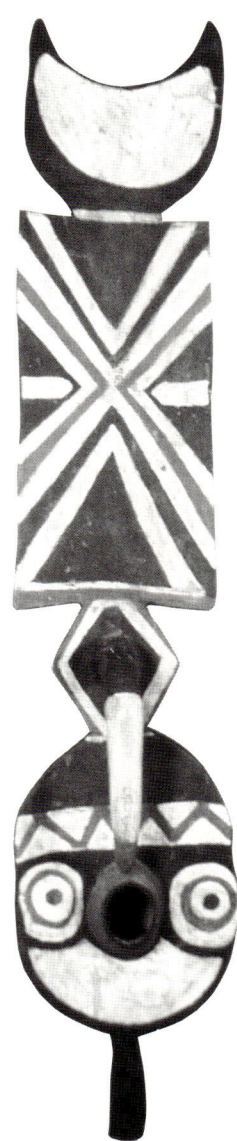

Fig. 4
Mask, Bwa, Burkina Faso, wood and pigment, H. 45 in.

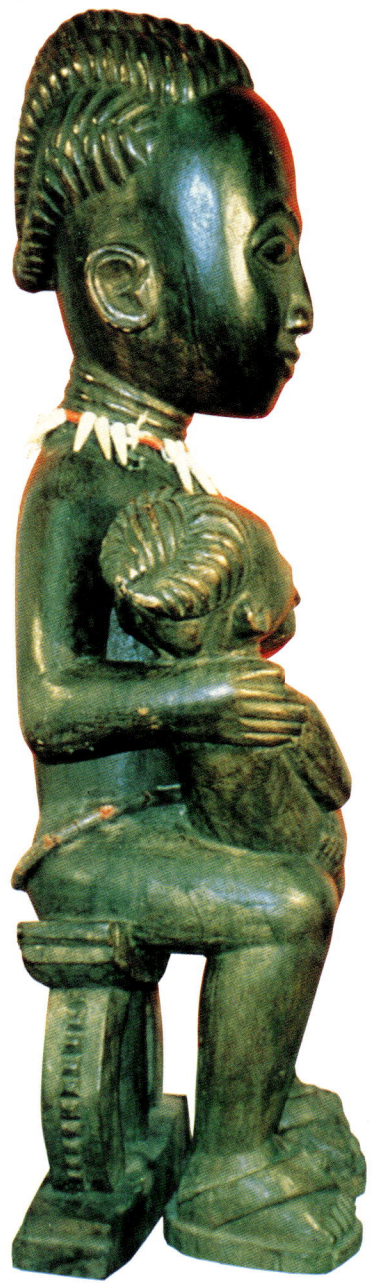

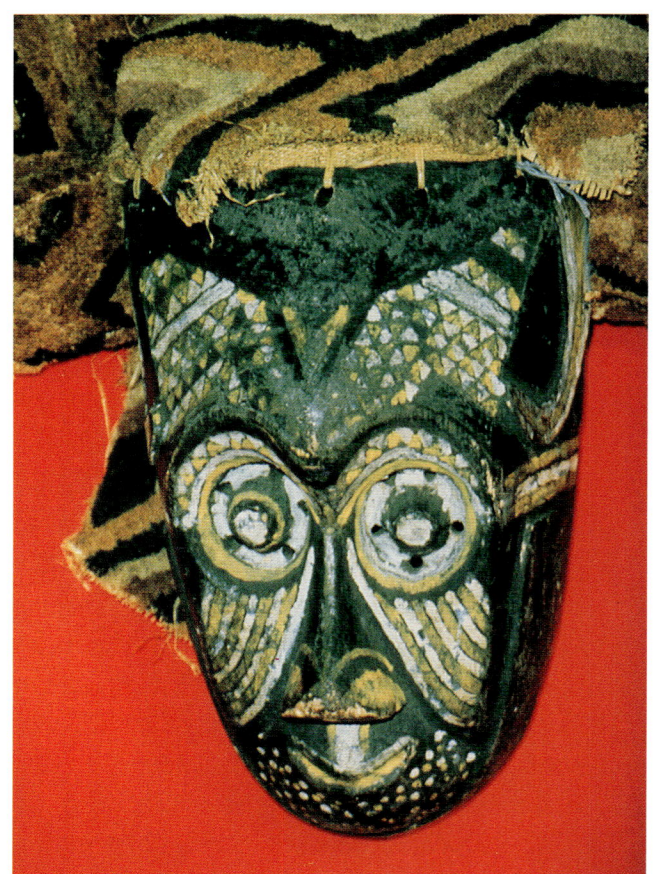

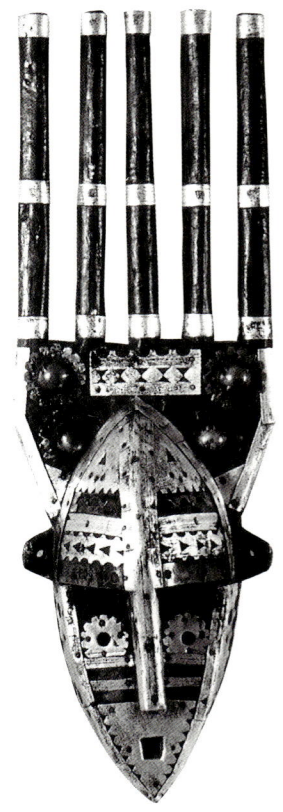

*Fig. 3
Female figure holding a
child, Asante, Ghana,
wood with shell and bead
necklace, H. 37 in.*

*Fig. 6 (Top right)
Mask, Kuba, Zaire,
wood, cloth,
H. 16 ¼ in.*

*Fig. 5 (Bottom)
N'tomo mask, Bamana,
Mali, wood and metal,
H. 23 in.*

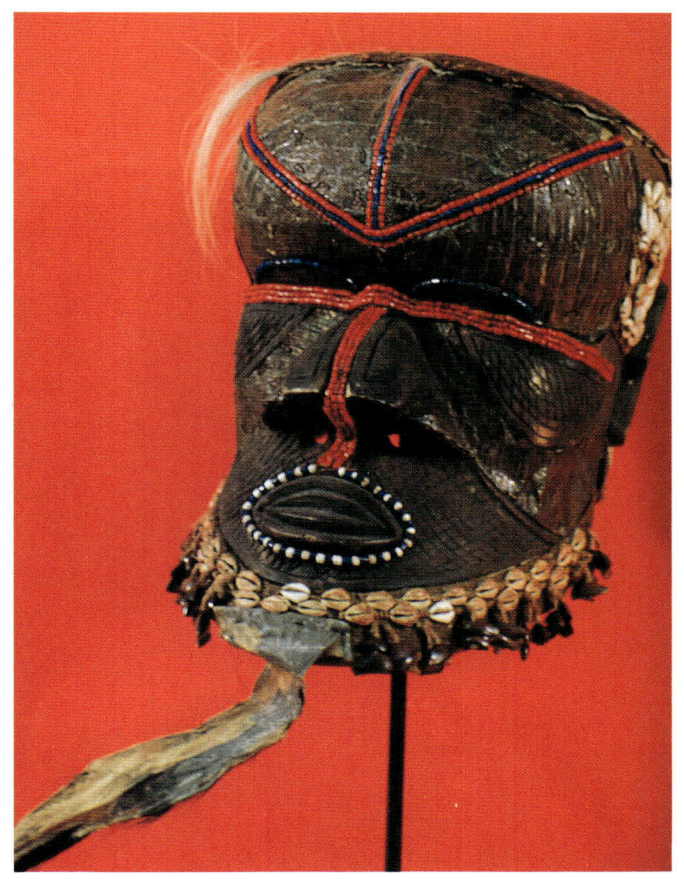

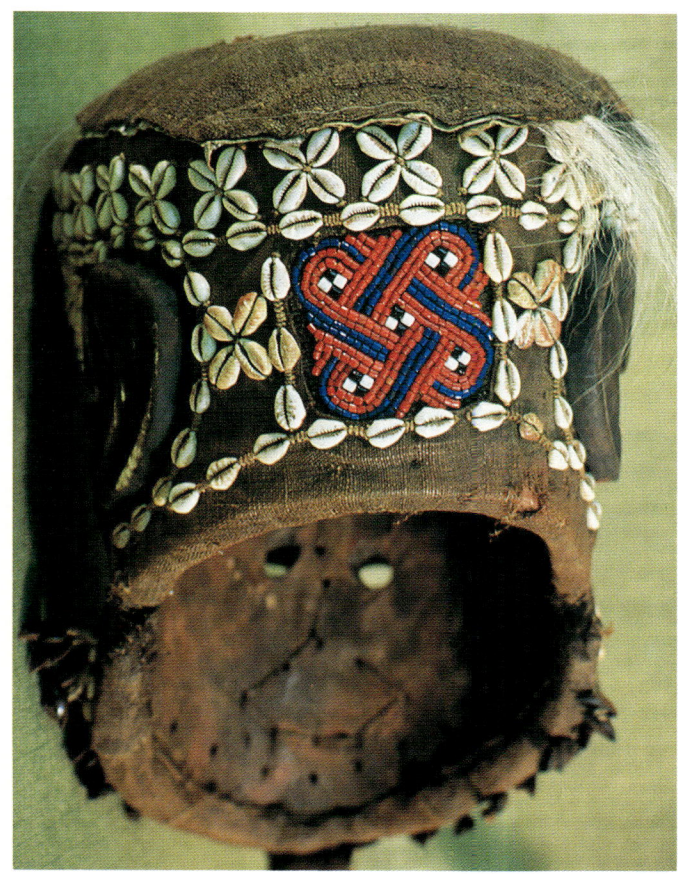

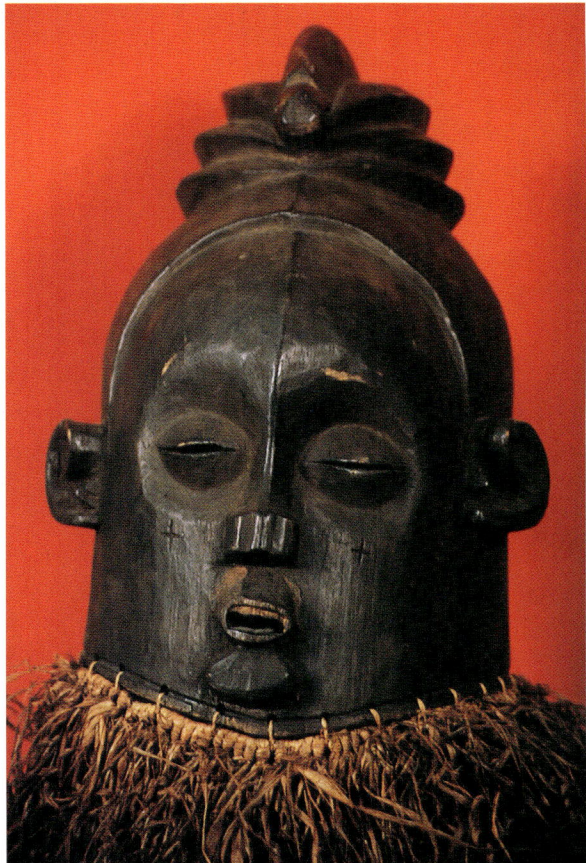

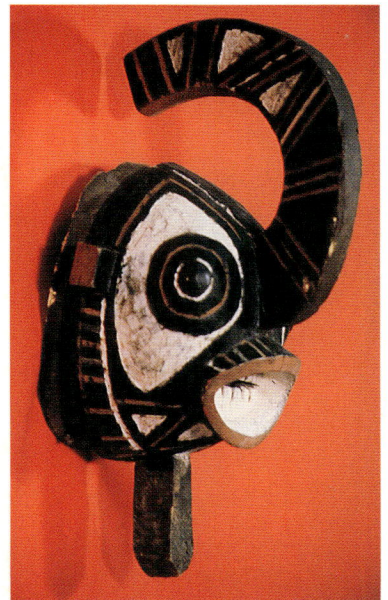

Fig. 8 (Top left)
Mboom *mask (front),*
Kuba, Zaire, wood, glass
beads, cowrie shells, antelope
skin, tufts of hair,
feathers, H. 19 in.

Fig. 10 (Bottom left)
Mask, origin unknown,
wood, raffia, H. 21 in.

Fig. 9 (Top right)
Detail of Mboom *mask*
(back) 8.

Fig. 11 (Bottom right)
Mask, Bwa, Burkina Faso,
wood, pigment,
H. approx. 24 in.

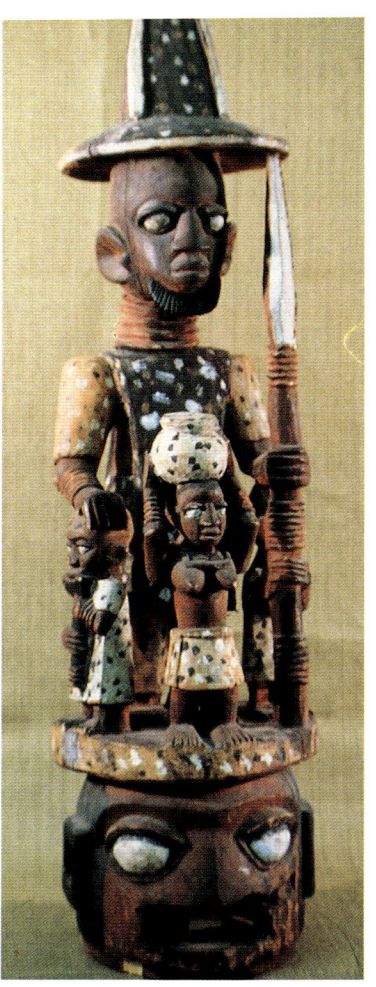

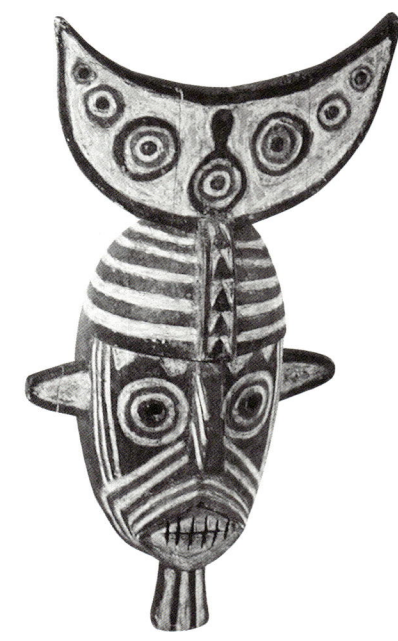

*Fig. 13 (Left)
Epa mask, Yoruba,
Nigeria, wood, pigment,
H. 44 in.*

*Fig. 12 (Right)
Mask, Bwa, Burkina
Faso, wood, pigment,
H. 25 1/4 in.*

the verb *muru* meaning "to open" or "to discover."[6] This is the beginning of the educational system that leads to initiation in the men's Poro Society. When junior masquerades are held, the boys make most of their costumes without adult help. This imitation of their older relatives is described as "free play." The youngsters assemble grass skirts, steal rags in the village and take them to their own "pretend Poro house" where the scraps are converted into the appropriate apparel.[7] This helps to keep alive the knowledge of traditional ceremonies and the appropriate masks and costumes that will be passed from generation to generation.

Like the figurative sculptures that are smoked, rubbed with soot, and carefully polished until they seem to shine, masks are often completed in the same manner; however, many are painted. If the mask is to be given color, the carved wood must be allowed to dry thoroughly. After the drying process is finished, the features are sharpened and defined with a knife or scraper. In the past, the wood was first coated with a gessolike substance on which colors made from ground minerals or clays of red, ochre, gray, and white were painted with fiber brushes.

Black was ground from charcoal. Today, tempera paints and oils are usually purchased at a trading post or store. Masks are often elaborately decorated with a veritable collage, ranging from feathers, beads, and cowrie shells to bits of glass, mirrors, polished strips of leather and metal, tusks, teeth, hair, and animal skins (figure 8). Messenger explains that in the past the raffia, attached to holes in the lower portion of a mask to disguise the neck and shoulders of the wearer, was added by the carver (figure 10); now, when the mask is finished it is turned over to a specialist for the addition of the long grasses.

Masks vary in size and proportion. Some cover the face and frontal hair (figure 12); others are topped with tall headdresses that rise high above the human head like the Epa mask of the Yoruba (figure 13). If the size is larger than the wearer's head, the eye openings are cut into a lower portion of the mask instead of the eye sockets. An open mouth may allow the wearer to see. To steady and balance a large mask during a masquerade, a taut rope is stretched across the inside of the carving. The wearer grips this in his teeth to help control the gyrations of the cumbersome carving.[8] With care, a mask can last for several decades. This necessitates oiling the carving each year, repainting it when necessary, and hanging it in a storage hut well above ground level to keep it from attracting a trail of termites.

Some masks and many figurative sculptures are made of metal, which is the next material to be investigated.

II

Working with Metal

When they fire the high furnace,
One transforms another into a hoe.
When they fire the high furnace,
One transforms another into a pretty
little mortar.
Real smiths are the masters of sorcery.

Lines from a masquerade performance,
translated by PATRICK MCNAUGHTON

Although the craft of iron is not represented in the collection of western sub-Saharan African objects at the Museum of Texas Tech

University, iron smelting and forging cannot be ignored any more than it is possible to omit the significance of the blacksmith in ethnic societies. Figures M and 14 illustrate the results of forging iron. The man and his horse (figure 14) made by Mamade Konnah (figure N), a blacksmith in the Liberian village of Naama, is from the collection of John O. Evans. The grass-roofed smithy where Konnah worked is shown in figure O.

Whether a smith worked metal at a smelting furnace in a thatched rectangular shelter, in a conical clay tower, or in a subterranean pit, his first duty was to serve the people by making weapons for hunters and warriors and supplying the agriculturists with farm implements. Lines from an epic poem proclaim:

> The world . . . begin[s] with farming
> And it will end with farming.[9]

Today, as in earlier times, just before the rains arrive to herald the approach of the new planting season, people go to the blacksmith to have old hoes repaired or new ones made. The blades range in size and shape and are hafted to wooden handles. The blacksmith is responsible for crafting spades, picks, and cutting tools for the harvest.

Over and beyond the practical skills that give importance to the blacksmith's work, he is believed to have powers not possessed by ordinary humans. His work causes him to go into the bush to get wood for the fire; this means that there is a risk of encounters with the frightening and capricious spirits that reside in the thick underbrush. The awe with which the blacksmith is viewed is associated not only with an ability to overcome danger but because he possesses *nyama,* a potent energy present in organic and inorganic matter. *Nyama* is released at the furnace and anvil of the blacksmith as he controls the flames that transform the flow of matter from an incandescent fluid to the heaviness and mass of iron.

Fire is a servant of man, but it is also an enemy. When lightning strikes in the heart of the forest, fire may spread in a raging sheet, devouring everything in its path. Among the Yoruba, Shango was revered as the mythic third king and the god of thunder and storms. Some believe that when Shango blinks, a lightning bolt will crash down to earth.[10] Shango's mate was Oyo, goddess of the Niger River. Thus, fire and water were united, just as both are essential at the blacksmith's forge.

One of the Dogon's mythical ancestors was a smith, and all later smiths are believed to be his descendants. Wrought iron objects hammered out at the forge are found at shrines dedicated to Shango. In Mali, forging ceremonial staffs topped with iron sculpture is an important

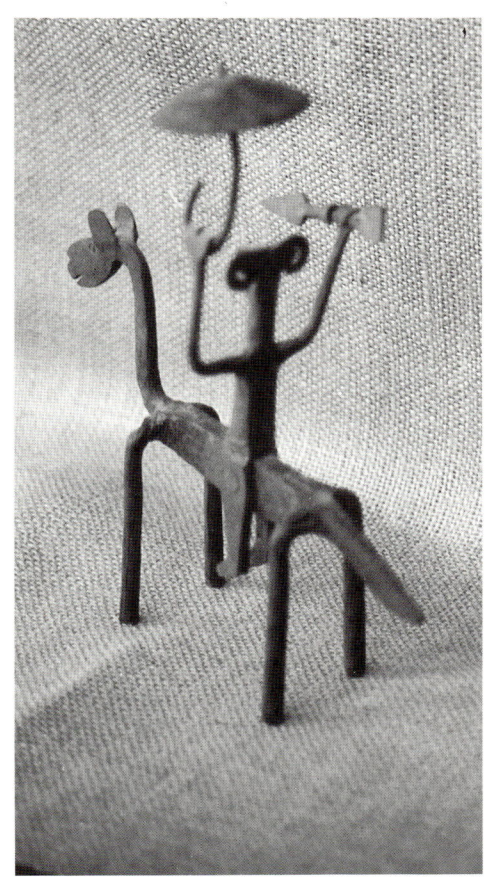

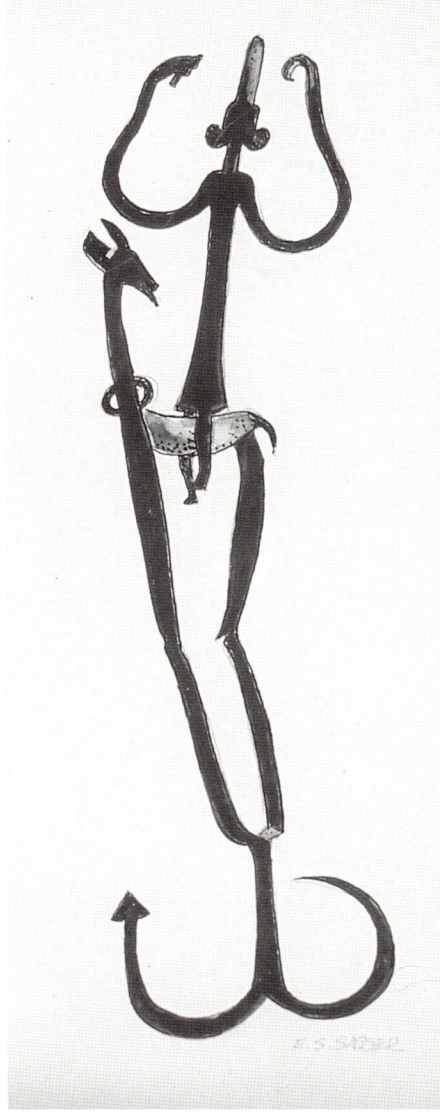

Fig. 14 (Top left) Equestrian, Liberia, forged iron, H. approx. 8 in. (Courtesy of John O. Evans III)

Fig. M (Top right) Bamana equestrian figure, wrought iron sculpture. Source: Patrick R. McNaughton, The Mande Blacksmiths. Sketch by E. S. Sasser.

Fig. N (Bottom left) Mamade Konnack, blacksmith in the Liberian village of Naama. (Photo by John O. Evans III)

Fig. O (Bottom right) Smithy at Naama, Liberia. (Photo by John O. Evans III)

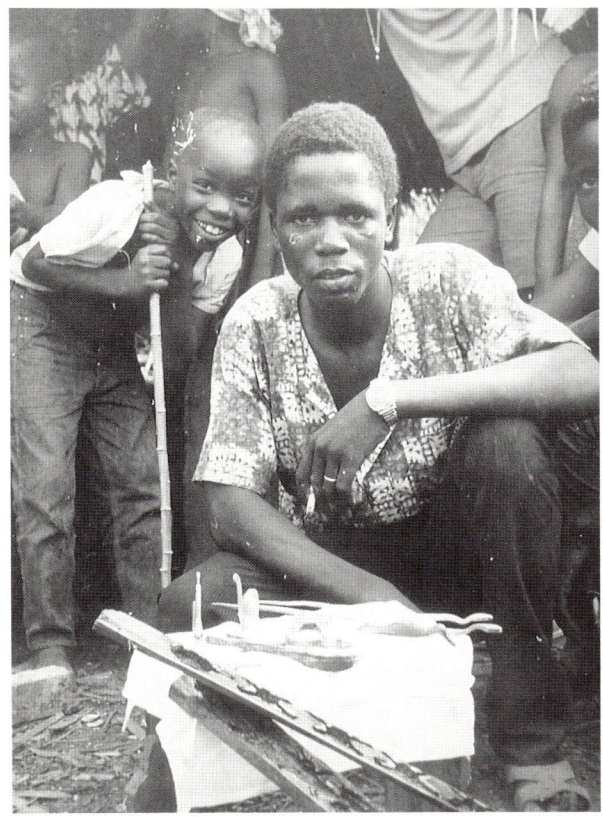

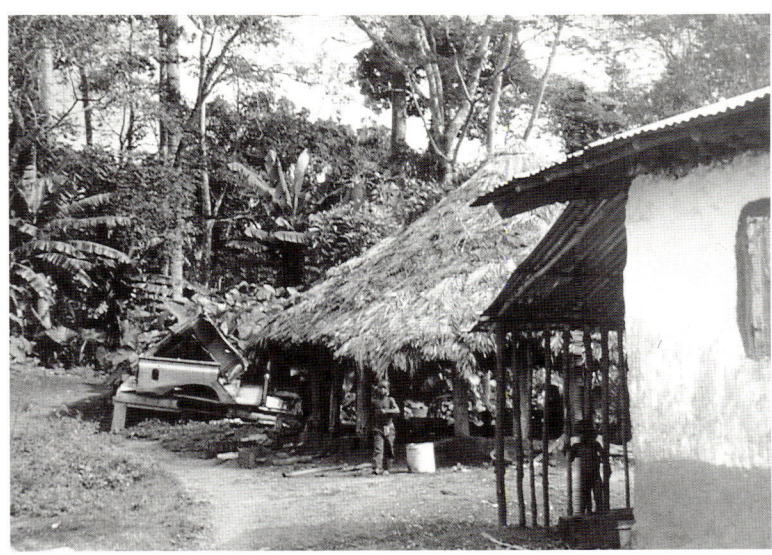

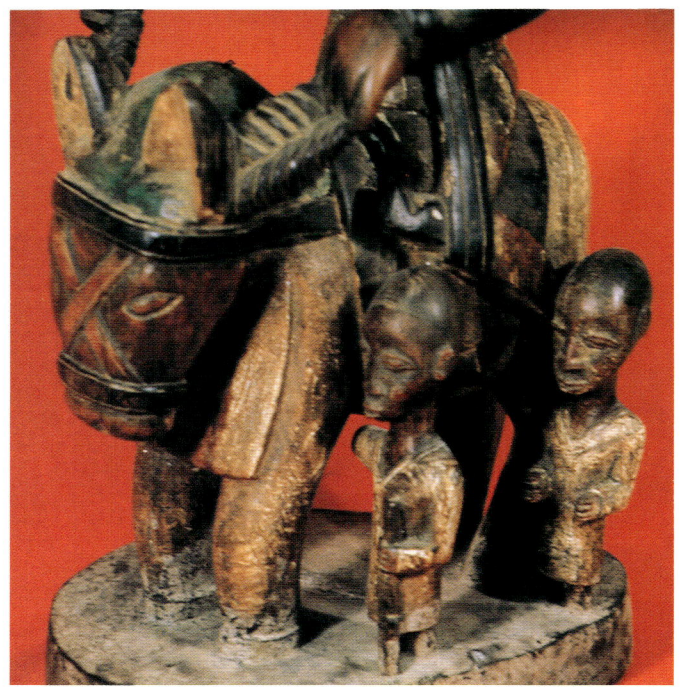

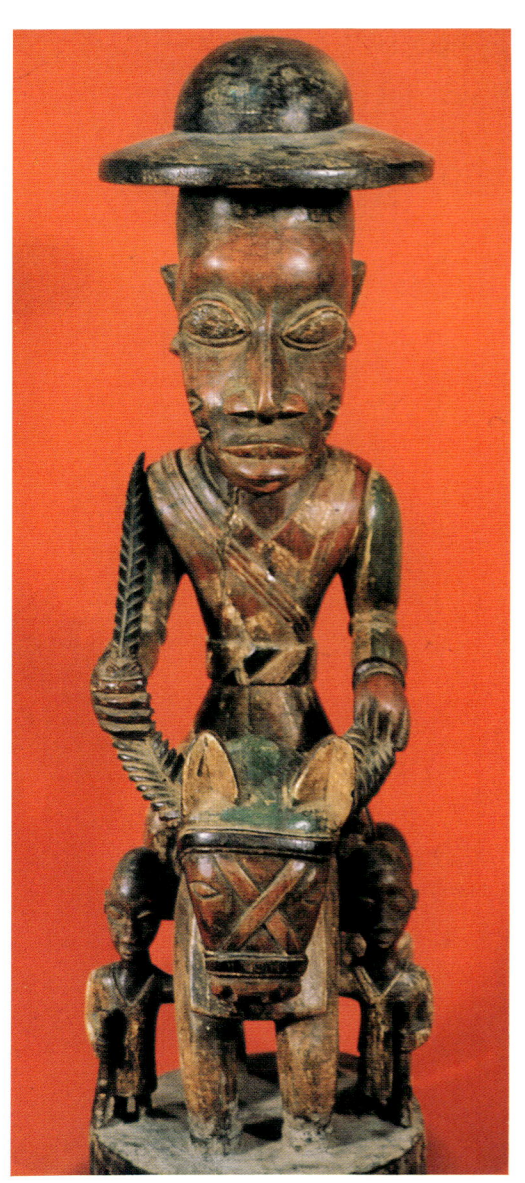

*Fig. 16
Detail of equestrian 15.*

*Fig. 15
Equestrian, Yoruba, Nigeria,
wood, pigment, H. 27 in.*

responsibility of the blacksmiths. Such staffs are made for leaders of sacred cults, or for the *hogon,* an important priest. Town officials also own staffs that indicate their rank, but these are of wood, tipped with small conical iron sleeves.[11] The importance of iron compared with wood lies in its aggressive power and in its association with the weapons carried by warriors. A staff's effectiveness was enhanced by the addition at its apex of the image of an equestrian figure, a symbol of prestige and position, because only the wealthy could afford to own such a valuable animal.[12]

Forged by the blacksmith, the representation of a horse and rider (figure 14) differs dramatically from equestrian subjects carved in wood (figures 15, 16). Wood retains a suggestion of the shape of the block from which the carving emerged. The same subject made of iron is essentially linear, that is, metal drawn out like three-dimensional calligraphy. The process of working with iron at a simple forge necessitates the elimination of details. Wooden pieces are frequently embellished with delicate incised lines or raised relief. Metal sculpture stands on the edge of the action and thrust—this is the difference between a club for bludgeoning and a sword's lightning stroke. It has been suggested that the life force in a wood carving is inherent in the wood, whereas in iron, the *nyama* is "imposed by the blows from the hammer that extend the iron into lines moving through space."[13] The metal produces a linear sign or an ideograph for the subject. Born from the fire and hammer blows, Dogon metal pieces have been called "writing in iron."[14]

Iron is not the only ore of importance to the Dogon and to other inhabitants of Africa. Copper is regarded as the metal of the sun. "The sun is said to be made of molten copper which throws off rays that draw up moisture into the sky."[15] Therefore, it has a luminous essence.[16] Perhaps some of the values associated with copper can be attributed to the limited number of African sites where copper has been found—for the most part in Mauritania and in the Nioro region of the Sudan.[17] The importation of copper, first by caravan route and then in the sixteenth century by European sea trade, made it a luxury in the western sub-Saharan African region. It was the metal of choice for the most prestigious objects.

Rarely used in a pure form, copper was combined with tin to produce bronze; the combination of zinc and copper resulted in brass. Evelyn Fischel has pointed out that in the literature of African art, the term *bronze* has been a designation for copper-alloy castings, even though some of these may actually be brass.[18] The problem of identifying brass and bronze objects is still subject to some confusion.

The western sub-Saharan African methods practiced in working with metal are like those used in other civilizations. Small solid pieces, like the wonderful array of brass weights for weighing gold, are cast directly in clay or wooden molds. Solid metal sculptures are heavy; enlarging the size increases the weight and the expense of the metal required. Casting larger pieces that were lighter and less costly led to the development of the lost-wax method perdue (*ciré perdue*). *Ciré perdue* is initiated with a clay model of the design to be reproduced. The subject is coated with thin layers of beeswax, an application that determines the thickness of the finished casting. Working over the outer layer of wax, the sculptor sharpens and refines the details and features of the figure. If the finished result is to represent a man or woman, small rolls of wax might be applied for the eyebrows; elaborate hair coils and patterns of scarification are carefully detailed in the same way. After the final touches are completed, clay slip is poured over the beeswax. When the clay dries thoroughly, the mold is turned upside down and heated to allow the beeswax to melt and run off through ducts of wax, added for this purpose. A space, stabilized by wooden pins, is left between the

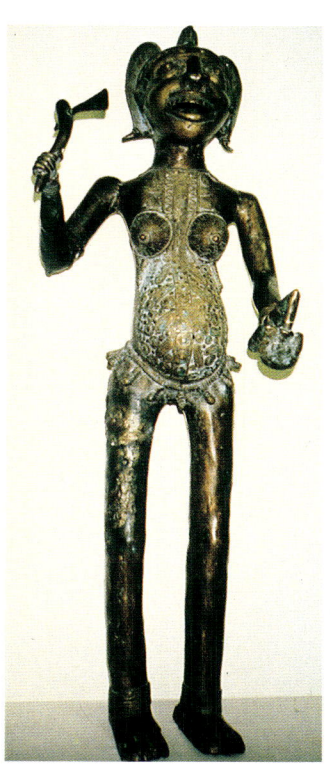

*Fig. 17
Standing female figure,
Fumban, Cameroon,
brass, H. approx. 36 in.*

inner core and the outer investment to maintain a separation. Molten metal is introduced into this space through a funnel-shaped opening. After the metal cools, the outer cast is removed and the rods (originally of wax) that channeled the overflow of metal are trimmed. The core is broken up and taken out through the openings left after the rods and funnel have been cut away. To complete the cast piece, the holes are patched, irregularities smoothed, and the surface is polished and burnished with great care.

The direct method of casting allowed a number of objects to be made from the same mold except in the case of a wooden mold that was charred by the molten metal; *ciré perdue* resulted in one figure only. A figure of a Fumban woman stands three feet in height; her skin is covered with refined scarification and she brandishes an ax with feeling (figure 17). This figure is an example of the lost-wax technique. The body parts—the arms, legs, and head—appear to have been cast separately and soldered to the torso. The best known sub-Saharan bronzes are those associated with southern Nigeria, with Ife, and the old Kingdom of Benin.

Gold was not used as a monetary exchange by the sub-Saharan Africans. It was reserved for jewelry and the personal adornment of rulers and their courtiers. Europeans, visiting western sub-Saharan Africa in the eighteen hundreds, were awestruck by the beauty of the golden ornaments that they saw. Excerpts from a description written by T. E. Bowditch, leader of an expedition in 1819 to the territory of the king of Asanti in what is now modern Ghana, mentioned the king's royal apparel which included "a necklace of golden cockspur shells . . . [and] his bracelets were the richest mixture of beads and gold . . . he wore a pair of gold castanets on his finger and thumb, which he clapped to enforce silence. . . . [His] various attendants were adorned with large stars, . . . crescents, and gossamer wings of solid gold."[19]

The trade in African gold and gold dust goes far back in history to Egypt's sixth dynasty or earlier. In the ninth century A.D., the land that is present-day Ghana was referred to by astronomer El Fazari as "the land of gold."[20] Gold was found in riverbeds and in pits where rocks had disintegrated. Among the Baule peoples, men excavated large lumps from the pit bottoms; the women pounded the rock to powder and washed away the impurities, leaving the pure gold. The precious metal was a trade item for export to North African countries along the rim of the Mediterranean. Its desirability contributed the name "Gold Coast" to the land on the Gulf of Guinea's north shore between Ivory Coast on the west and the so-called Slave Coast on the east. To the western sub-Saharan Africans, copper, the material of the shining disk that sent streamers of heat to earth, was far more symbolically significant than the gold that whetted European greed.

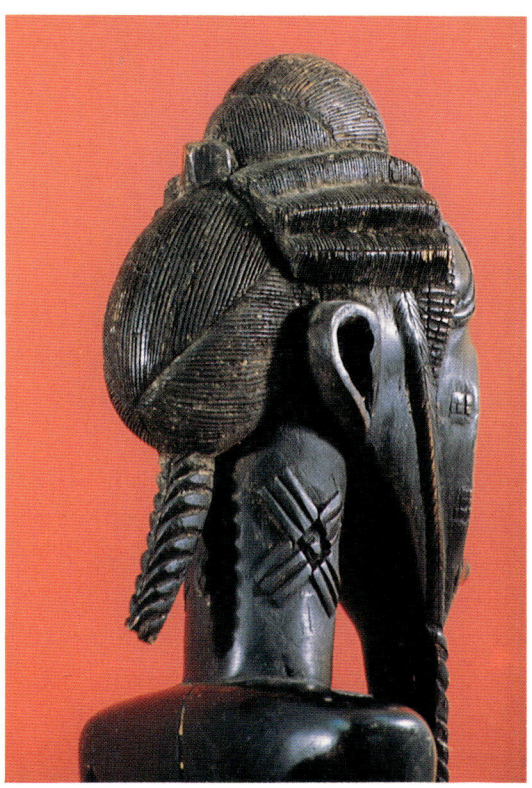

Fig. 18
Detail of seated male
figure (back view),
Baule, Ivory Coast,
wood, H. 32 in.
(see figs. 1, 22).

III

Some Peer Standards of Evaluation

Anybody who meets beauty
and does not look at it will soon be poor.

from the oral literature of divination,
(Beier and Gbadamosi 1959)

Throughout the early part of the twentieth century, the question of aesthetics plagued scholars and critics writing about African sculpture. Was function the primary criterion for the consideration of masks and figurative sculptures made by African craftsmen? Should artists and writers of nonAfrican countries view traditional African art from the perspective of their own culture and its values? Should the emphasis rest on the powerful African carvings that influenced the work of European painters and sculptors during the early decades of the twentieth century? Should African art be viewed primarily in the context of its meanings to the ethnic groups for whom it was made? Is it possible for those without African roots to understand this kind of ethnic significance? Fortunately, in the last several decades, spearheaded by anthropologists and joined by art historians, black and white, there has been a growing

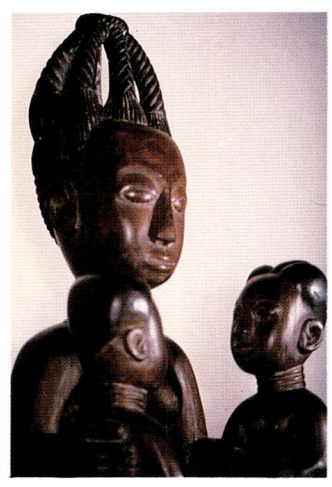

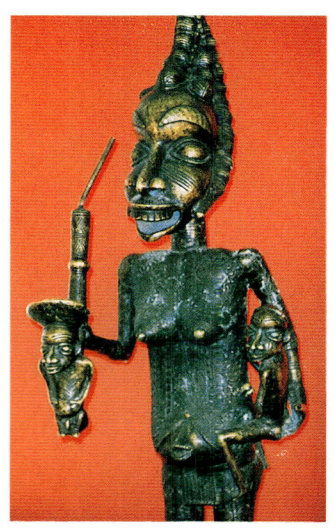

*Fig. 19
Mother with twins,
Yoruba, Nigeria, wood,
H. 18 in.*

*Fig. 20
Standing female figure,
Fumban, Cameroon,
brass, H. 46 1/4 in.*

recognition of the need to develop an awareness of the viewpoint of the Africans who continue to be involved in the traditional arts. Craftsmen have been asked what *well made* means to them. The Chokwe believe that "knowing how to make an object well includes knowing how to make it beautiful."[21] But what is meant by *beautiful?* The answers differ from one African society to another, but many concepts are repeated in answers given to questions asked by informants who represent different regions and countries.

Important information, gathered at a conference held in 1965, has been published under the title *The Traditional Artist in African Society,* edited by Warren d'Azevedo. The discussions with African artists from western sub-Saharan African countries have helped make art forms that have seemed difficult to understand, except at an intuitive or emotional level, more accessible. This does not imply that interpretations have been "westernized" for nonAfrican consumption, but that the African point of view has been presented with new insights provided by craftsmen strongly involved in the process of adding to and preserving a remarkable heritage.

From the beginning, there has been no difficulty in acknowledging that African masks and figures cannot be understood as "art for art's sake." Some of the purposes of African carvings, those not associated with utilitarian objects, are: communication with the ancestors and supernaturals; appeasement of menacing spirits; elimination of threatening witchcraft. African carvings may act as entreaties for spirit participation at ceremonies celebrating the stages attained by initiates in secret societies, help in the seasonal progress of agriculture, success in the hunt, and the maintenance of a harmonious balance between man and nature.

If effectiveness in the performance of required rituals and positive responses in answer to requests from the supernaturals are criteria for judging the merits of carvings, the essays assembled by d'Azevedo indicate that traditional African artists also have other standards that are applied when assessing excellence in the arts. Illustrating this, Robert Farris Thompson, in his essay, "Yoruba Artistic Criticism," cites the appraisal of the face and hands carved by a superior craftsman. If these "are carved with proper conscientiousness," his informant told him, "the carving will become readily visible and therefore good and therefore beautiful." He adds that clarity and visibility are particularly appreciated. This becomes meaningful to those who live in an environment dominated by the deep shadows of the woodlands. Closely related to visibility, sheen and luminosity are admired in a finished work (figure 18). The wood "should be so smooth and polished that it not only reflects light but seems to glow with an inner light."[22] The more the

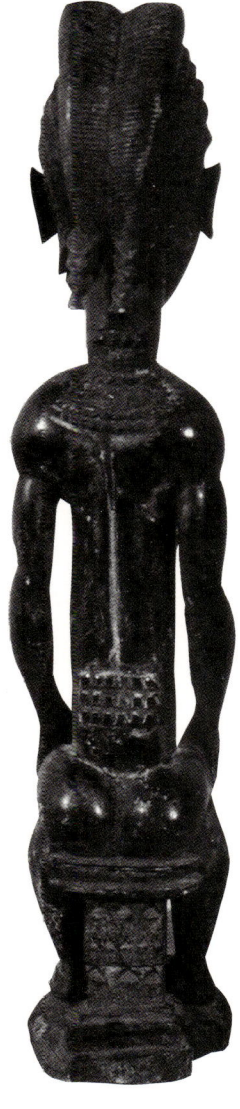

surface gleams from meticulous polishing, the longer the life of the piece will be—in one hundred years it will still be "shining."[23] When a smooth surface is juxtaposed with the patterns of cicatrization, the textural effect is enriched (figure 18). A carving is praised if the shadows within the incised lines are crisp and well-defined; designs that are small and tightly spaced, as in many hair arrangements, are considered admirable.[24] Roundness and fluid linear transitions from one mass to another are favored by some ethnic groups (figure 19). But angularity is recognized for certain desirable effects (figure 20). A pointed chin gives intensity and purpose to a heroic pose.[25]

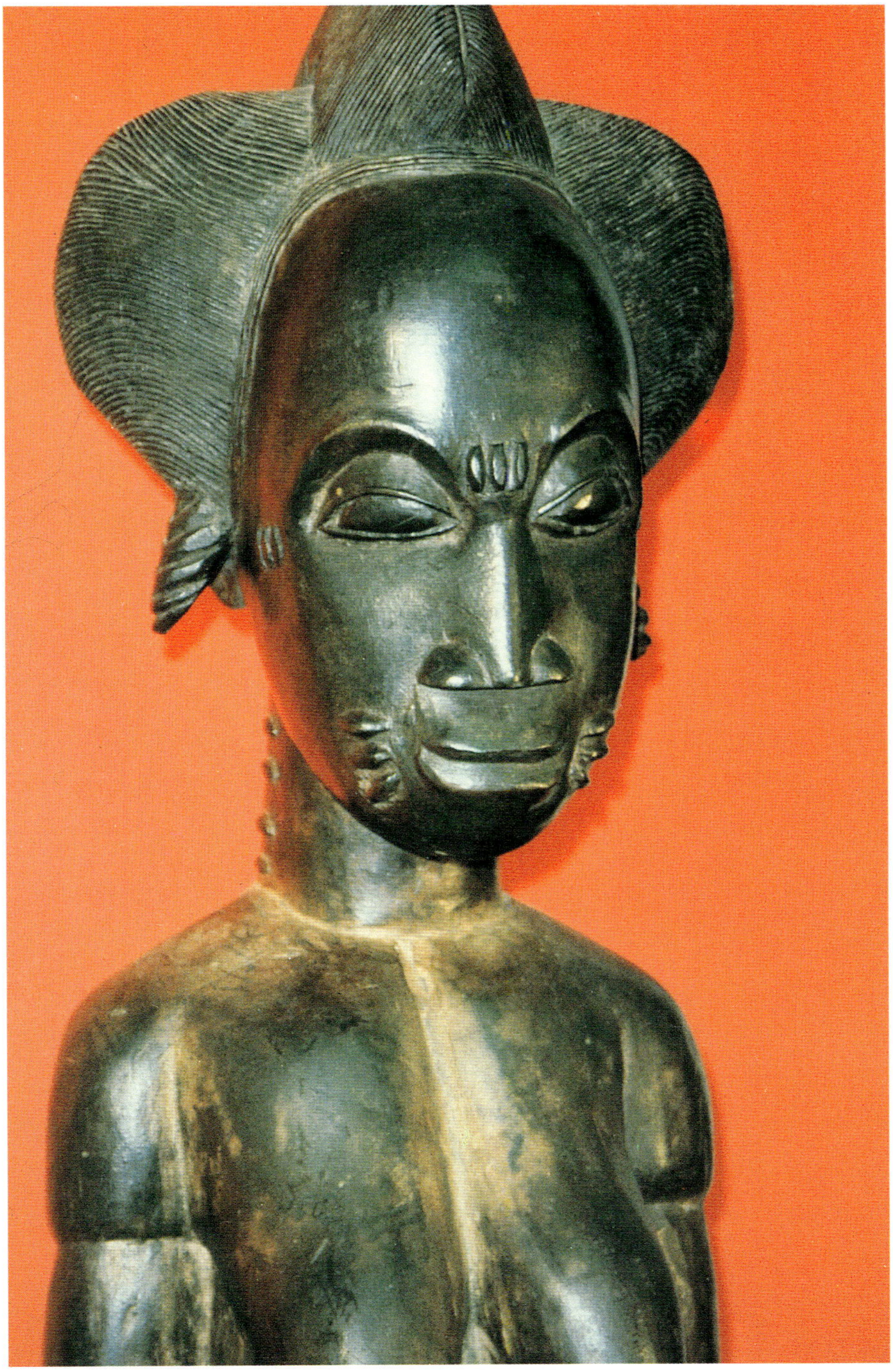

Symmetry and the balance of parts are equated with serenity and calmness,[26] the opposite of the wild aggressive forces unleashed by the

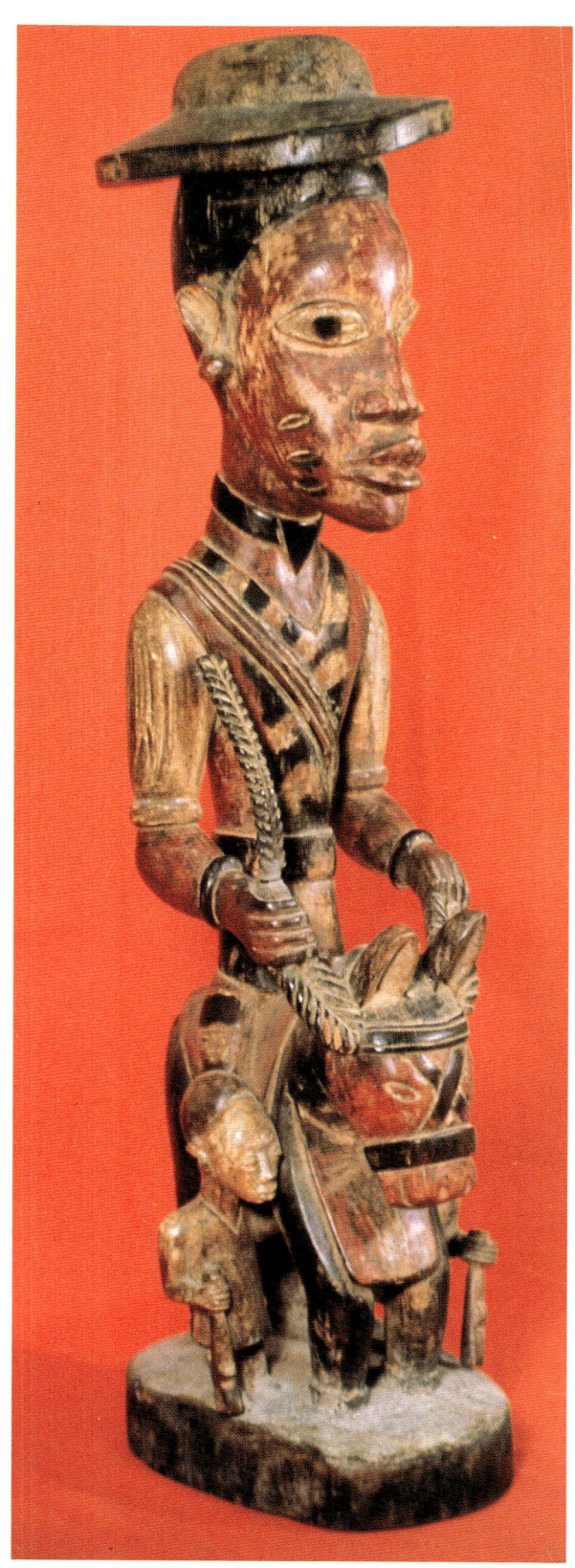

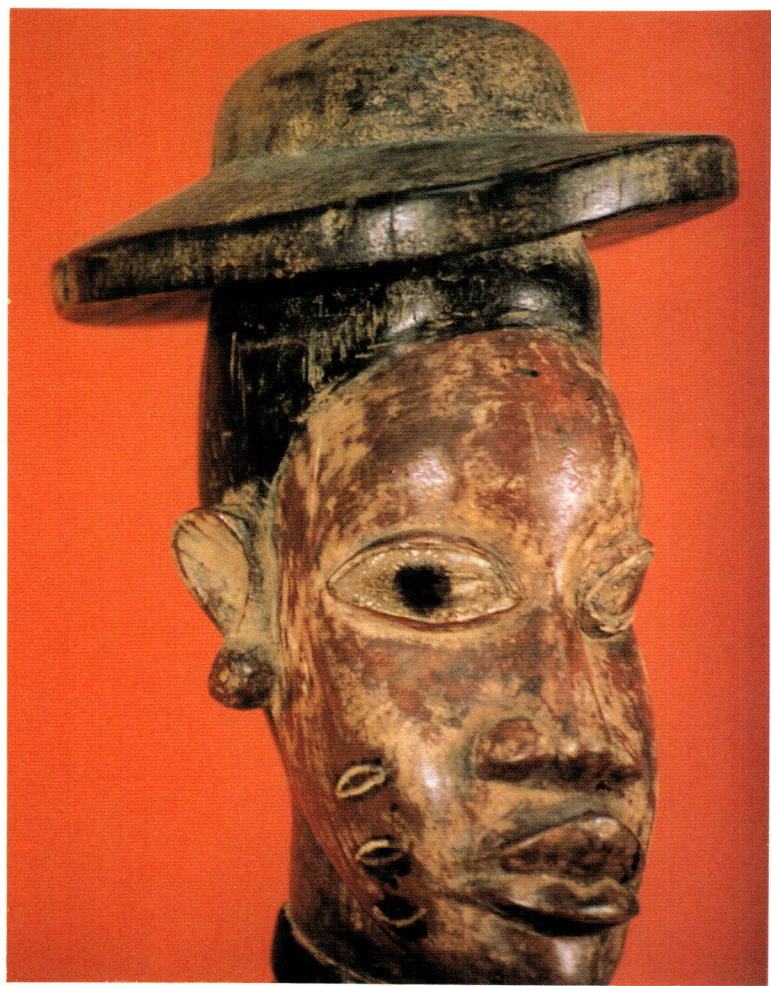

*Fig. 23
Equestrian, Yoruba,
Nigeria, wood, pigment,
H. 34 ¾ in.*

*Fig. 24
Detail of equestrian
head, 23.*

creatures of the bush. The idea of serenity and strength is contained in the Yoruba desire to portray people in their prime (figure 21). Realism in the Western sense is not an aim. Because seniority is idealized, Thompson writes, ". . . what could be more appropriate than to flatter the moral beauty of the elders with the physical beauty of the young?"[27]

Straightness is another virtue addressed by African artists. It is thought of as an upright position—the straight back of a woman sitting on a stool (figure 22), or a horseman on his mount (figure 23). Scale is another way of indicating importance. Just as in ancient Egypt a king was represented larger than those who attended him, a wealthy Yoruba landowner astride his horse towers over the diminutive servants who walk along beside him (figure 23). An enlargement of the head in proportion to the body acknowledges that the head is believed to be the seat of character. "Heads as wisdom symbols mark the visual climax [of the body]"[28] (figure 24). In the masquerades, masks are often much larger than the bodies that support them, thus becoming the focal point of the dancer.

But compared with carved figures, mask designs and constructions reveal a different aspect of African art. Many carved figures express an ideal that has been described as an "economy of form, gesture," and "facial expression," that results from an "inward directed energy . . . and control."[29] Masks, participating in the coalescence of art, music, dance, and speech, are emotionally charged. Integrated into a choreographed whole, masks empower their wearers to attract a supernatural energy that is thrust outward toward the throngs of people that come together. Until the masks are awakened, they are quiescent. Once the performer places the mask on his head, its inertia is jolted by a potent force that bonds the people to the mythic spirits and to the ancestors.

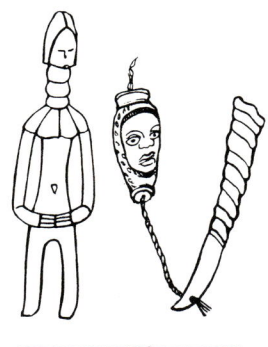

FOUR

Masks

*To have music
without dance
is unthinkable . . .*

from *When the Devil Dances*
by HARRISON OWEN

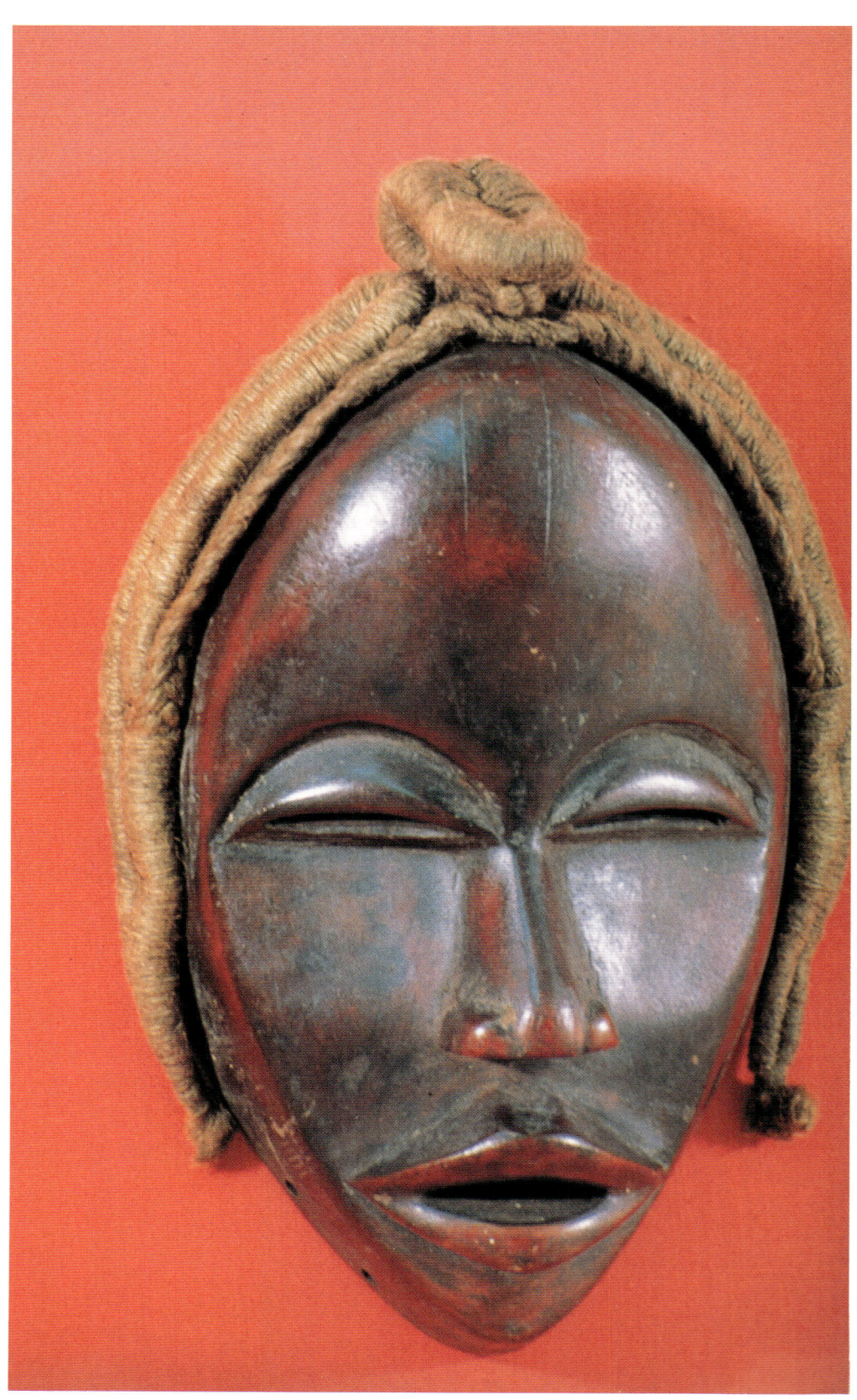

Fig. 25
Mask, Dan,
Ivory Coast/
Liberia, wood,
fiber,
H. 13 ½ in.

Francois Neyt has observed, "a mask that does not dance . . . is no more than a piece of dead wood."[1] It is impossible to bring the masks in museums to life except in the imagination, but it must be constantly remembered that each played a part in an elaborate ceremony of vital importance to the well-being of a family or a group.

When the masks appear, the bodies of the masked dancers are usually concealed or partially covered by elaborate costumes. To induce awe or fear, some maskers are lifted on stilts as much as fifteen feet above the ground. The movements, progressing slowly or swirling rapidly, are joined by the throb of drums and the rhythms of chants. Many masquerades take place at night in the light of a bonfire where the leaping flames and eerie shadows produce unearthly effects. The intensity of the drama springs in part from the common knowledge that the rituals taking place have been performed in the same way for many generations. An awareness of the fragility of life is alleviated through the bonding of the present to the past and future. The visible and audible repetitions of the ceremonies contain the continuity that connects the generations. The masked dancers invite the spirits to descend into the masks that are their homes; like the watchers, those who dance are transported away from the profane world into the sacred realms.

To consider the hundreds of ethnic masquerades held throughout western sub-Saharan Africa, each accompanied by its own traditional costumes and masks, would require a lifetime of travel and study. In this chapter, some of the masks from the Collection at the Museum of Texas Tech University are used to illustrate the striking varieties of subjects, designs, and materials that give masks an endless fascination for people of all backgrounds and cultures.

Although purpose, mythic background, design, scale, colors, and textures differ dramatically from one ethnic society to another, the mask makers, who work in wood, usually receive similar training. Discussed in the preceding chapter, the instruction of the wood-carver need not be considered in detail; suffice it to say, in most cases a teenager who shows promise is apprenticed to a master carver. The young apprentice is already familiar with prototypes through repeated attendance from infancy at village masquerades. Segy points out that a reason for the repetition of a style associated with a particular mask is "the concept that the spirit would not recognize his abode if it [the mask] were different from the conventional forms."[2] When completed, and after it is consecrated by the shaman, a mask is believed to become the dwelling place of a particular spirit.

The tools with which an apprentice gradually becomes skilled include the adz, used either with a handle for roughing out massive forms, or, if the handle is removed, as a knife for carving fine details. For the most refined touches, tools and knives may be purchased at a store. The crosscutting ax is employed when deep cuts are needed to outline the features or emphasize details on a large mask. Hollow chisels are useful for carving the inside surfaces of masks. Sharp iron tools are employed to penetrate the wood when the holes are made around the rim of the carving in which fibers are inserted to hide the wearer and maintain his anonymity. This helps to reinforce the illusion of a supernatural being.

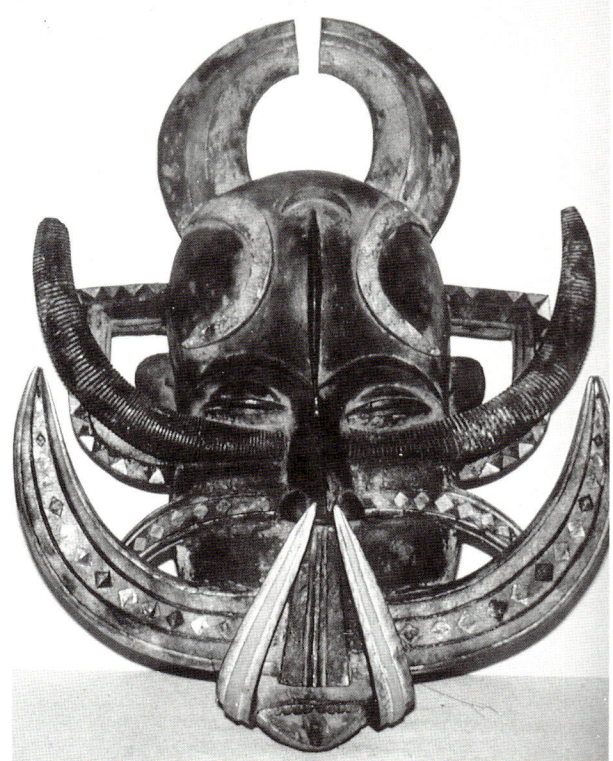

*Fig. 26
Mask, Bete, Ivory Coast,
wood, pigment,
H. 15 1/4 in.*

Upon the death of a master carver, it is not unusual for his best student to inherit his tools. These are believed to retain some of the artist's skills.[3] Tools have often been regarded as having their own spirit or power, just as wood is associated with the spirit of the tree that must be propitiated before it is cut down.

The subjects for masks fall into two general categories: (a) masks with features based on those of humans and (b) animal masks. There are also hybrids that combine both human and animals motifs. The division is useful and will be followed in this chapter by considering:(a) masks representing the supernaturals but related in concept to human features (figure 25) and (b) masks representing animals or composite creatures (figure 26).

I

Masks with Human Features

The object that is sculpted with love be-
comes the carrier of presence, communication,
participation; every decoration becomes a sign,
and the sign is the carrier of the message . . .
the object is presented as an ideogram; its
image and sign are visible and its beauty can
be appreciated, but its language is not accessible
to all.

FRANK WILLETT in *African Art*

Like all masks, those that represent ancestors, supernaturals, or symbolic concepts conceived in terms of the human face are separated from a realistic approach by stylization, color, or by the materials used. Some masks depend upon unpainted wood or fibers; in many cases ruffs or streamers of raffia are attached (figure 10). Other masks rely upon paint, either lavishly applied in striking patterns (figure 12) or in a subdued manner (figure 7). A third type may become a collage of applied substances: fibers, fur, beads, bark, metal, mirrors, fabrics, or any other texture that enhances the design (figures 8, 9). Other masks are made of leaves, woven of yarn or fibers, for example, the fiber masks of the Salampasu people (figure 27).

Among the unpainted masks at the Museum of Texas Tech University there is an example of one of the largest mask types found in western sub-Saharan Africa; this is a *nimba* shoulder mask of the Baga.   Illustrated in figure 28, it is four feet in height. The Baga inhabit a formidable region in the Republic of Guinea. The land is interfaced with swamps, which make it hard to distinguish where the land begins and the watery surface ends. The tangles of mangroves attract primarily crabs and swarms of mosquitoes. The difficulties are challenged, however, and partially overcome by the human occupants who busy themselves reclaiming marshes that are turned into rice fields. It is not surprising to find that the *nimba* mask appears in rituals associated with agriculture. The mask is a wood carving of an enormous female head and bust mounted on four prongs used for steadying and steering. The mask may weigh as much as thirty pounds. The masker sees through an opening pierced between the breasts of the carving. The body of the dancer is concealed by a long fiber cape. The design of the mask is monumental and stark with a clarity of features allowing maximum visibility against a matting of tropical plant growth. The hatchet-shaped nose, sharp jawline, and crested hair create an awesome profile that proclaims the power of the female guardian of the harvest and the one who receives the appeals of women for many offspring.

A smaller mask of unpainted wood, with some Yoruba characteristics, but as yet unidentified, is both beautiful and curious (figure 29). The crisply defined features of a man's face end in a short stylized beard. The mask is surmounted by what at first glance seems to be a serpent with phallic implications. Upon closer inspection the fluid curve becomes the figure of a man who kneels on the forehead of the mask. His attenuated arms terminate on either temple; each hand holds a knife. Is this a threatening gesture or a protective one?

Some masks that are not painted take on a handsome patina that may resemble bronze so closely it is difficult to believe they are actually made of wood. The carving in figure 30 is a Luba helmet mask. The Luba occupy a large area in Zaire, not far from the territory of the Songye. A nineteenth-century helmet mask of the type in figure 30 is an admired possession of the *Musée Royal de l'Afrique Centrale* at Tervuren in Belgium. (This is illustrated in *The Art of Africa* by Elsy Leuzinger, plate 58.) The wood has a remarkable sheen and the features are subtle and elegant. The horns that curve around the head in the nineteenth-century carving are freed from the mass, whereas in the later sculpture in the museum collection, the horns are attached and carved in high relief. Both masks have ceremonial beards; a fringe of fibers remains in place in the Belgian-owned piece.

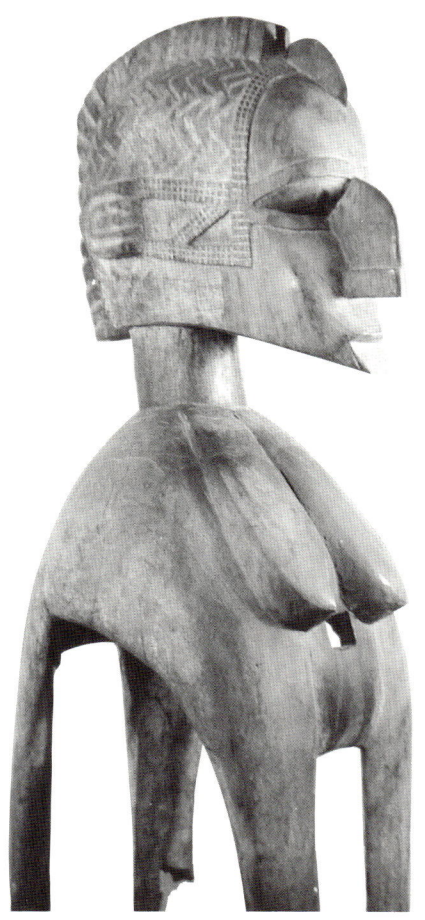

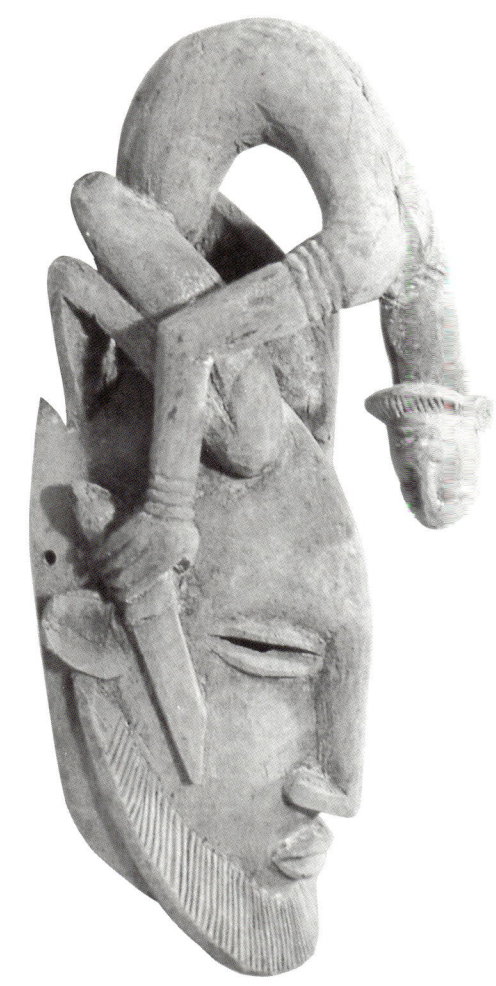

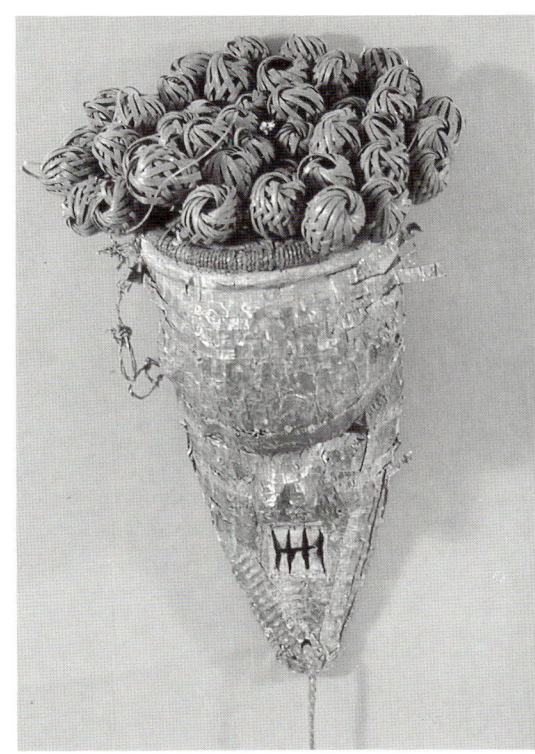

Fig. 28 (Top left)
Nimba *mask, Baga,*
Republic of Guinea,
wood, H. 48 in.

Fig. 29 (Top right)
Mask, possibly Yoruba,
Nigeria, wood, H. 14 in.

Fig. 27
Mask, Salampasu,
Congo, wood, rattan,
H. 26 in.

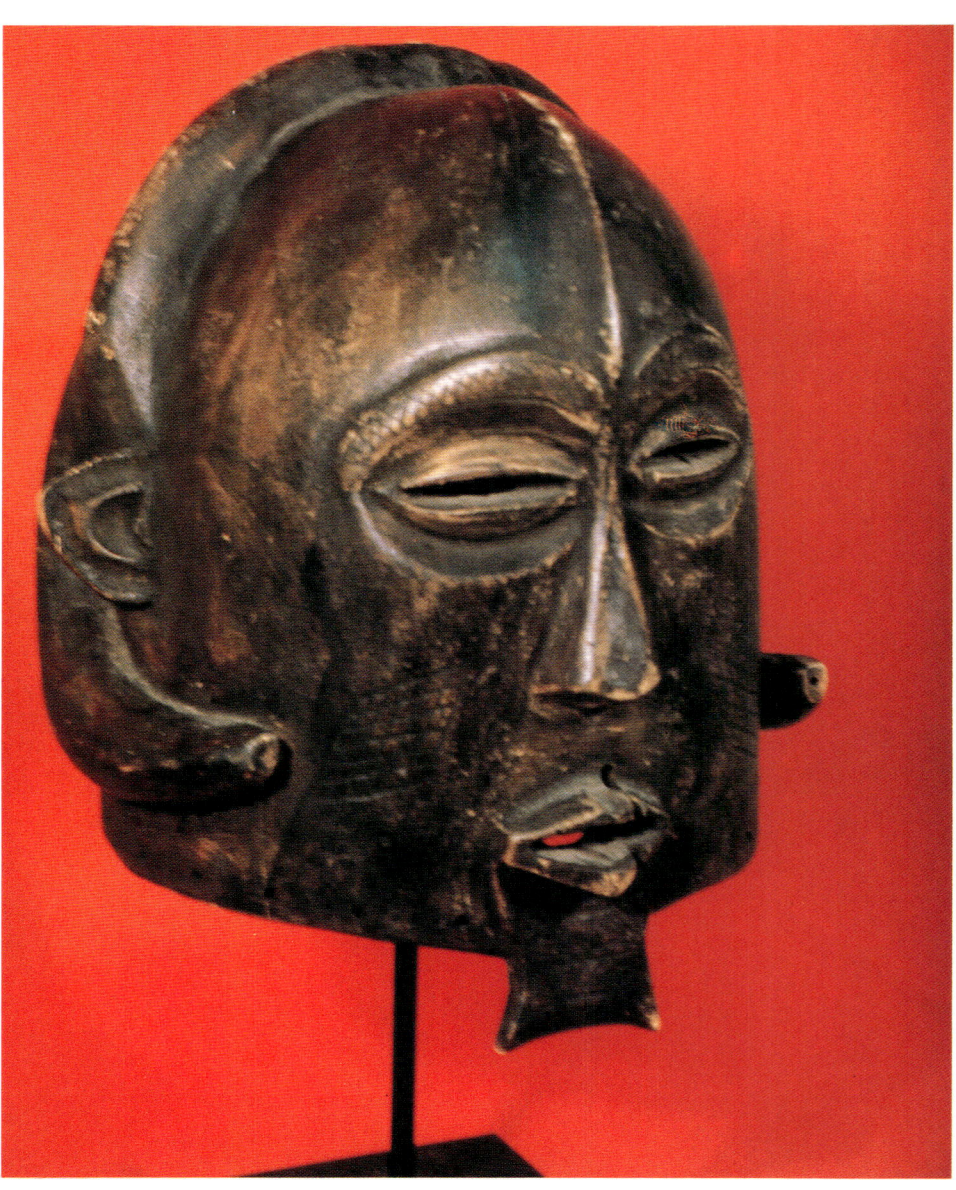

*Fig. 30
Mask, Luba, Zaire,
wood, H. 14 in.*

Two blackened wood masks from the Museum of Texas Tech University include a Bekom piece from the Cameroons (figure 31) and a Bete mask from Ivory Coast (figure 32). The Cameroon mask has the typical heavy jowls, large oval eyes, and small projecting ears. The decorative cap is a distinguishing feature of men of high rank in the social structure of the grassfields. Masks are not always completely hollowed out, because the carving may be intended to rest on a bamboo structure surrounded by a tufted collar of palm fibers that conceals the masker's head and face.[4] Much of the art produced by the Bekom is associated with the court. Masks are used for commemorative death celebrations, as well as the King's annual masquerade and a new king's installation ceremonies.

The Bete who live in the southwestern part of Ivory Coast are agriculturists existing in a subsistence economy. They place particular importance on the hunt. To overcome hostile forces that hunters encounter in the underbrush and forests, their masks offer magical protection by instilling fear and terror in potential enemies.[5] Tusks curve

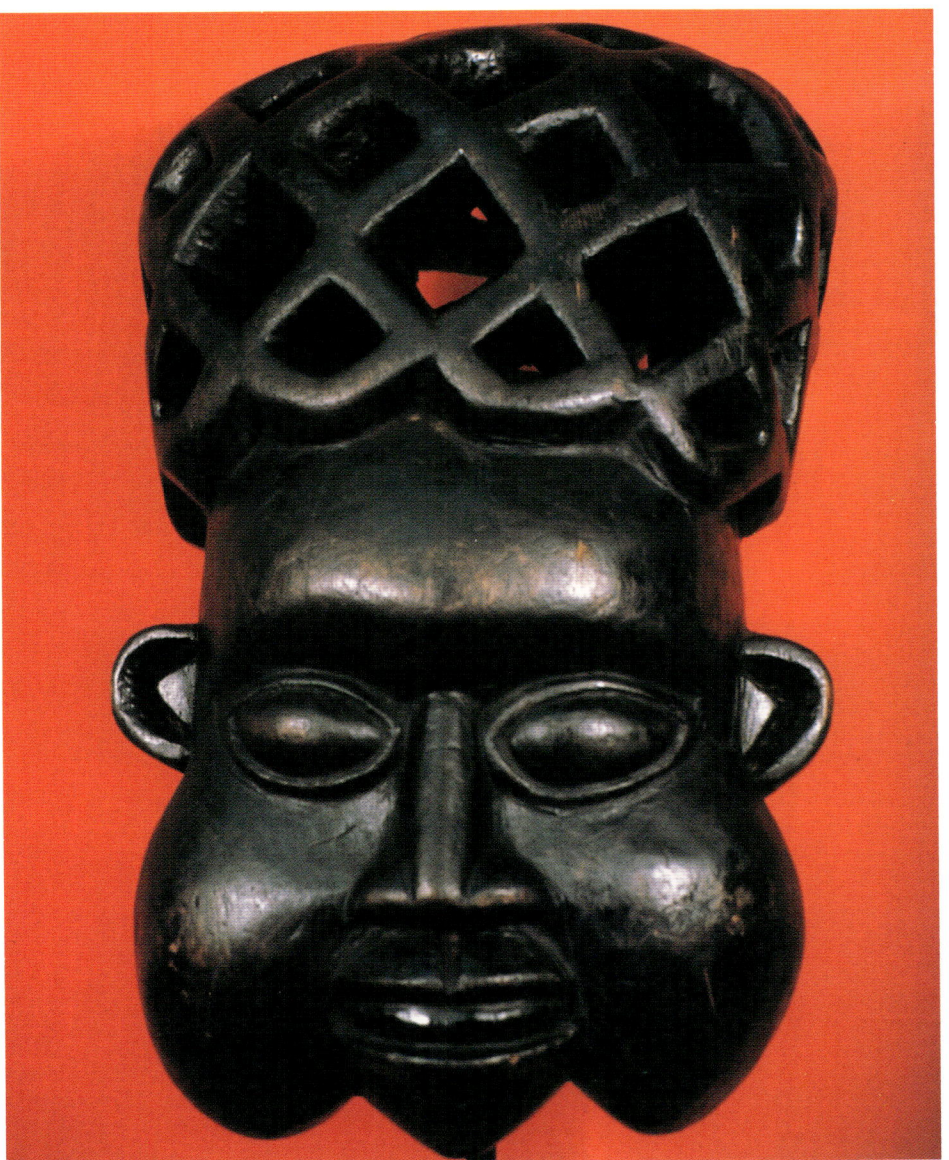

Fig. 31
Mask, Beken,
Cameroon wood,
H. 19 1/2 in.

out from the nose like a gargantuan handlebar moustache (figure 32). The bulging protuberances, deep-set eyes, and texturing of nailheads reinforce the ferocious appearance. Raffia is still attached to the lower portion of this carving.

One of the most pleasing small masks in the collection is a circle with eyeholes like freckles dotting the cheeks. The patina gives the impression of bronze (figure 33). The provenance is unknown, but it is said to have been used in initiation rites.

Less difficult to identify are the masks of the Dan people, who live in northeastern Liberia and northwestern Ivory Coast. Their homelands range from forests in the south to savannas in the north. Farming is a way of life, but in the past the Dan have been recognized as fearless warriors, waging battles with their neighbors. Independent and acknowledging allegiance to no central authority, the Dan by the end of the nineteenth century took a step toward unity with the formation of the leopard society, called the *go*. Power remained the aim of clan chiefs, but this could no longer be satisfied by war and the acquisition of land.

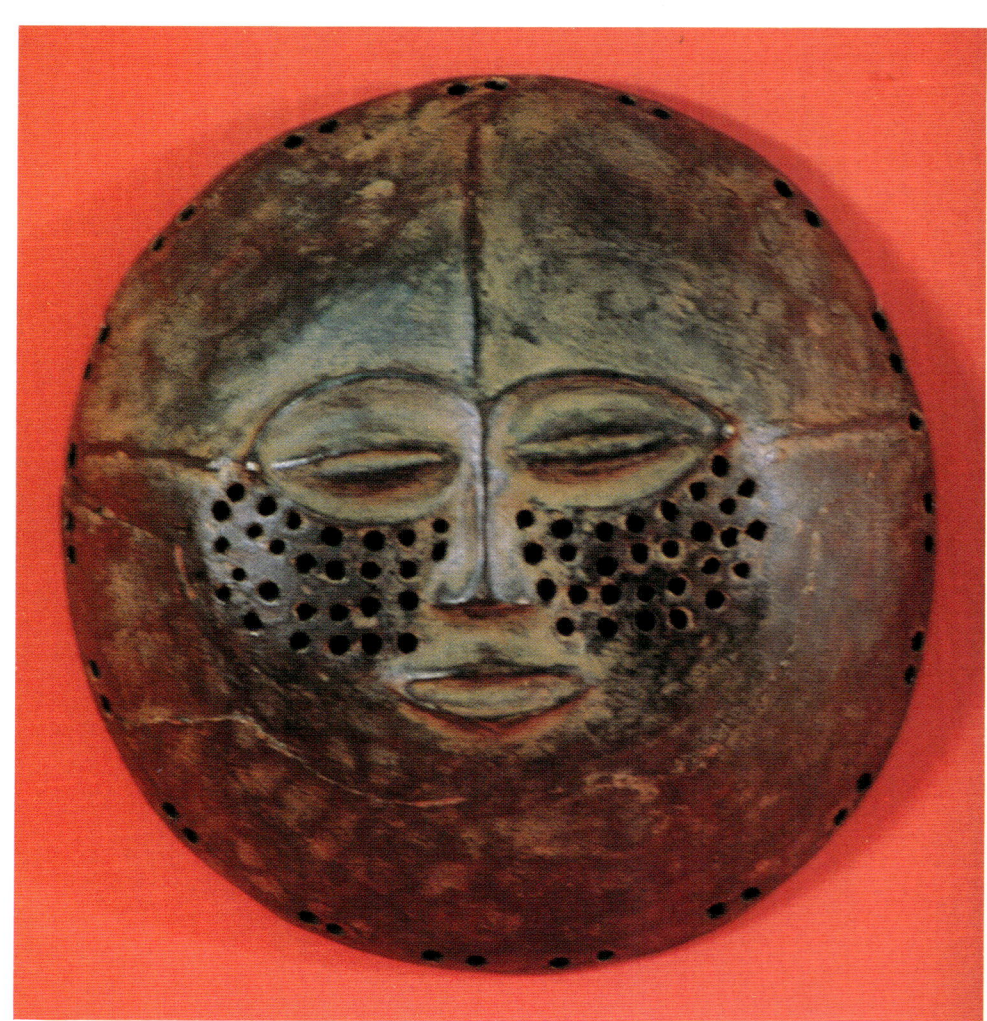

*Fig. 33 (Top)
Mask, origin unknown,
wood, diameter, 6 in.*

*Fig. 32 (Bottom)
Mask, Bete, Ivory
Coast, wood, raffia,
nailheads, H. 17 in.*

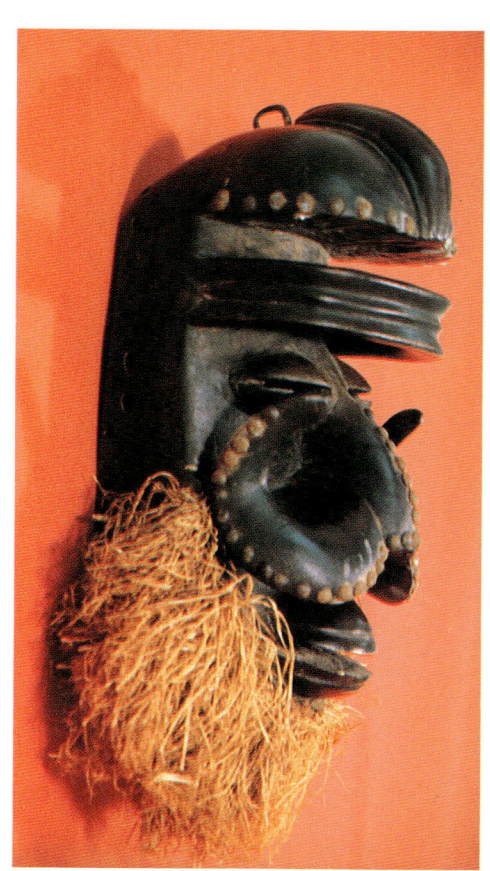

As a substitute, goals centering on prestige were satisfied by membership in the secret societies and through associations with dancers and elder statesmen. Status could be increased by the ownership of masks worn in initiation rituals and ceremonies.[6]

Masks among the Dan serve a variety of purposes, but there are characteristics held in common. The masks are usually blackened and often meticulously polished. The forehead is high and domed; the eye sockets may be round or treated as slits. The nose and lips are pronounced, but refined in shape. Contrasting with the shining surface of the face, a braided fiber or yarn wig is added and a beard is often applied (figure 34). The use of the masks is determined by the master of the *go* (leopard) society. It is the *go* master's hut that protects the most potent fetish from which power is drawn. This shelter is also the place where prominent persons are buried and where other masks of the highest rank are kept.[7]

To the Dan, masks are materializations of supernaturals who live in the bush. These spirits reveal themselves to individuals to whom they express the wish to become a part of the lives of humans.[8] Masks are classified according to their importance, but these classifications are not necessarily static. The status of a mask may be increased at the death of an owner who has gained esteem and position among his peers. On the other hand, a mask that is not effective can be demoted. If it is damaged, it is often sold to Europeans or Americans.[9]

One mask plays an important part in settlements on the edges of the forests or close to the bush and grasslands. It is called *sagbwe*. Its function and that of its wearer is to protect a community from fire hazards, particularly in the dry season when the *harmattan* blows. A masked watchman patrols the village between sunrise and sunset to make sure fires are not left unattended. Preparing food may be done outside the house or inside beneath the thatched conical roof; a ceramic cooking pot is lifted on three stones above a small fire. Even a few embers whipped into a tongue of flame can send the fire licking at huts throughout an entire village. A careless cook who is discovered with a fire left unattended is severely reprimanded, her pot tipped over, and she is given a few strokes with the switch carried by the masked "fireman." If the foolish woman were not punished sufficiently by scolding, a light beating, and a loss of the meal being prepared, there was a further punishment. An object in the household was confiscated, and only the woman's husband could recover it by paying a stiff fine.[10]

Among the Dan some carvings are known as "passport masks" (figure 35). They are small and fit like credit cards into the palm of the hand. Francoise Stoullig-Marin says that these "identifications" were "attached to the arm."[11] William Bascom states that a Dan man might also carry a miniature replica of a family mask in order to benefit from its power. "These masquettes," Bascom continues are thought to have "power of their own and the sections of kola nuts used in divination were touched to them before being cast on the ground."[12] Other ethnic groups own similar miniature masks. The Pende carve small masks of ivory or wood about two inches long. They are decorated with markings like those on the large masks. Worn suspended around the neck, they represent a badge of initiation and function as protective amulets.[13] According to Christopher Roy, a pendant with a small mask, or *ikhoko*, attached was worn by those responsible for guarding ceremonial masks from theft or vandalism.[14] Another purpose served by the miniature masks was associated with healing rituals. A "mask" might visit a person suffering from an illness; after the appropriate rites were performed, the curative forces released were prolonged if the patient wore an *ikhoko* like the "mask" worn by the shaman during the ceremony. Small pendants were worn by men, women, and children but with a difference—those of the men were usually carved of ivory, whereas the women and young ones wore masks carved from wood.[15]

Other masks worn as adornment or as emblems of prestige included small gold masks fastened to the swords once carried by kings among the Baule of Ivory Coast. The Yoruba tied face pendants of bronze to belts. Susan Lerer includes in her book *African Metalwork and Ivory* a photograph of a seventeenth- or eighteenth-century Benin leopard head worn as a hip mask.[16] In the Texas Tech Museum collection there is a metal casting of the head of a leopard with a small loop for hanging (figure 36). This later piece appears to be influenced by the early designs. At the courts of the ancient City of Benin, the leopard was a symbol of royal power. Its energy and force made the jungle creature a metaphor for the ruler, or *Oba*. Warriors in the service of the *Oba* were distinquished by their leopard tunics; certain other officials, among them horn blowers, were identified by leopard masks.[17]

In contrast to the metal masks and those that remained unpainted or carefully blackened, many receive added visibility and meaning by an application of paint (figure 37) and painted designs. The paint may either be lavishly applied or restrained in its use. The Suku mask from Zaire (figure 38) is called *kakungu*, it appears at the circumcision ritual and the initiation of young boys. Painted a dark reddish brown, the mask is held by a grip under the chin and it is surrounded by thick raffia. One of the largest African masks, sometimes five feet in height, the *suku* has inflated cheeks, bulging forehead, and a projecting lump of a chin. An object of terror, it is regarded as a protection against witches that might enter the initiation camp and harm the young candidates. The mask has

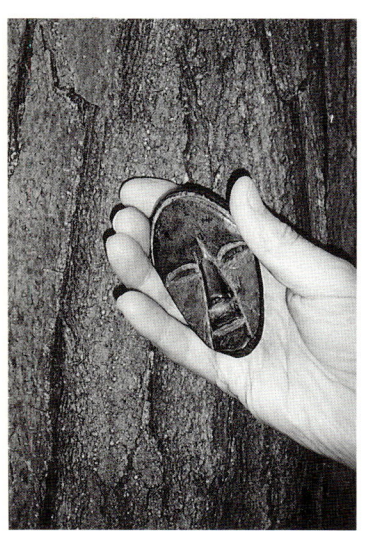

*Fig. 35
"Passport" mask, Dan,
Ivory Coast/Liberia,
wood, H. 3 1/4 in.
(Courtesy of John O.
Evans III)*

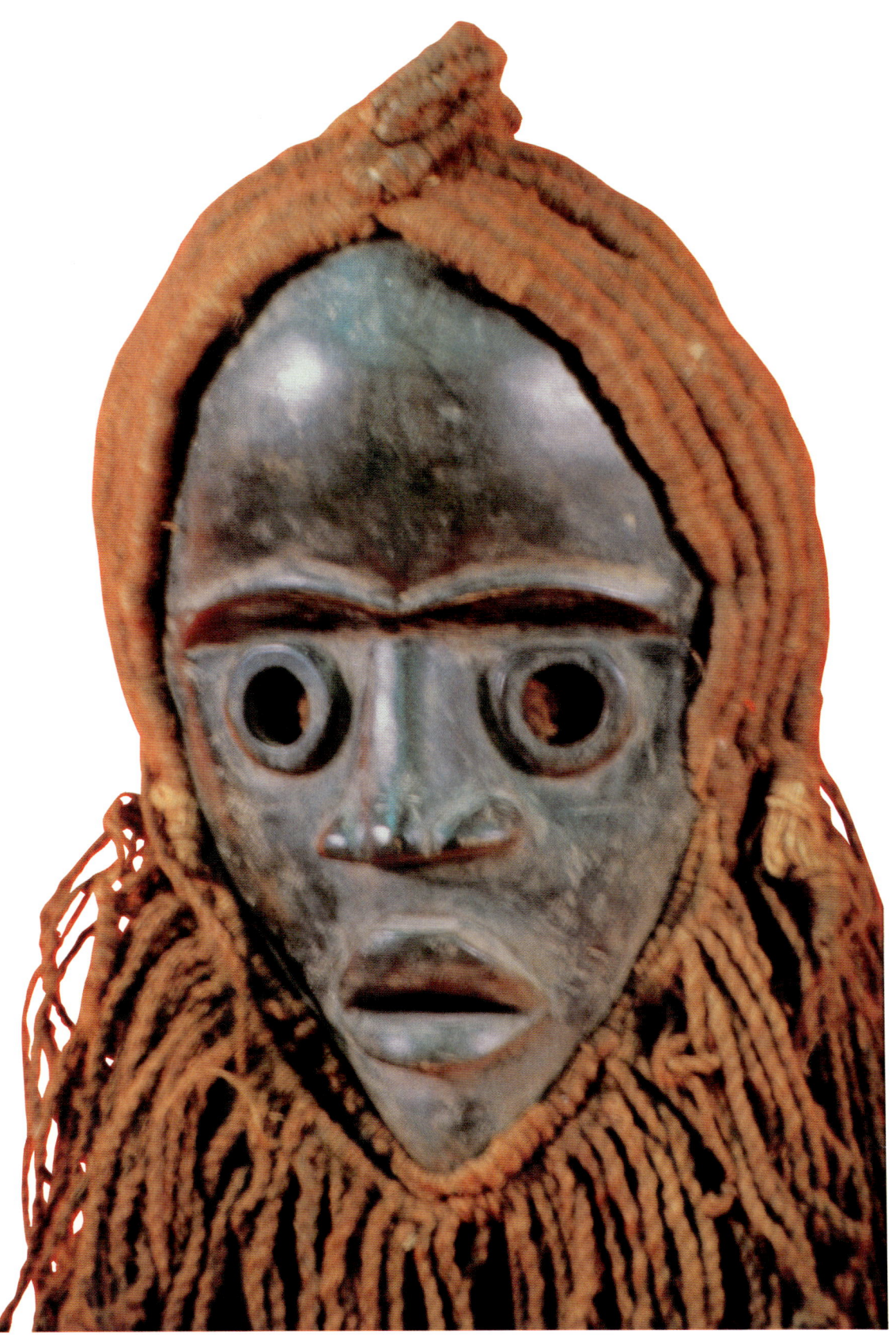

Fig. 34
Mask, Dan, Ivory
Coast/Liberia, wood,
yarn, H. 26 in.

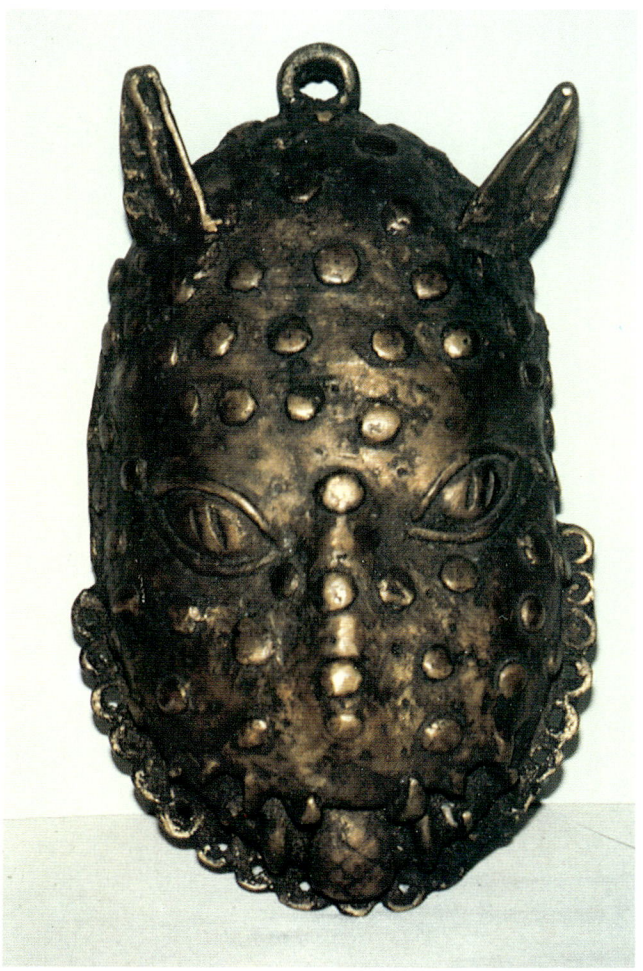

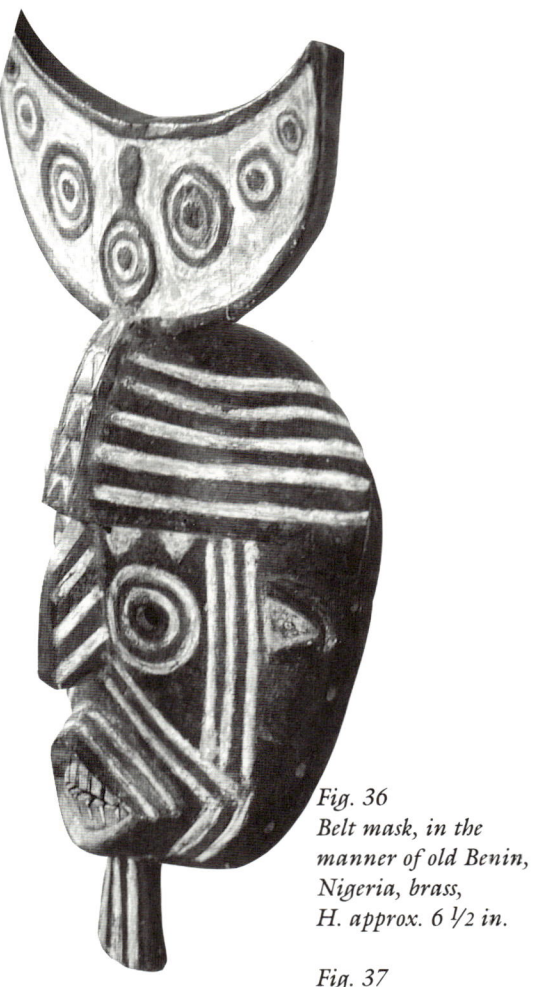

*Fig. 36
Belt mask, in the
manner of old Benin,
Nigeria, brass,
H. approx. 6 1/2 in.*

*Fig. 37
Mask, Bwa, Burkina
Faso, wood, pigment,
H. 25 1/4 in.*

another remarkable attribute; it is believed to be able to jump enormous distances, leaping over huts or into the midst of the forest.[18]

A Bwa mask from Burkina Faso has a strongly accented and dramatic design (figure 37). The markings are painted in contrasting black and white. There is a crescent moon boldly resting on top of the head like that which appears on the tall Bwa board masks. The eyes are surrounded by circles to concentrate and enhance the sight. Ringed circles are painted on the crescent, perhaps suggesting the full moon. By the diminishing scale of the circular forms toward the cusps, the waning or waxing of the moon may be intended.

One of the most curious masks in the museum collection is constructed on a domed wicker framework, which is a reminder of the framing used for shelters among many ethnic peoples (figures 39, 40, 41). Of undetermined origin, this mask is decorated with designs painted vigorously in red and black on a white ground. The boldness of the painting suggests the influence of the Igbo who settled on the plateaux

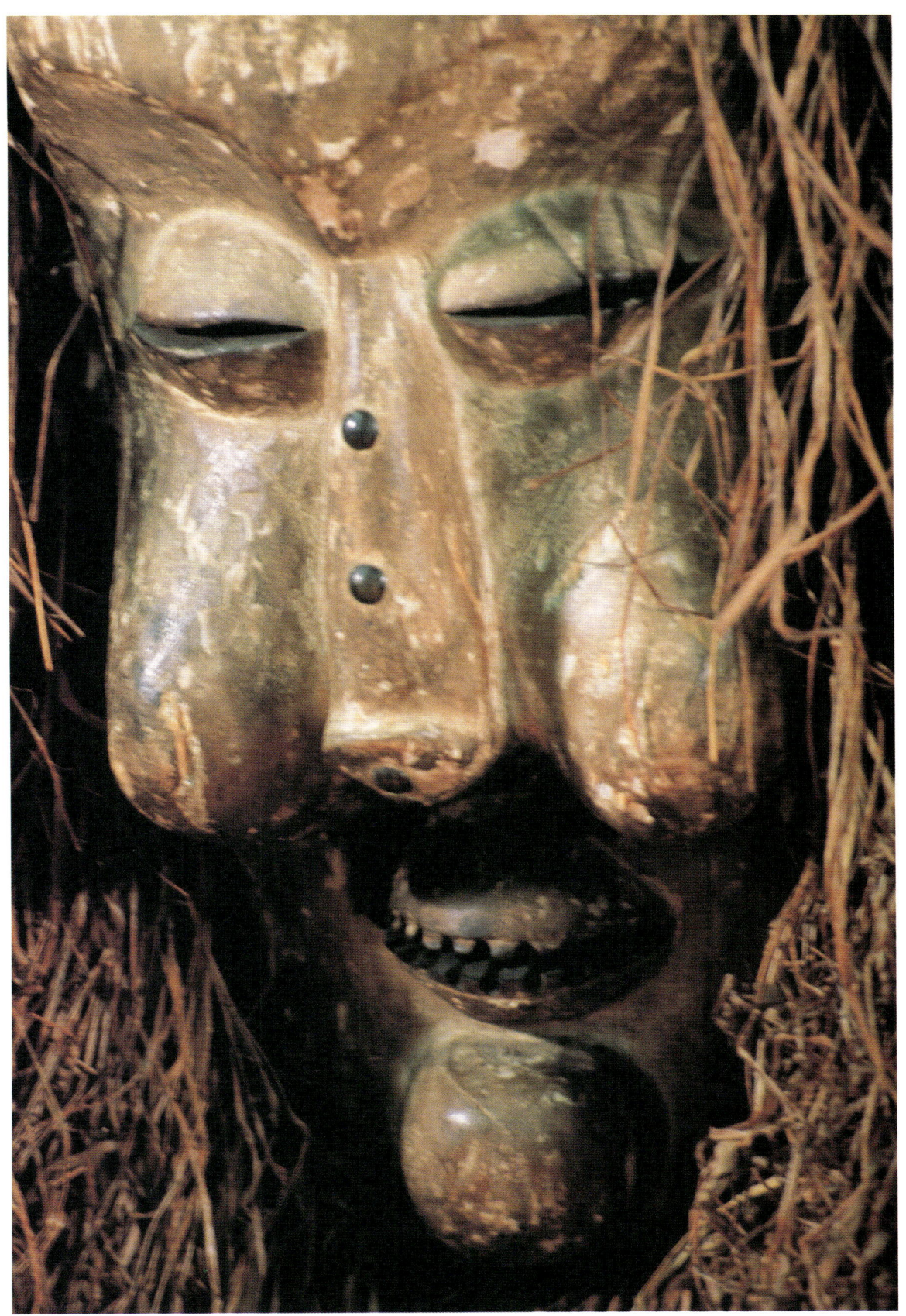

Fig. 38
Kakungu *mask, Suku,*
Zaire, wood, raffia,
H. 29 *in.*

of eastern Nigeria on either side of the Niger River. The Igbo living close to the Niger have invisible gods related to rivers and an earth goddess.[19] An association with water is apparent in the fish penetrating the mossy textured hair of the mask. There is a finny projection over the painted ears; the nose resembles a sharp fin, even the mouth pouts like that of a fish (figure 41).

A smaller mask with an elaborate headdress composed of three black semicircular crestings, possibly representing combs—the center one decorated with knobs—is Igbo in style (figure 42). The face has parted lips revealing the teeth. Four segments of scarification stand in raised relief in front of each ear; a series of barely visible painted dots move from the nose to the forehead. Painted scarification is indicated on both cheeks—a line on one and an X on the other.

Corresponding to the Igbo "notion of complementarity,"[20] another mask has two faces connected back to back. Attached to arched structures that rise from the top of the large heads, two small masks bind the profiles together (figures 43, 44, 45, 46). The arrangement of two faces looking out in opposite directions, a recurrent treatment in African sculpture, is usually referred to as a "Janus" head. The term is borrowed from the Roman god who gave his name to the month of January. One head looks backward into the past and the other forward into the future, thus profiting in the New Year from past mistakes. The classical device does not seem to have influenced African usage; instead the interpretation centers around the joining of opposites, that is, masculine-feminine, light-dark, the civilized and the demonic. In this case the small masks at right angles to the large faces reflect the patterns of scarification on the cheeks of the larger masks. One of the major faces is darker than the other. The lighter mask has a hair arrangement with a twisted shell motif on either side of the face that resembles certain feminine coiffures.

Often spoken of as the N'gunie River style, a white-faced Punu mask is illustrated in figures 47 and 48. It is made by equatorial forest people to the south and southwest of Gabon. Although white masks are present throughout Gabon, the Punu masks are more naturalistic. The face is oval with a rounded forehead often marked with a diamond-shaped scarification. The hair is dressed in a mounded or looped fashion and resembles the hair arrangement of the women of the region. The realistic effect is rapidly dispelled when the mask is worn by a stilt dancer lifted in the air to a height of fifteen feet. A vivid description relates, "In this context the mask appeared tiny, out of proportion with the rest of the body. The effect was unearthly, as was suitable for masks said to represent the spirits of beautiful young women who have returned to the world to participate in funerals. The elaborate three part coiffure and the diamond shaped marks on the forehead indicate that the spirits

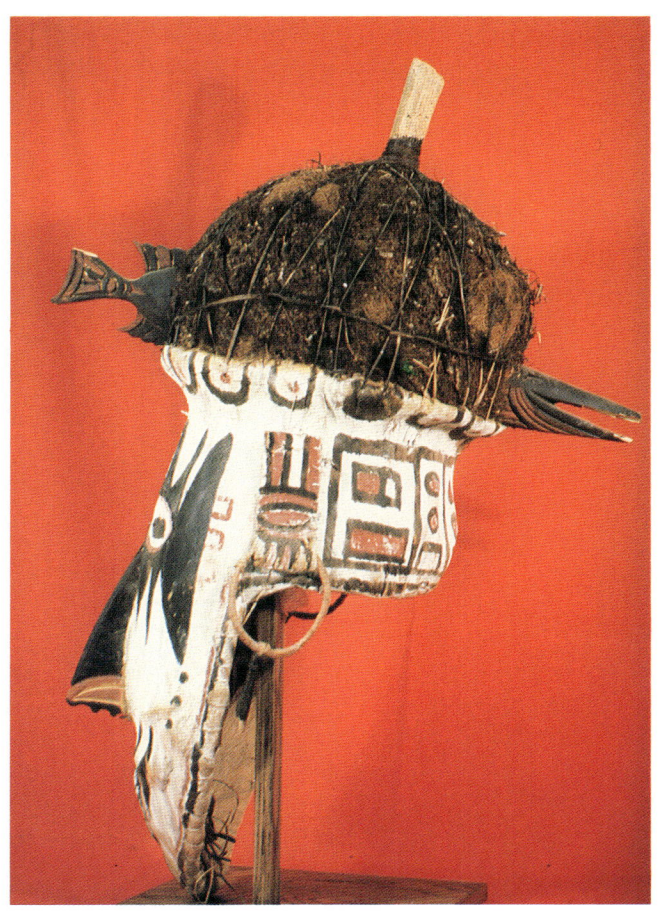

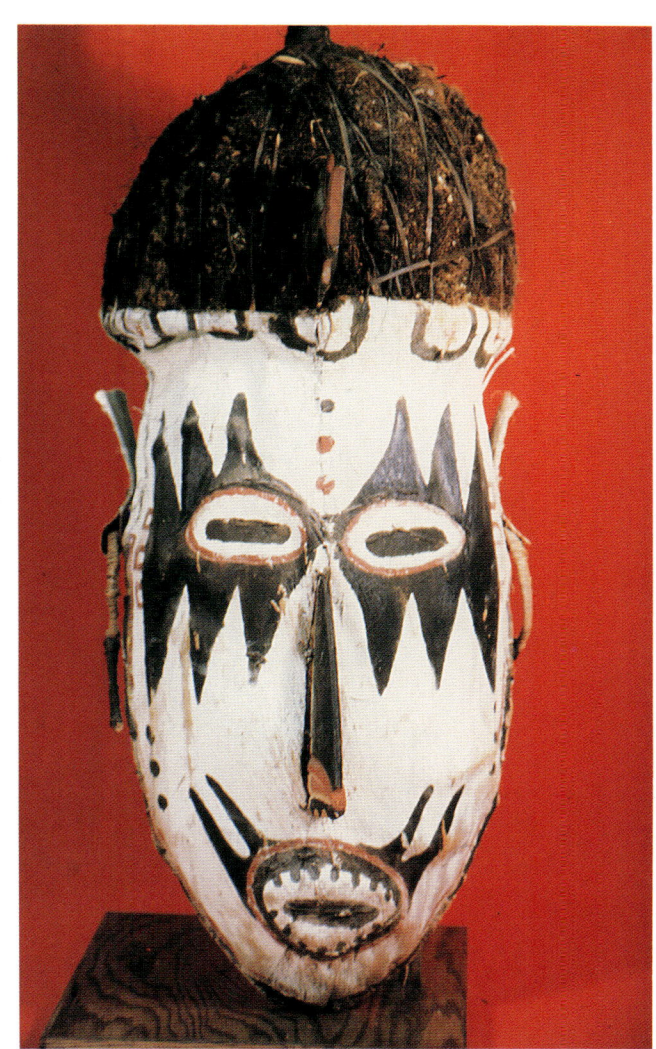

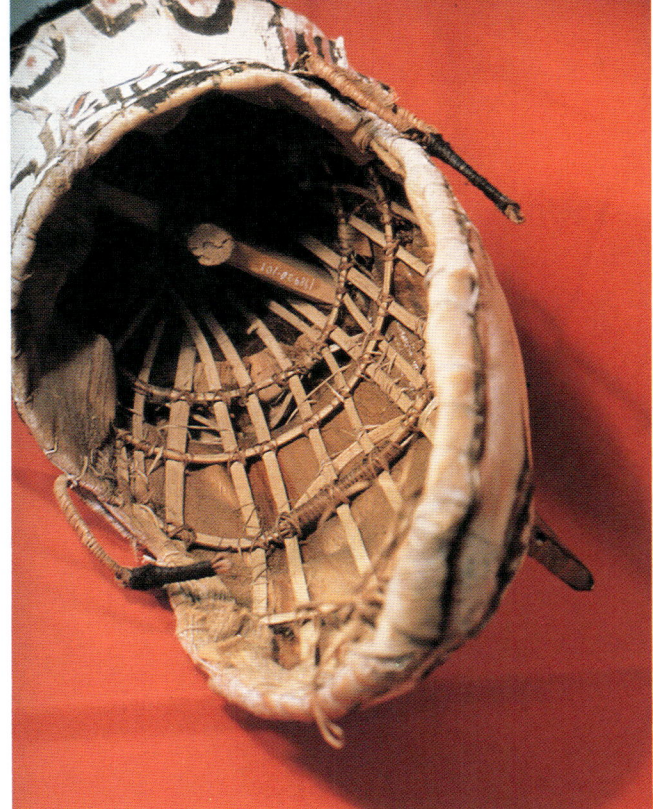

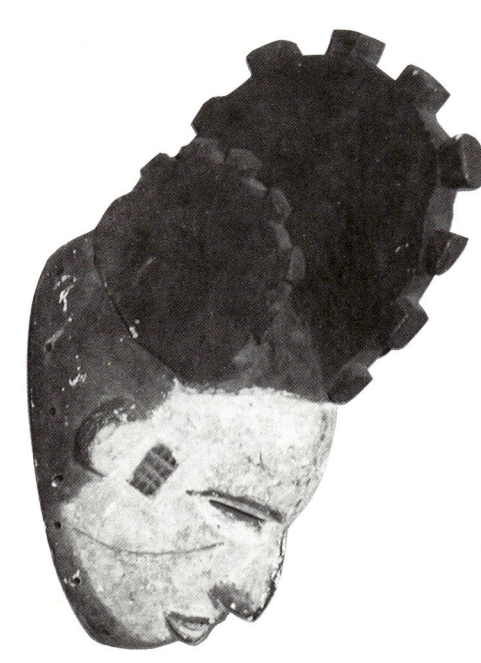

Fig. 41 (Top left)
Detail of mask 39.
Fig. 39 (Top right)
Mask, origin unknown,
Igbo(?), Nigeria, wicker,
wood, fibers, paint,
H. 33 1/4 in.
Fig. 40 (Bottom left)
Detail of mask 39.
Fig. 42 (Bottom right)
Mask, Igbo, Nigeria,
wood, pigment, H. 19 in.

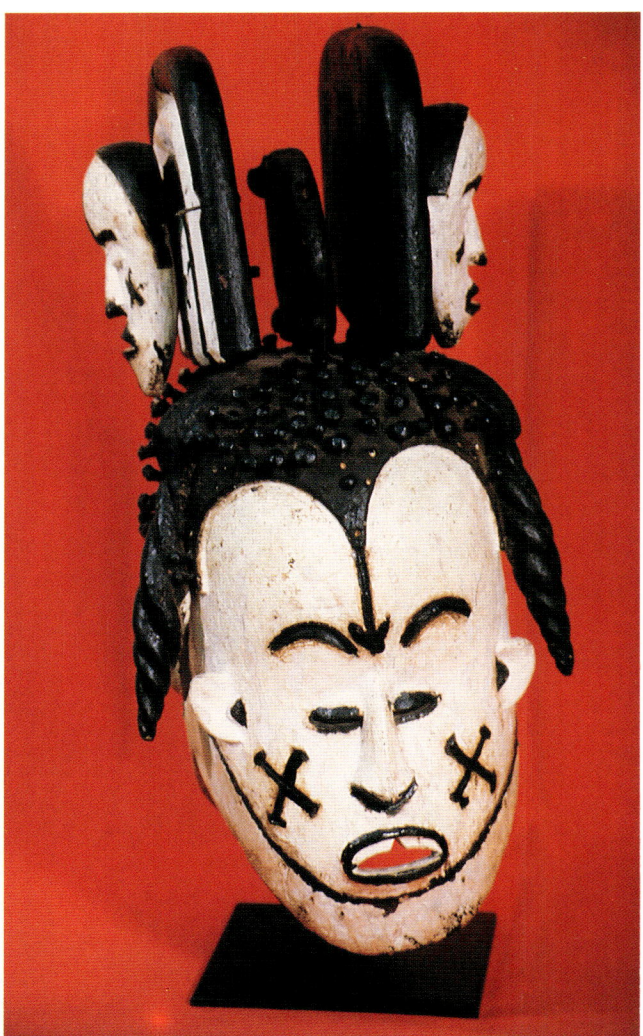
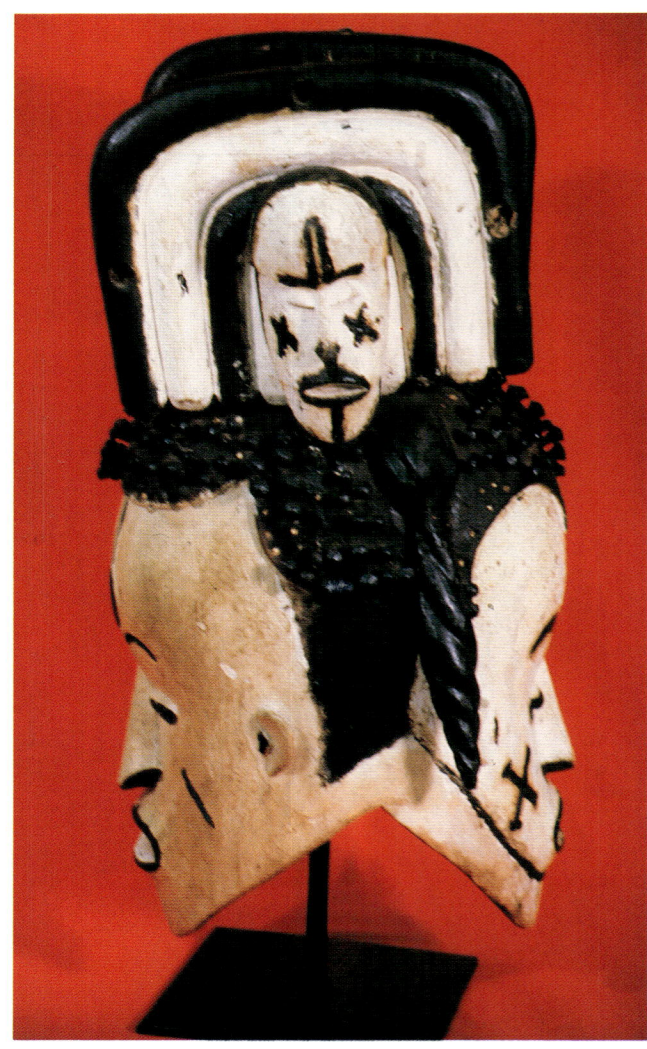

Fig. 43
Mask ("Janus" type),
Igbo, Nigeria, wood,
pigment, H. 21 in.

Fig. 44
Detail of "Janus" type
mask 43.

are still members of their ethnic group even after death."[21] The white face is an indication that a spirit is represented. The eerie drama is intensified because the maskers often dance at the time of the full moon.

There is a curious resemblance between the Gabon Punu mask with its slightly slanted eyes and pale flesh tones and Japanese stage make-up that whitens the skin with rice powder. This tempting analogy has never been substantiated, but in *African Masterpieces* by Suzanne Vogel and Francine N'Diaye, a small block in the puzzle of contact with the Japanese is suggested. Vogel and N'Diaye point out that it is known that some Africans from the mouth of the Niger sailed to Japan as crew members on Portuguese vessels during the seventeenth century. 22

White for the face is the only paint visible on a curious mask similar to those made by the Wurkum, an ethnic people living in the Nigerian province of Bauchi north of the Benue valley (figure 49). Associated with fertility rituals, the Wurkum mask has an easily remembered shape. A head, held on a long neck, rises from a round tirelike collar (in this instance decorated with very small carved masks). Curving over the head from the back to the front, there is a projecting crest. The figure has a

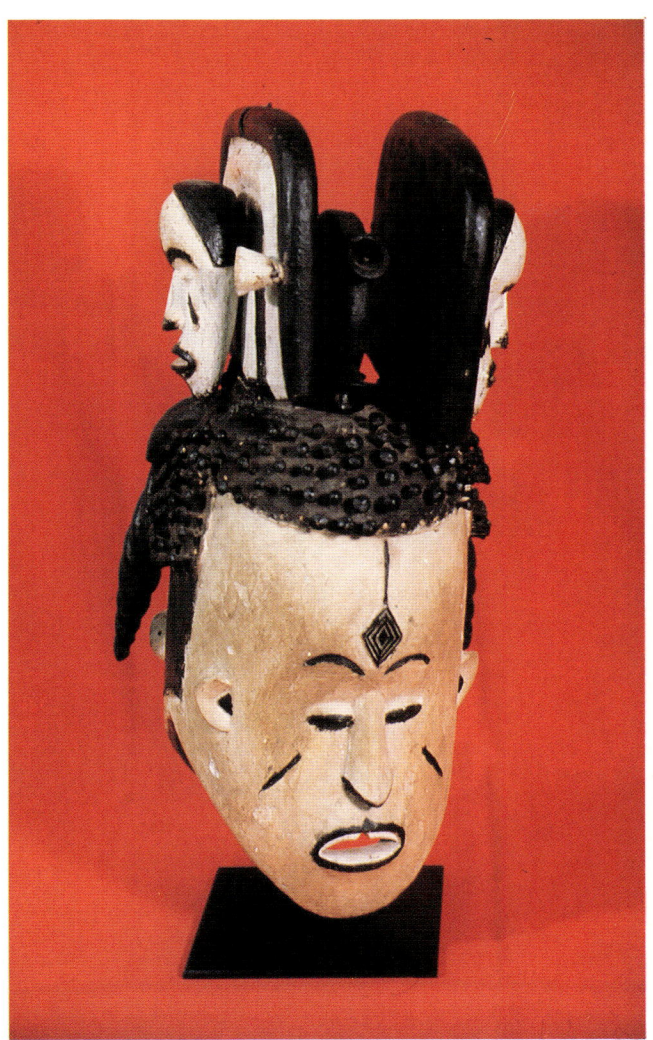
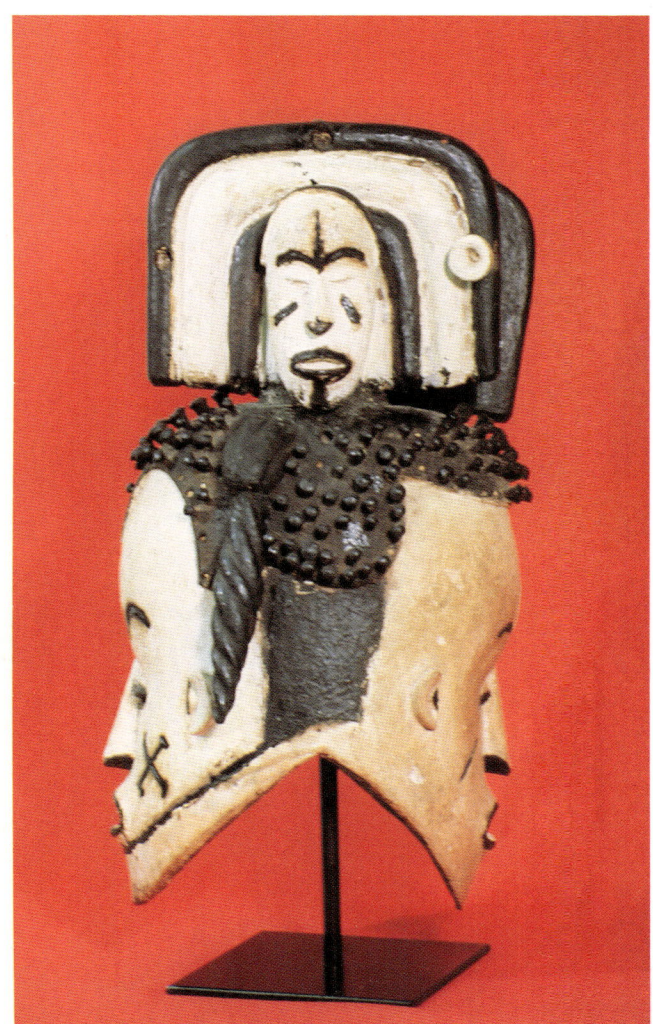

slightly concave face to which white paint has been applied; nose, eyes, and mouth are in low relief. The nose, extending like a bird's beak associated with the typical mask, is omitted in this example. The carved head, neck, and circular ring are attached to a wooden helmet. Rounded and domed, the hollow interior accommodates the masker's head; his body is hidden by a raffia skirt attached to the lower part of the wood.[23]

Large and dramatic painted masks are made by the Yoruba who live in northwestern Nigeria and the Republic of Benin. These play an important part in the Epa masquerades during festivals celebrating the social interplay of people living in the northern Ekiti towns. The masks also call attention to the hierarchy that interlinks ranks and occupations: the work of the farmer, the hunter, the shaman and herbalist, the warrior. But of greatest importance to the stability of all, the harmonious relation between male and female is stressed.[24] Two excellent examples of Epa masks are shown in figure 50. The tallest mask is forty-four inches in height. On top of the wooden headpiece worn over the masker's face, a platform displays a man accompanied by three

Fig. 45
Detail of "Janus" type mask 43.

Fig. 46
Detail of "Janus" type mask 43.

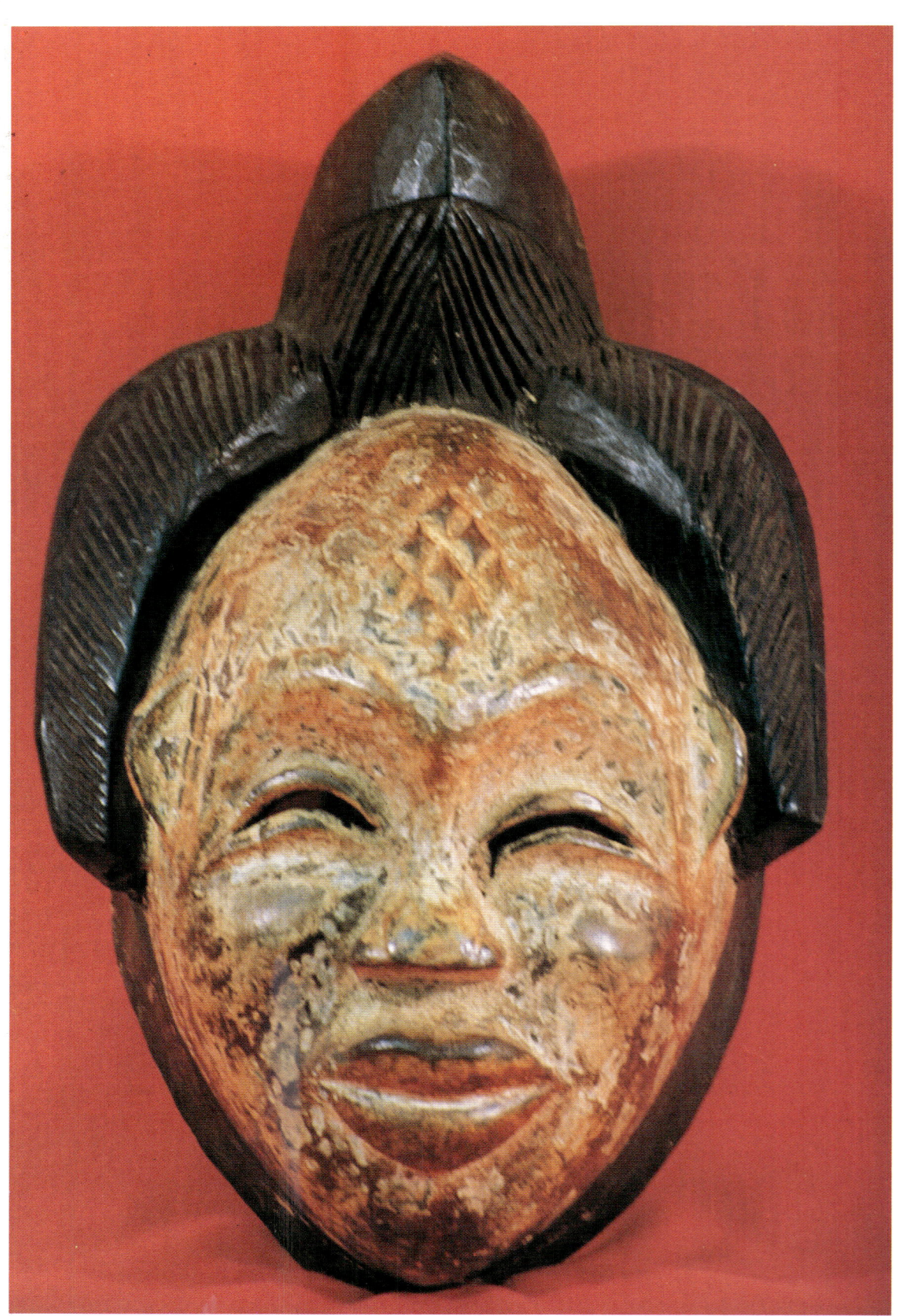

Fig. 47
Punu mask, *Gabon,*
wood, pigment,
H. 16 in.

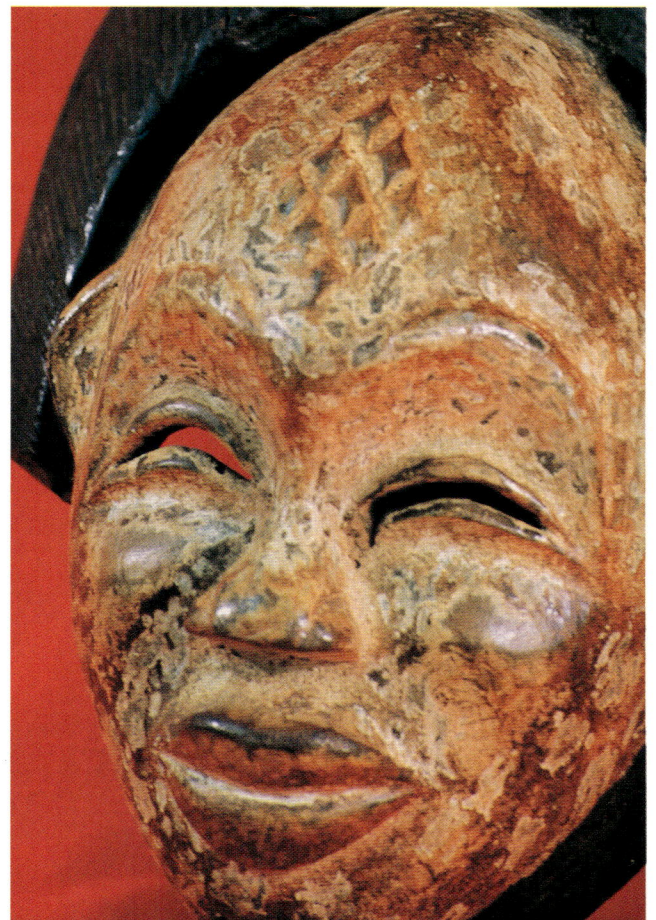

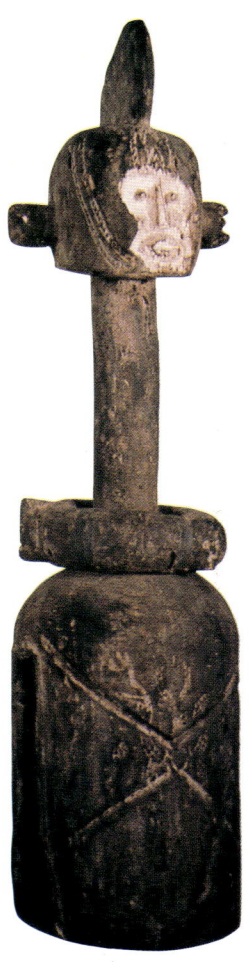

Fig. 48
Detail of Punu *mask 47.*

Fig. 49
Mask, Wurkum, Nigeria, wood, pigment. H. 43 in.

figures. The second mask, forty inches tall, has a superstructure occupied by a woman with her children.

The composition of an Epa mask is, thus, divided into two parts. A helmet covers the dancer's head. This is shaped like a pot with twin faces, carved in a "Janus" arrangement (figure 51). The bulging eyes have no openings. Instead, the masquerader looks out from an open mouth. Square ears at the sides are shared by both faces. Palm fronds or cloth fastened at the base of the mask hide the figure of the dancer. The second division of the mask rises above the headpiece and is a stage for multiple figures that form a tableau.

The principal male carved on the Epa mask in the museum collection is mounted on a horse; he carries a spear, suggesting the occupation of warrior-hunter. Smaller figures on foot accompany him: a flute player upon whose head the horseman rests his hand (figure 52), a woman with a jar, and a girl who holds on to the lower part of the spear. Each of these wears multiple carved bracelets indicating that they may be members of a prominent family rather than servants.

A maternal presence is dominant in figure 53. Surrounded by smaller figures, the mother, her hair dressed in a central crest, stands

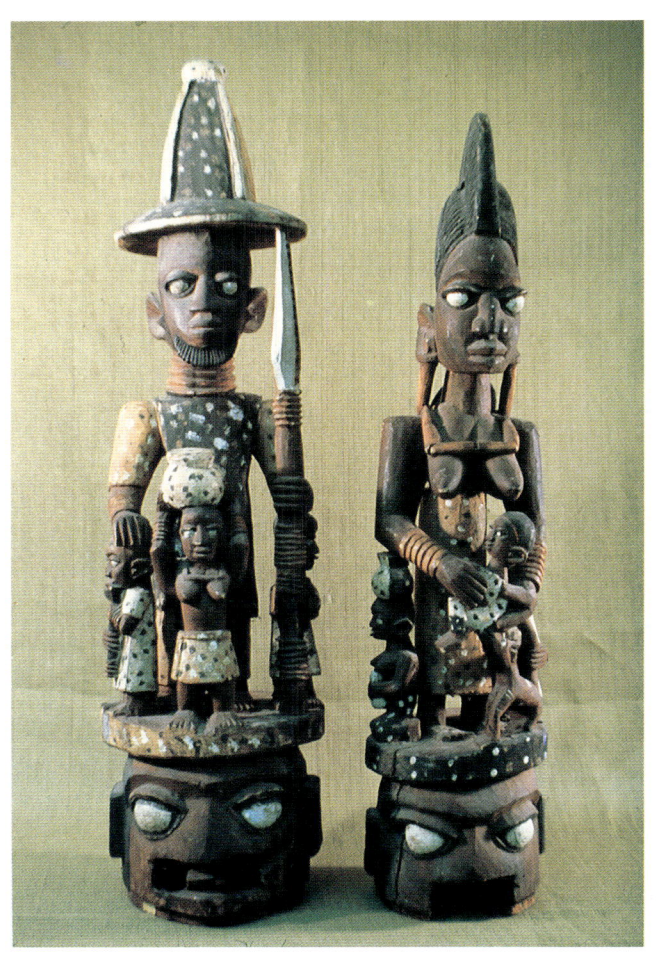

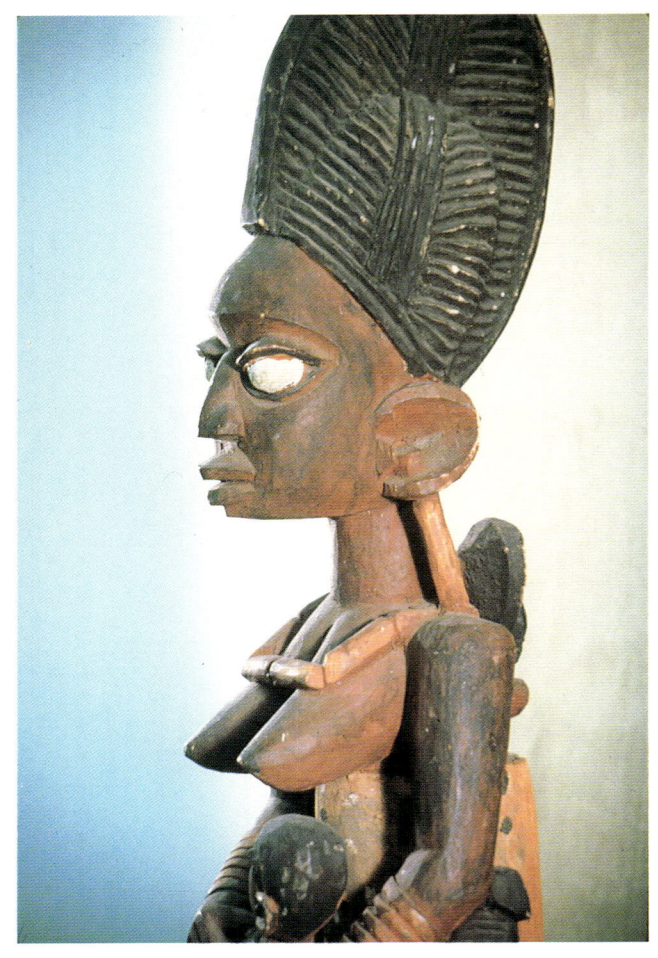

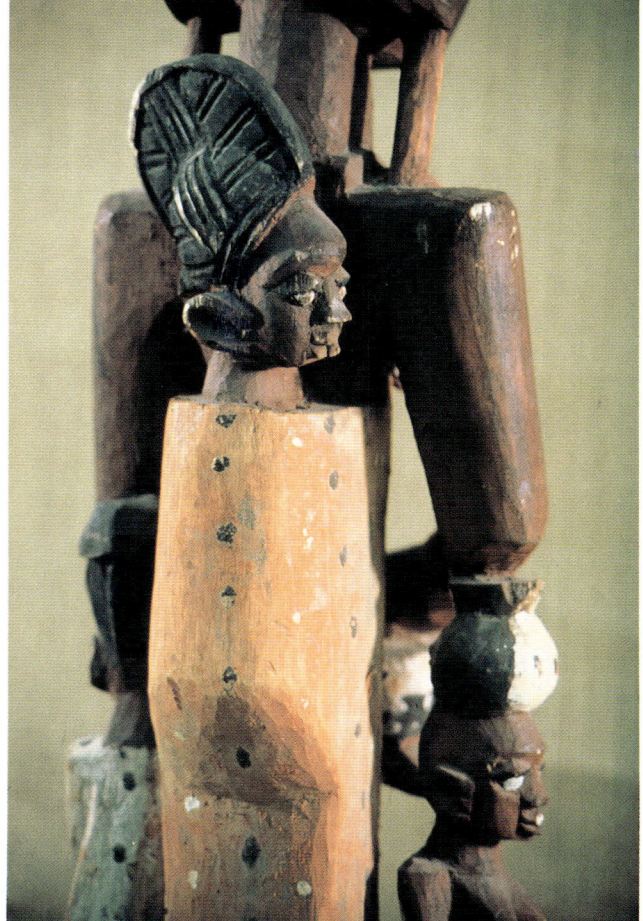

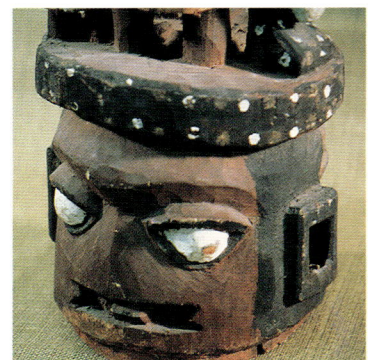

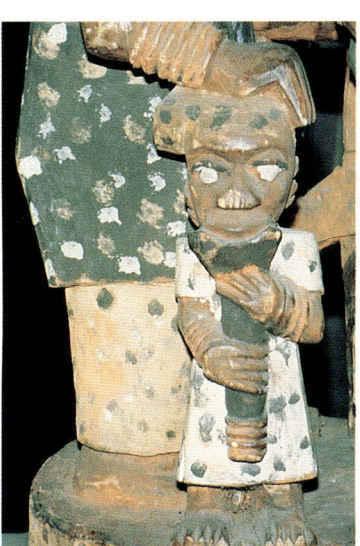

Fig. 50 (Top left)
Masks, Epa, Yoruba, Ni-
geria, wood, paint:
man, H. 44 in.;
woman, H. 40 in.

Fig. 53 (Top right)
Detail of head and shoul-
ders, woman's Epa mask
50.

Fig. 54 (Bottom left)
Detail of baby on
mother's back, woman's
Epa mask 50.

Fig. 51 (Middle right)
Detail (helmet) of
man's Epa mask 50.

Fig. 52 (Bottom right)
Detail, child with musi-
cal instrument on man's
Epa mask 50.

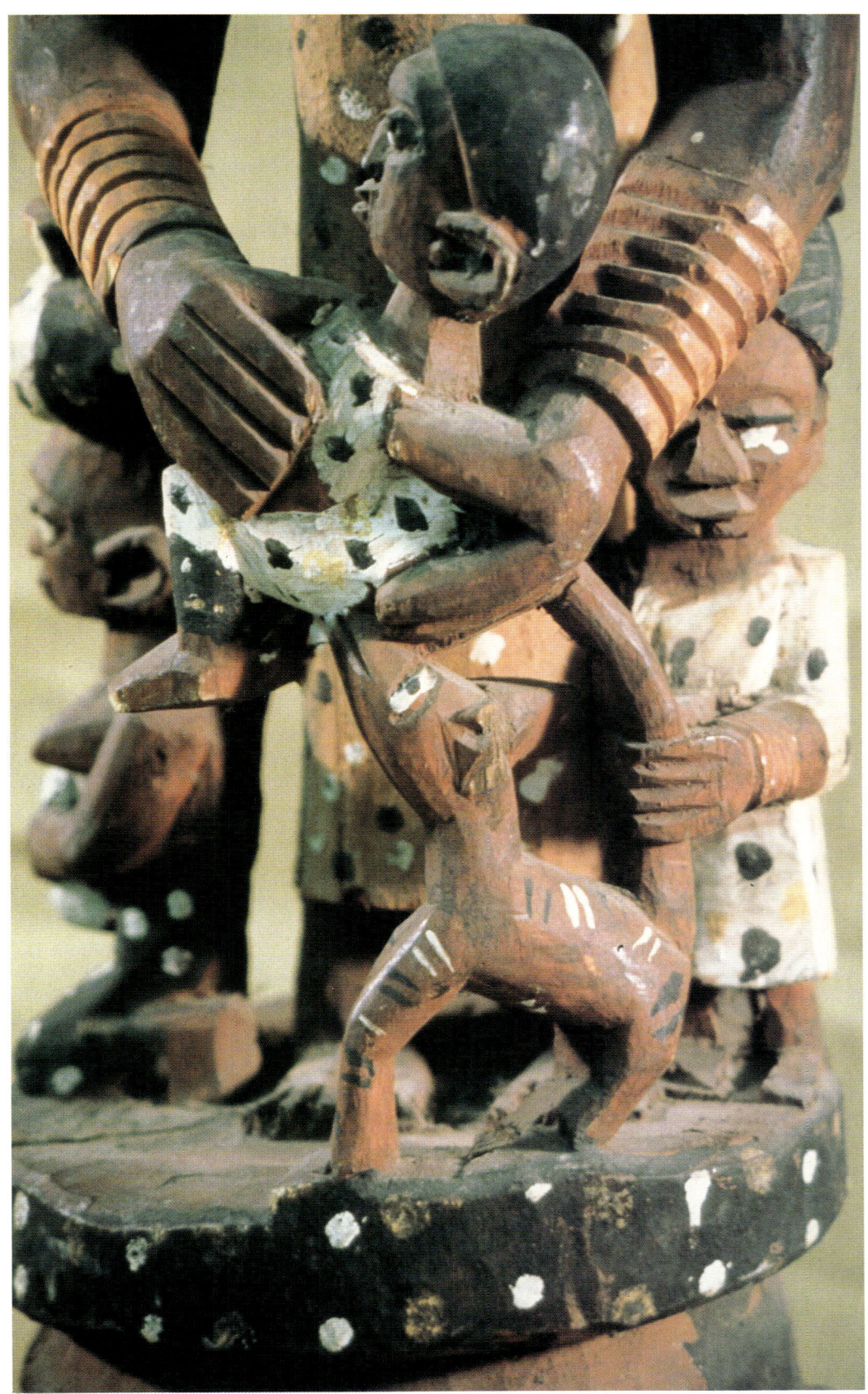

Fig. 55
Detail of children on woman's Epa *mask 50.*

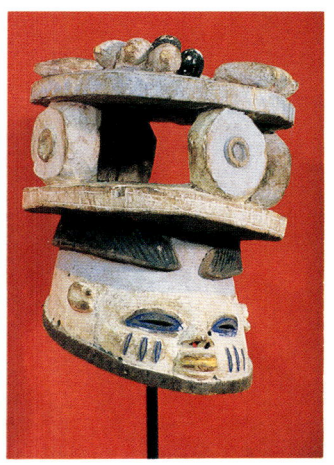

*Fig. 56
Gelede mask, Yoruba,
Nigeria, wood, paint,
H. 15 1/4 in.*

arrow straight. A bright-eyed baby is tucked into a carrying wrapper on her back (figure 54). An older child hides behind the mother's skirts while craftily pulling a dog's tail (figure 55); the dog retaliates by nipping a youngster cradled in its mother's arms. Despite such diversions, the tall woman is unflappable.

At the Epa festivities, the wearer of one of the towering masks must rush into the dance square and leap onto an earthen mound more than three feet high. Should he stumble in this attempt, it is a message that the offerings that have been made are not satisfactory to the deities and ancestors.[25] It is appropriate that the name of Epa, a venerated woodcarver, has been given to this annual celebration distinquished by its intricately carved and painted masks, which tilt high above the crowded plaza. During most of the year, the Epa masks are kept in a shrine. Only when they are removed and animated by the movements of the dancers do the masks become complete in the eyes of the villagers.

The Gelede mask also plays an important role among the western Yoruba. The Gelede masquerades were first initiated toward the end of the seventeenth century. The important ceremonies honor the "spiritual power of elderly women" known as *awon iya wa,* or "our mothers." The celebrations are intended to honor and please the powerful old ones and to persuade them to use their influences for the good of the people and community. The concept of "the mothers" contains elements of both good and evil. The harmful aspect comes from the practice of witchcraft; the positive influence channels forces that will benefit the people.[26] The identity of the wearer of the Gelede mask is not hidden. The painted mask is worn on top of the dancer's head with only a gauze cloth covering the face (figure 56). The carvers have a wide range of subjects from which to choose: they may select familiar proverbs, animals treated metaphorically, fruits, or other agricultural products.

Both painted patterns and textures of all kinds are used on masks made by the Kuba who live in Zaire. The Kuba kingdom originated in western Kasai at the beginning of the seventeenth century. At its height in the second half of the nineteenth century, craftsmen fostered an art intended to increase the prestige of the wealthy and powerful. Sculptors enjoyed a privileged position in society. It was their responsibility to make the elaborately decorated masks required for initiation rites and for funerals.

The *bombo* helmet mask in figure 57 is referred to by William Bascom as *Mboom* and described as a representation of a rival, possibly a Pygmy, who desired the sister-wife of a Kuba ancestor known as Woot.[27] This mask appears at initiations and is distinguished by a rounded overhanging forehead and unusual beaded bands and patterns of shells. Cowrie shells border the mask and form a design at the back

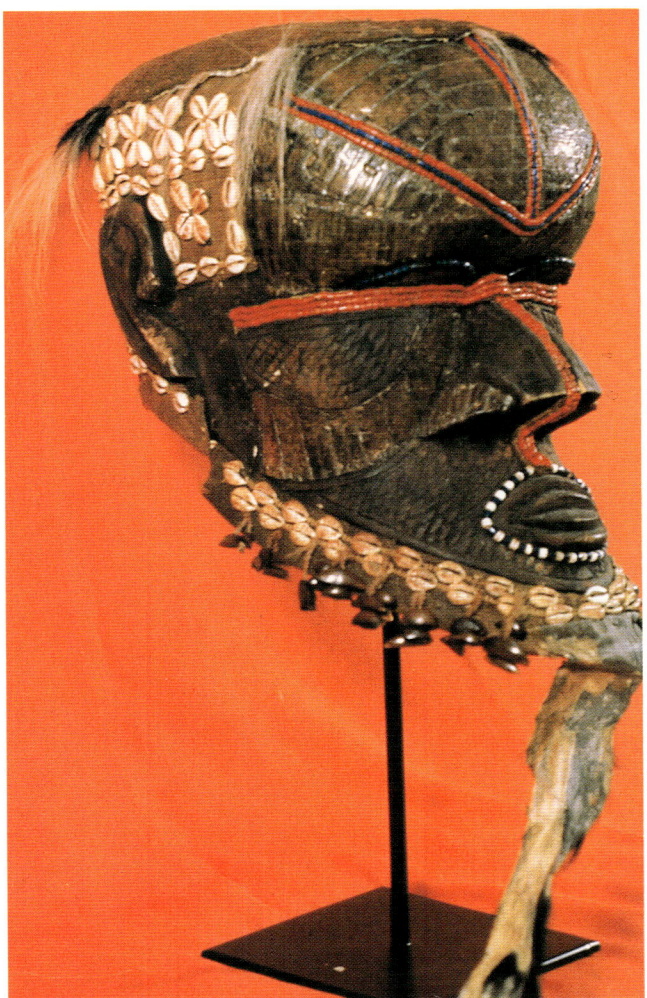

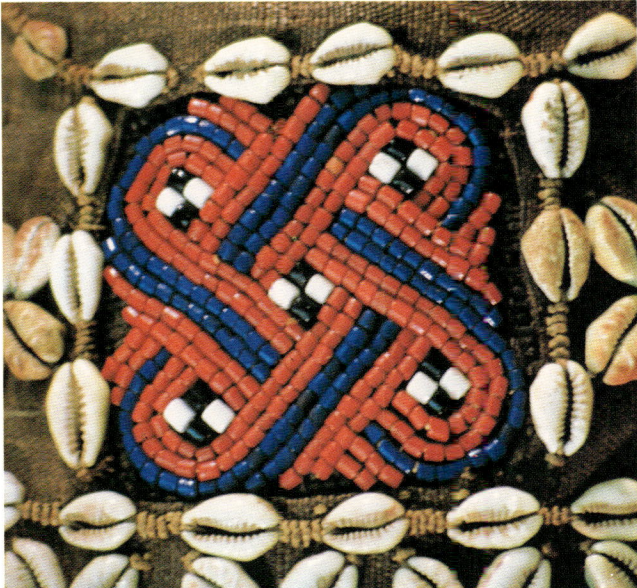

Fig. 57
Mask, Mboom, *Kuba, Zaire,*
wood, glass beads, cowrie shells,
antelope skin, tufts of hair,
feathers, H. 19 in.

Fig. 58
Detail of Mboom *mask 57.*

of the helmet (figure 58). The intertwining motif is used by many western sub-Saharan people. It appears as a carving, for example, on Yoruba doors. Associated with the Yoruba deity Ogun, it possesses an affinity with the circle of life that is interwoven endlessly, and with the idea of mystic support and psychic sustenance. It is also interpreted as representing the coils of serpents. The forehead is trisected by bands of red glass beads that move down the nose across the mouth; an additional line of red beads bandages the eyes. Sealing the eyes may symbolize the secrecy involved in initiation and its accompanying rituals. The mouth is outlined by alternating white and black beads. A narrow beard, possibly of antelope skin, is attached to the chin.

Another Kuba mask has eyes that are formed of conelike projections. Koloss has pointed out that they resemble the eyes of a chameleon.[28] Painted with colored segments, the cones are surrounded by perforations acting as openings through which the masker can see (figure 59). Some masks are made without eyeholes and are placed on the points of the timbers used for the initiation wall built on one side

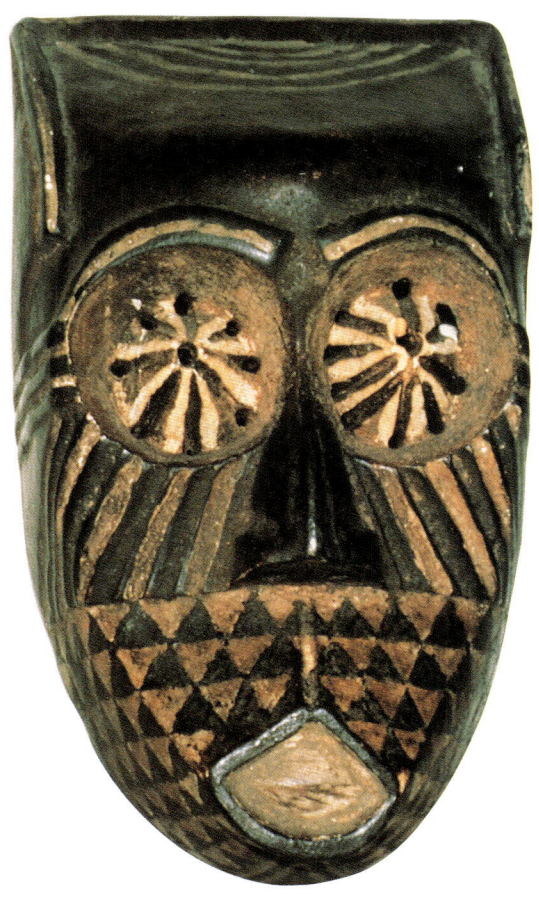

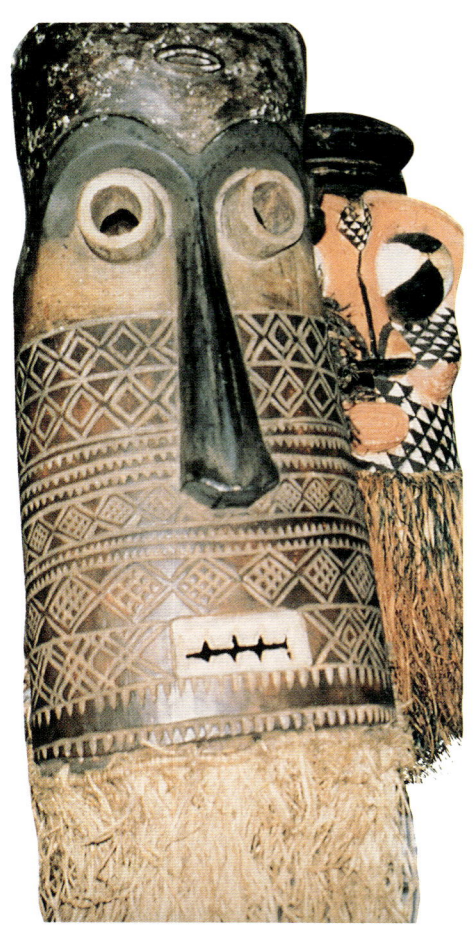

Fig. 59
Mask, Kuba, Zaire,
wood, pigment,
H. 12 in.

Fig. 60
Mulwalwa *mask in*
background, Kuba,
Zaire, wood, paint,
fiber, H. approx 19 in.;
Pumbu *mask in fore-*
ground, Eastern Pende,
Zaire, wood, fiber,
H. approx. 24 in.

of a village during the period in which the rituals of passage take place.[29]

There is a mask called a *Mulwalwa* that is barely visible at the far right in figure 60. The "chameleon eyes" and a pot on top of the head help in its identification and place it in the realm of male activities. The inverted container refers to the men who carry stacked pots to collect the palm wine consumed with relish and in large quantities during initiation related activities. The pot suggests that *Mulwalwa* may be "a palm wine drinkard," in the words of Amos Tutuola, therefore, dangerous to anyone coming too close. "The unpredictable persona of this mask," Koloss says, "is evident during masked dances when a member of *Mulwalwa*'s entourage controls its aggressive nature by restraining the masked figure with a rope tied firmly around its waist."[30]

The larger mask in the foreground of figure 60 is a *Pumbu* mask of the eastern Pende from Zaire. In *Secrecy, African Art That Conceals and Reveals,* a similar mask is illustrated and described as the most dangerous of the masks, one reserved for only a few of the most powerful chiefs of the region. The description continues:

> Unlike most masks, it dances rarely—and only in the event of special problems, such as a chief's serious illness, or a regional epidemic or famine. Pumbu represents the executive branch of the chief's office, which must sometimes deal with

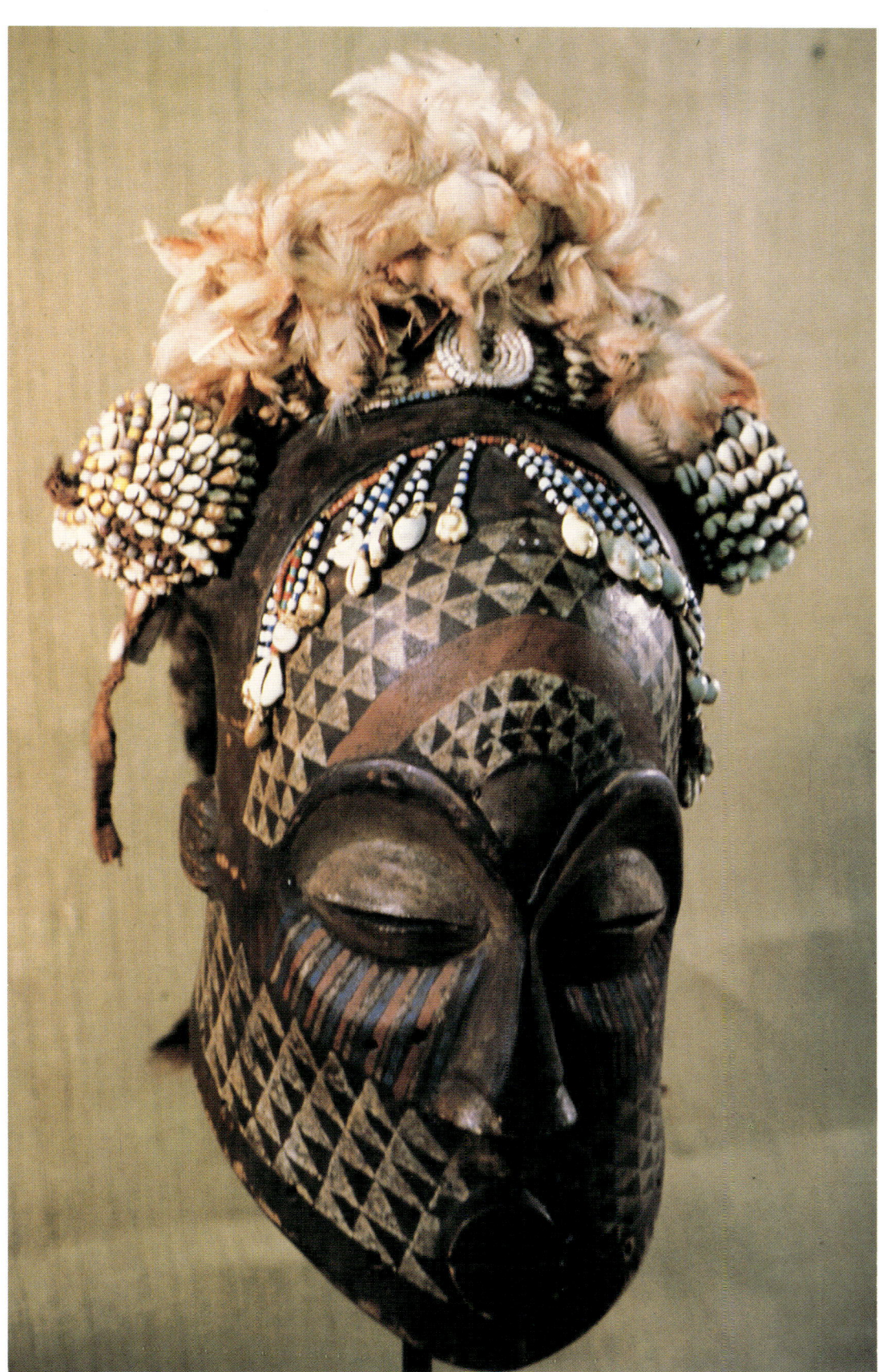

*Fig. 61
Mask, Kuba, Zaire,
wood, paint, shells,
feathers, fur, H. 23 in.*

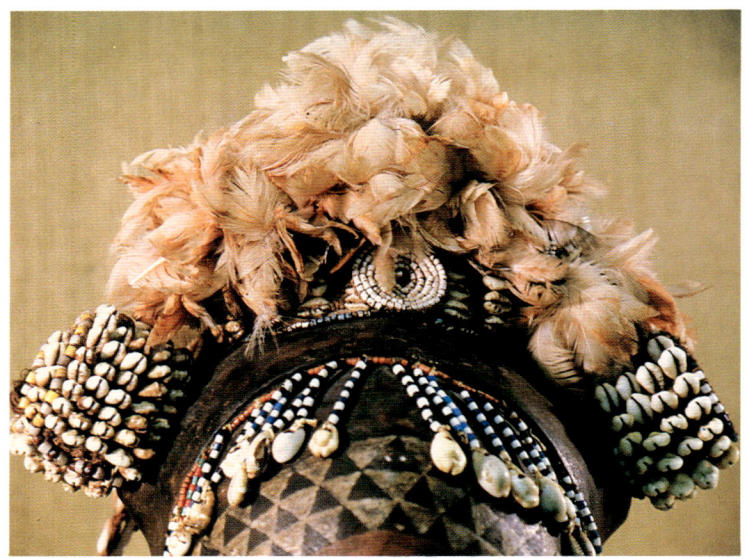

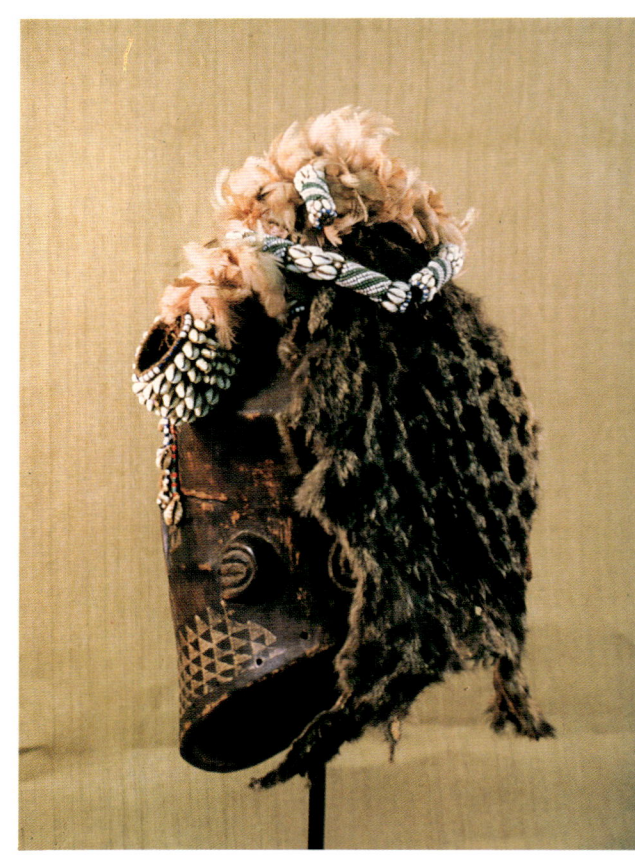

*Fig. 62
Detail of Kuba mask
61.*

*Fig. 63
Detail of Kuba mask
61.*

war or execution. The Pende associate a wide-open eye showing lots of white with uncontrolled anger; hence Pumbu's protruding white-rimmed eyes express an aesthetic of fear.[31]

One of the finest masks at the Museum of Texas Tech University is a helmet with many Kuba features (figures 61, 62). It has painted triangular markings on the chin and arched bands of triangles on the forehead overlaid by a fringe of beads ending in cowrie shells. Cowries are also used to fashion circular lobes on either side of the elaborate headdress. Crowned by fluffy reddish tan feathers, the arrangement is climaxed in back by a piece of leopard skin from which slivers of fur dangle like the beast's legs (figure 63).

Difficult to identify precisely, figure 64 exhibits Kuba characteristics. There are parallel stripes on the cheeks and on the forehead, where they are centered by a clan marking and a dangling string of cowries. The lines descending under the eyes are interpreted as tears shed on the death of an initiated man. The tears relate to the context in which the mask is worn, because the same mask serves for both initiations and funeral occasions.[32] A strand of cowries and cluster of fibers descending from carved and coiled ram's horns are present on either side of the face.

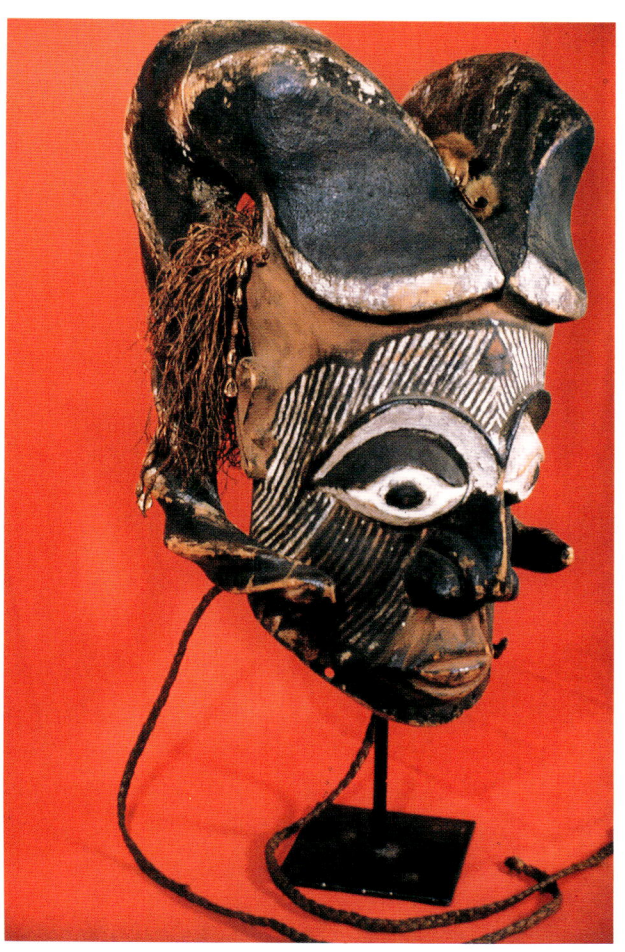

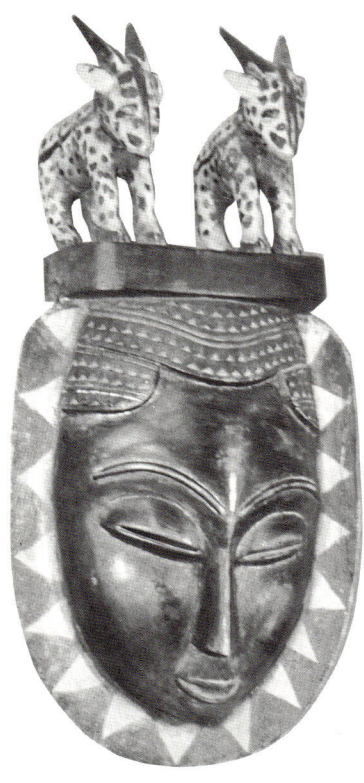

The mask, eyes wide open, has an arresting character that is not easily forgotten. The colors used are primarily black, white, and reddish brown.

These colors appear frequently among various ethnic groups, but they differ in interpretation. White, for example, is associated by the Punu with the land of the dead, spirits, and clairvoyance. Among the Kongo white represents health and a harmonious life. Black is the opposite of harmony and suggests disorder and misfortune, whereas red is filled with vitality and possesses magical powers.[33]

Made of blackened wood accompanied by light brown and black paint, the mask in figure 65 shares design qualities with the Yaure (or Baule). The stylized hair framing the face supports a platform on which two horned animals stand. Painted around the face of the mask, there is triangular pattern in a beige tone; a similar design is often done with cutwork. The same yellowish color is applied to the animals that resemble goats; their bodies are splattered with black dots. Animals and birds are frequently subjects for western sub-Saharan African masks, indicating the close relation between people and the creatures that share their environment.

Fig. 64 (Left) Mask, Kuba charac- teristics, Zaire, wood, paint, fiber, beads, H. 22 in.

Fig. 65 (Right) Mask, Yaure (or Baule), Ivory Coast, wood, pigment, H. 18 in.

II

Animal Masks

*If you follow an elephant
you don't have to knock the de
from the grass.*

An Asante Proverb

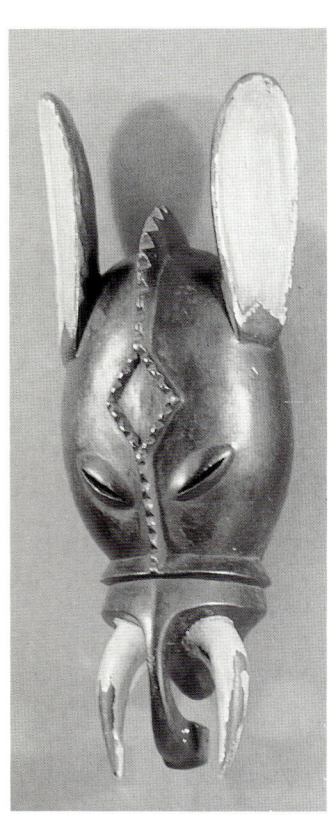

*Fig. 66
Elephant mask, Guro,
Ivory Coast, wood,
H. 19 in.*

In myths and legends animals are the helpers of the ancestors and are honored and respected by later generations. Wild animals are hunted for food and hides; domesticated ones not only supply nourishment but are sacrificed in honor of the supernaturals and ancestral spirits to bring benefits for the village people. Like the spirits of some ancestors who roamed angrily about in the world of the living believing that they were neglected by their kinsmen, an animal killed by a hunter who does not perform the proper ritual may lay in wait to take revenge. A mask could entrap the animal's spirit enabling the wearer to cause the creature to submit to his authority. When a shaman or masker puts on an animal mask, he absorbs something of the animal's power—the antelope's grace and speed, the leopard's strength and majesty, the ram's bravery in head-on combat, the cunning of the wily hare, the magic of the bird's flight, or the elephant's ponderous endurance.

In Benin, where the village of Oregbeni was the center of the guild of elephant hunters, the elephant was linked to the chief's power.[34] A familiar figure and the goal of hunting expeditions, the elephant was represented with great accuracy. This visual understanding is present in a splendid bronze plaque, now in the National Museum in Lagos, Nigeria. The elephant mask pictured in figure 66 was made by the Guro who live on the shores of the Badama in Ivory Coast, an area that ranges from heavily forested land to tree-filled savannas. The carving suggests an absence of face-to-face contact with elephants; the tusks that dwarf the small hooked trunk indicate that the Guro were better acquainted with ivory as a favored trade item than with the anatomy of the beast.

Another Guro example is the *zamble* mask, representing a polychrome carving that is both antelope and panther (figure 67).[35] At one time the Zamble secret society used this as a war-mask, but in recent times their dances are held in public and at dance competitions organized by villages.

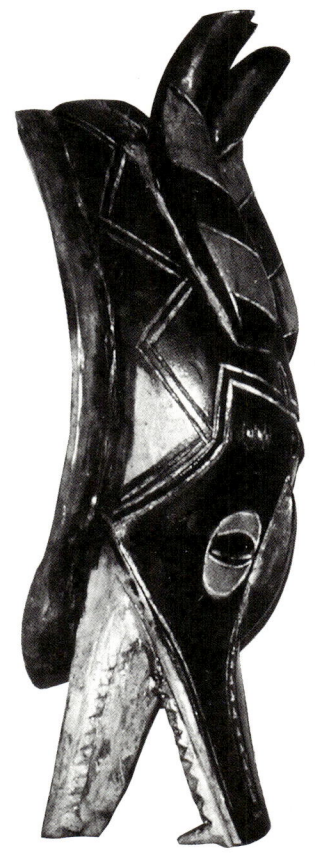

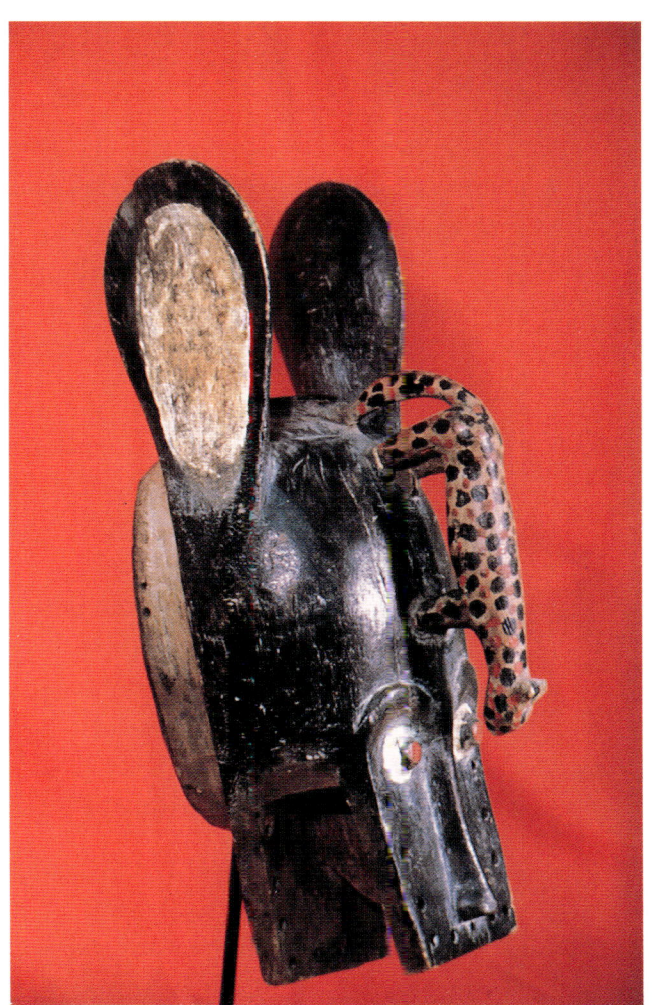

An as yet unidentified mask displays some Guro qualities (figure 68). Between the large ears, a spotted leopard climbs down the forehead to have a better look at the creature's red eyes, circled in black and placed over startling white outer rings. When there is a wide open mouth with a carved tongue, as in this instance, the opening may allow the wearer to see through the gaping jaws; otherwise, the mask is probably worn on top of the head rather than in a vertical position.

It is not surprising that animals represented on masks are closely bound to the land where they roam and where the people who see and hunt them make their homes. There are many antelope masks among the ethnic peoples of the steppe, dry savanna, and grasslands of Mali, Burkina Faso, and Niger. These semiarid land dwellers carry on dryland farming when the periodic rains fall and hunt during the rainless seasons. In southwest Mali, the antelope headpieces associated with the *tyi wara* performances of the Bamana are striking in appearance; the grace and noble bearing of the *dage*, or roan antelope, is captured in the stylized design. The male's tall, slender horns rise above a mane often carved in an openwork pattern. The female antelope is represented carrying a young one on her back. Oddly, the antelope with its

Fig. 67
Zamble mask, Guro,
Ivory Coast, wood, pig-
ment, H. 14 1/2 in.

Fig. 68
Mask, Guro(?), Ivory
Coast, wood, pigment,
H. 25 3/4 in.

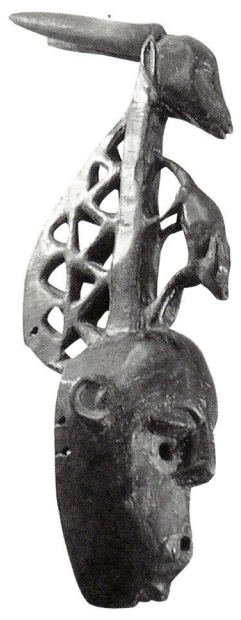

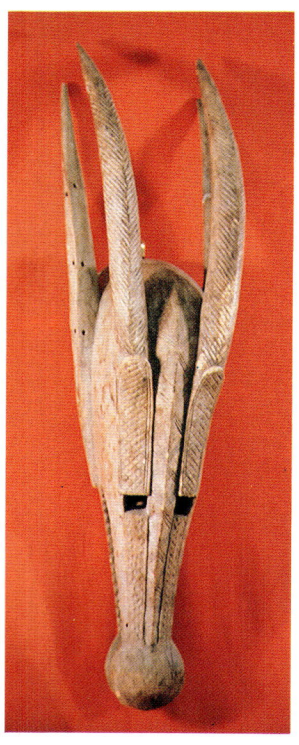

Fig. 69
*Mask, Bamana, Mali,
wood, beads, H. 25 in.*

Fig. 70
*Mask, Bamana, Mali,
wood, H. 33 in.*

speed and elusiveness symbolizes the Bamana farmer's skills. The seeming paradox between the antelope's swiftness and evasiveness in contrast to the plodding laborer working in the fields is discussed by Sarah Brett-Smith in *African Art*. She points to the timidity of the creature, "even the sadness of an animal on the alert for its pursuer," who shares with man the fragility of life in the "harsh Sahel environment." She continues:

> Like the antelope, the Bamana farmer must remain ever alert to evade the alternate waves of flooding and drought that imperil his life. Poised to meet any emergency, he must alter his farming tactics to meet every change in the weather, just as the antelope zigzags to and fro to escape the hunter. In some years a Bamana farmer may sow five times to reap even a small harvest; one small mistake and the family starves the next year. The farmer's muscular strength can vanish in a few months of famine, just as the *dage* falls reeling from the hunter's shot. Both human and animal life are surprisingly fragile.[36]

It is the antelope that is believed to have taught the people to cultivate the land with digging sticks. Today when new land is ready to be cleared, two members of the *tyi wara* association come to the fields wearing the antelope headpieces. The male and female carvings are fastened to basketry caps worn on top of the heads. Bending over the sticks held in their hands, the dancers imitate the frolicking of young antelopes in order to propitiate the earth spirits and to insure the fertility and bounty of the new soil revealed. It is said that the body of the dancer represents the aardvark whose habit of burrowing in the earth is seen as mimicking the tasks of the farmers. The dancers celebrate in their dance the planting and the growth of crops. Women participate by forming a chorus that sings the praises of the ideal cultivators. During the masquerade, each man who wears the *tyi wara* headdress has a companion, a woman who dances behind him. This equates the male and the earthly female with the union of the sun, a male force, and the female earth who together produce fruitful fields and the crops that promise abundant food.[37] An account relates, "The zigzag of the [antelope's] mane parallels the zigzag path of the sun between the two solstices; the horns stand for the millet stalk [growing from the earth]. . . . The headdress is worn with a long flowing raffia fringe which represents water . . . necessary for the growth of the plants."[38]

A related mask of blackened wood, so smoothly polished it looks at first like pottery, has a cresting topped by a sensitively carved antelope's head and a body (or mane) fashioned in a zigzag pattern of openwork (figure 69). This is attached to a carved face mask that has circular openings for the eyes surrounded with reddish brown as are the small mouth and pronounced nose. A four-legged creature moves along the antelope's body and touches the mask's forehead. In the light of the symbolism discussed in the preceding paragraph, this may represent the aardvark.

Another Bamana horned mask, related to the antelope, is of unpainted wood (figure 70). The nose is long and slender ending in a slightly bulbous shape. The ears, with holes pierced in them for textured attachments, are almost as long as the curving horns and repeat the linear emphasis of the gracefully attenuated design.

Worn by a male society of the Bamana whose various grades of membership are based on age, the *N'Tomo* mask has a stylized and distinctive design. It is based on the human face and crowned by a band of tall horns that differ in number from five to seven or ten. One of the unusual features is the surface over the face that is decorated with cowrie shells, dried red berries, or aluminum sheeting cut in patterns (see figure 5). At the Museum of Texas Tech University, the *N'Tomo* mask has metal circles placed around the eyes. The metal is enlivened with incised details; metal also covers the bridge of the nose and the area around the mouth and chin. The masks are brought out at agricultural celebrations or to prevent illness.

Among the Marka who live across the Mali border in Burkina Faso, a similar mask, without the candelabra of horns, is worn by the *Ndomo* society members at the circumcision ceremony of adolescents and as men advance from one grade to another.[39] The face, sheathed in metal, is long like the nose of the antelope; oblong eyes are open under the overhanging forehead and two horns rise from the hairline. Narrow vertical rods of metal hang across the eyes; they end in small tassels of red cotton threads (figure 71).

The *Kurumba* antelope headdress from Burkina Faso is another mask that owes its beauty to a keen observation of the graceful antelope (figure 72). The long neck ends with ears, decorated with cowries that loop back to touch the slender horns. The exaggerated length of the nose is painted with bands and lozenges. The mask, which to an observer seems impossible for a dancer to balance, is fastened to the head with a plaited basket. Swaying above the throngs in a dusty plaza at the masquerades, *Kurumba* maskers create awe and a sense of the presence of the supernaturals. At funerals, following a period of mourning, the antelope dancers appear to make certain that the spirits of the dead are sent away from the village and will not harm the living. The fact that the mask has been commercially produced since World War II does not lessen the beauty of the design or the intuitive sense of the antelope spirit.

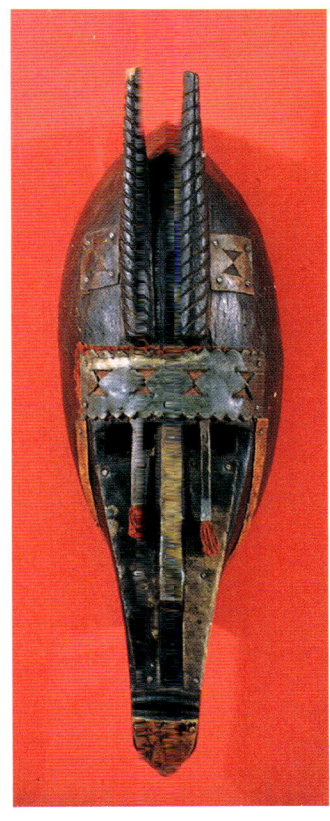

Fig. 71
N'tomo *mask, Marka, Burkina Faso, wood, metal, thread, H. 17 1/2 in.*

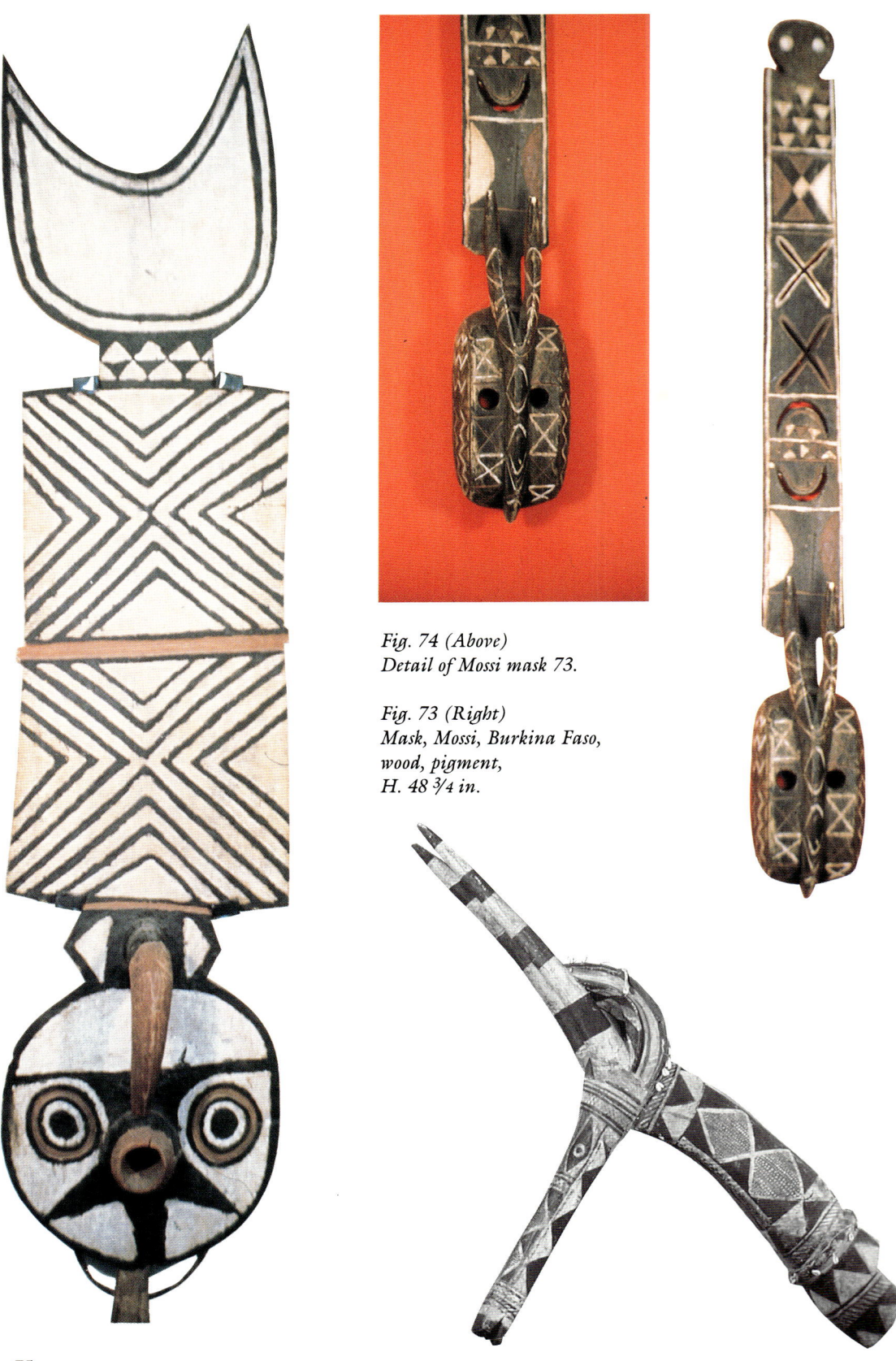

Fig. 74 (Above)
Detail of Mossi mask 73.

Fig. 73 (Right)
Mask, Mossi, Burkina Faso,
wood, pigment,
H. 48 ¾ in.

Fig. 75
Plank mask, Bwa, Burkina Faso, wood, paint, H. approx. 61 in. (Gift of Ambassador and Mrs. Julius Walker to ICASALS; now on permanent loan from ICASALS to the Museum of Texas Tech University.)

Fig. 72
Kurumba antelope headdress, Burkina Faso, wood, paint, cowrie shells, H. 56 in.

Another ethnic group in Burkina Faso, the Mossi, have several unusual antelope-inspired masks. In the Yatenga region the kob antelope is a powerful symbol. Although not illustrated, the University Museum collection has a mask of the Wango society. Vertically oriented, an oval carving with a shallow concavity forms an abstract antelope head that covers the face of the wearer. A spine with ladderlike notches divides the surface and small triangular openings on either side create eyeholes. Almost twice the height of the lower portion of the carving, a female figure, symbolizing an earth spirit, is attached to a decorative backing. The curvilinear treatment of the woman's body juxtaposes positive form and negative space, creating an unexpected harmony with the concave surface of the oval mask. A restrained use of scarification is repeated on the face of the woman. Worn at the annual festival of the ripening of certain fruits, a time when sacrifices are brought to the female deity of the fecundity of land, the mask is also present at the burials of older men of the village.

Verticality is stressed in another male antelope mask of the Mossi. Tall and narrow, the one in the Museum's collection measures 48 3/4 inches in height (figures 73, 74). A boxed head fits over the contour of the wearer's face. Horns spread out from a ridge that separates the face into two parts; round eyes are cut on either side of the raised marking. A design of repeated X shapes and bands are marked on the long, narrow plank above the face. The exact meaning of the recurrent Xs is unclear, but among the Bwa, they are said to refer to scarification on the faces of initiates.[40]

Burkina Faso's Bwa plank masks have a far more massive board rising above round faces with curling noses (figures 75, 76). Until the 1970s, Christopher Roy writes, these masks were identified as Bobo-Fing.[41] The misidentification was caused by the people in southern Bwa villages who borrowed the spectacular plank masks of their Bobo-Fing neighbors.[42] The masks usually make their appearance at the beginning of March and may be seen until May when the spring rains are expected. Susan Vogel and Francine N'Diaye describe the scene in these words, "The Bwa country during the hot, dry season when the masks dance is a monotonous rust color of the earth, with earthen houses of the same color and everything covered with a heavy layer of dust. The procession of masks with their bright black, white, and red paint gleaming in the tropical sunlight is truly dazzling."[43] Living in a harsh landscape that is parched for part of the year, the people must depend upon the infrequent downpours of rain to avoid near starvation. The masquerades are a means of establishing the necessary harmony between humans and nature. The masks are mediators when worn by maskers courting the goodwill of the supernaturals in behalf of the people; they

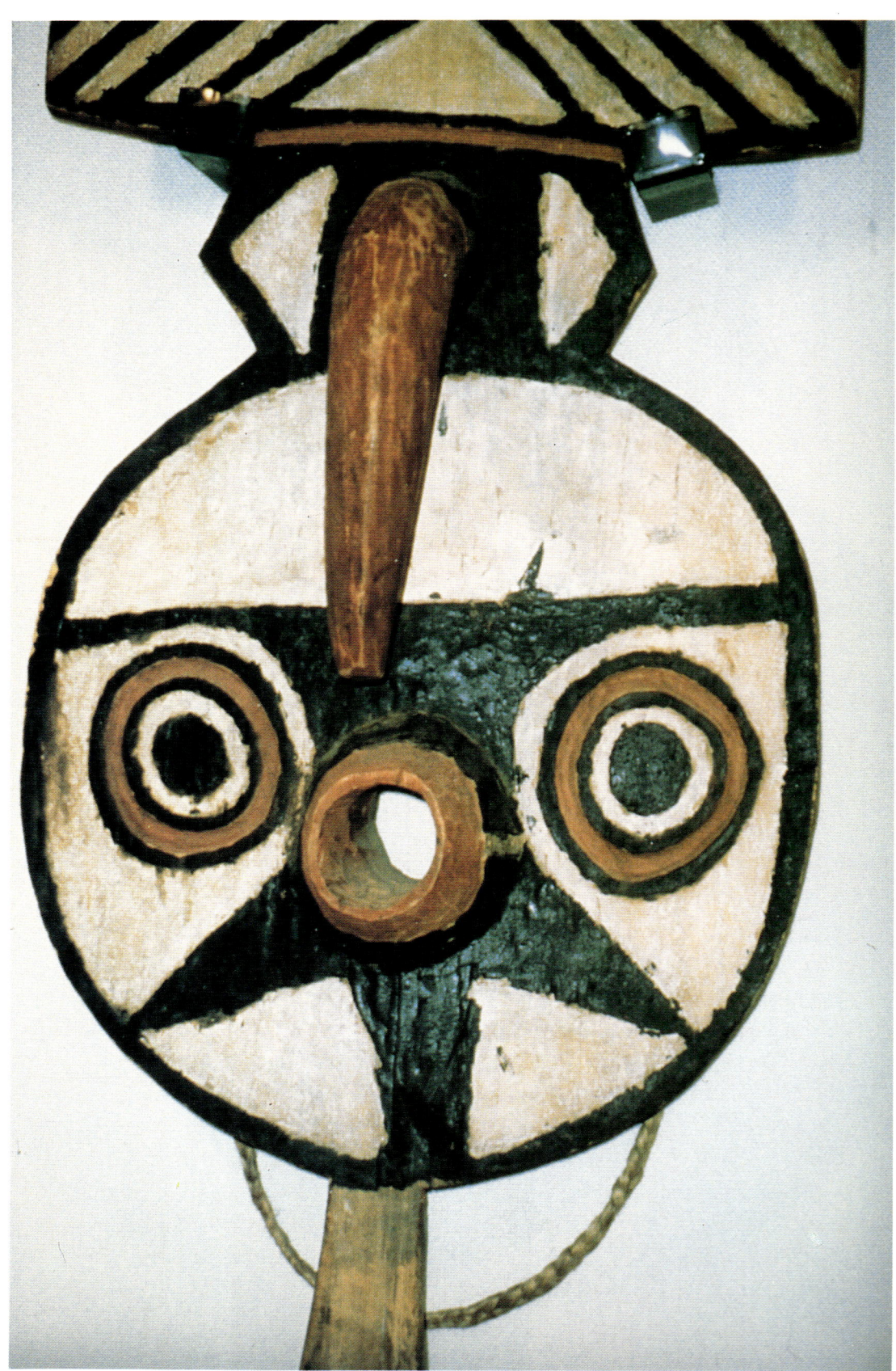

*Fig. 76
Detail of plank
mask 75.*

are the agents for cleansing and purifying the village, for chasing away the layers of evil that may have accumulated since the last planting season.

In the midst of the abstract design patterns of the Bwa masks, there are borrowings from nature and symbolic interpretations. The downward curving beak suggests a bird. The circles around the eyes are thought to intensify vision, therefore, adding to the power of the wearer. A crescent overhead is believed to represent the moon, perhaps in contrast to the round face at the base that resembles the moon when it is full. Masks must necessarily take into account practical considerations. To this end, the circle of the mouth presents a space through which the wearer can see. In order to steady the unwieldy structure an attached rope is held with the teeth.

Painted patterns on the board include light and dark squares like those associated with the funeral blankets of the Dogon as well as zigzags and diagonals. The X shapes refer to forehead scarification of the initiates. According to Anderson and Kreamer, preparation for initiation introduces the candidates to the meanings of the geometric shapes painted on the masks and to the moral lessons and mythical family histories encoded in the symbols.[44]

Christopher Roy writing the text on the Sudanese Savanna in *African Art from the Barbier-Mueller Collection*, equates the great plank masks with "supernatural flying spirits from the bush that provide their blessings and protection to the families that own them."[45] The Bwa butterfly mask fills this description (figures 77, 78). The handsome construction with outspread wings is worn horizontally. It is primarily black, reddish brown, and tan. The painted design depends partly upon remarkably inventive patterns of triangles, often joined to form "bow ties and hourglasses" that give variety to the overall design. At the midsection of the "butterfly" there is a dark panel with an open mouth revealing serrated teeth; eyes, circled in concentric bands, are painted on the wings outside of the central plane. Above the mouth on the black ground, there is, in high relief, a small head of a man with a stylized beard. The butterfly masks perform at spring festivals for the purpose of encouraging the fertility of fields, as well as of animals and humans.

Bwa mask makers, like their neighbors, adopted the antelope as a subject for their carvings. A large female kob antelope mask is called a *koan* (figure 79). Possibly representing a bush spirit, the *koan* is painted black, white, and red. A hollow triangular nose stands out three-dimensionally, the eyes are emphasized by circles within circles, and the tall horns are ringed with bands of alternating black and white. The masquerades in which the *koan* appears are held during the dry season.

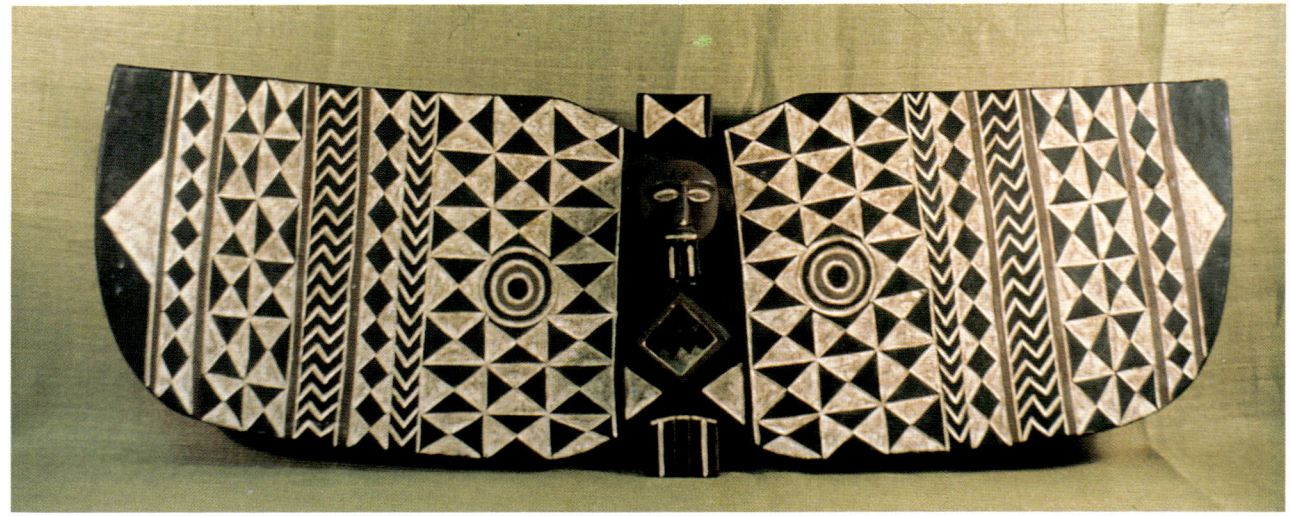

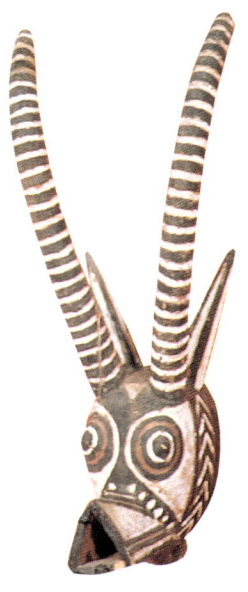

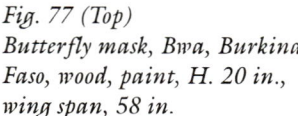

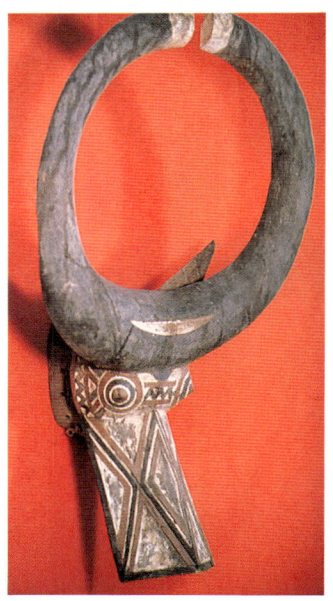

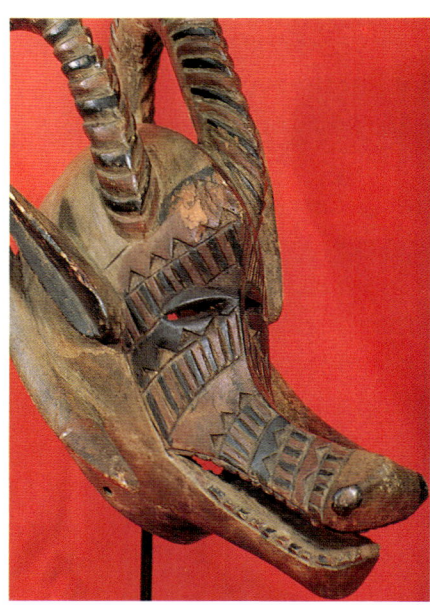

Fig. 77 (Top)
*Butterfly mask, Bwa, Burkina
Faso, wood, paint, H. 20 in.,
wing span, 58 in.*

Fig. 79 (Left)
Koan *mask, Bwa, Burkina
Faso, wood, paint,
H. 29 1/2 in.)*

Fig. 82 (Middle)
*Buffalo mask, Bwa, Burkina
Faso, wood, paint, H. 31 1/2 in.*

Fig. 80 (Right)
*Antelope mask, Bwa, Burkina
Faso, wood, paint, H. 10 1/2
in.*

*Figs. 79 and 82 are a gift of
Ambassador and Mrs. Julius
Walker to ICASALS; now on
permanent loan from
ICASALS to the Museum of
Texas Tech University.*

Like so many other masks, it takes part in the funerals of elder statesmen and participates in frightening away ill-natured spirits that might endanger the people.

Two antelope masks in the Bwa style illustrate other design treatments. In figure 80, the dramatic carving is painted in bands using vertical brush strokes in black, gray, and blue; the same colors alternate on the horns that loop back and join the body of the mask before sweeping forward to the jawline. The convex circle of the horns forms a striking contrast to the inverted curve extending from the forehead to the nostrils. The second antelope is blockier and left unpainted (figure 81). The surface planes are incised with barely visible textures and the curving horns are more deeply grooved providing a pleasing contrast for the simple mass of the head.

Bwa masks have another horned animal as a subject—a buffalo mask is worn by the Do Society. Unlike the antelope's horns that rise straight from the head or curve back with baroque amplifications, the horns of the buffalo describe an almost complete circle (figure 82). The

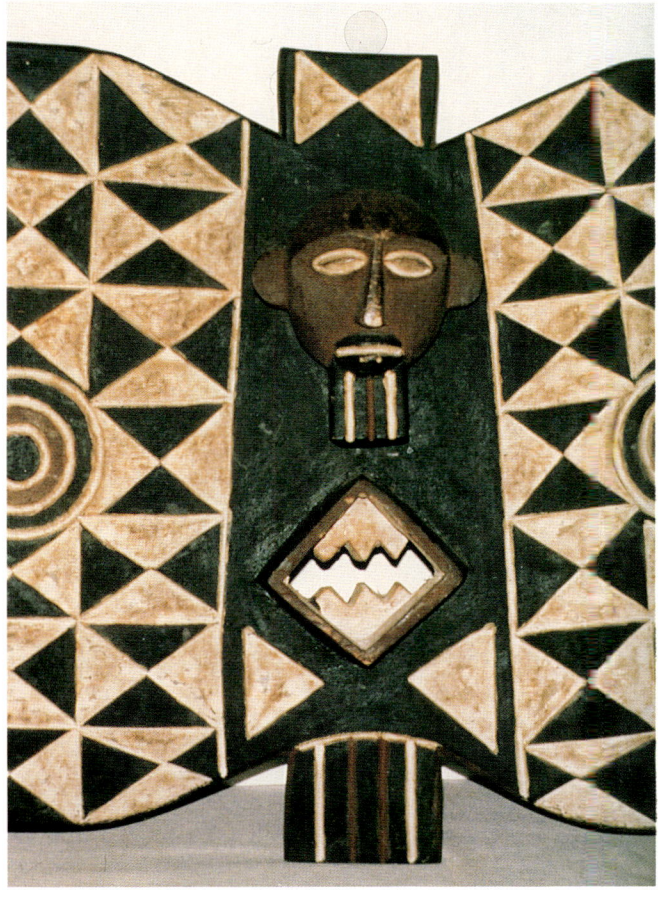

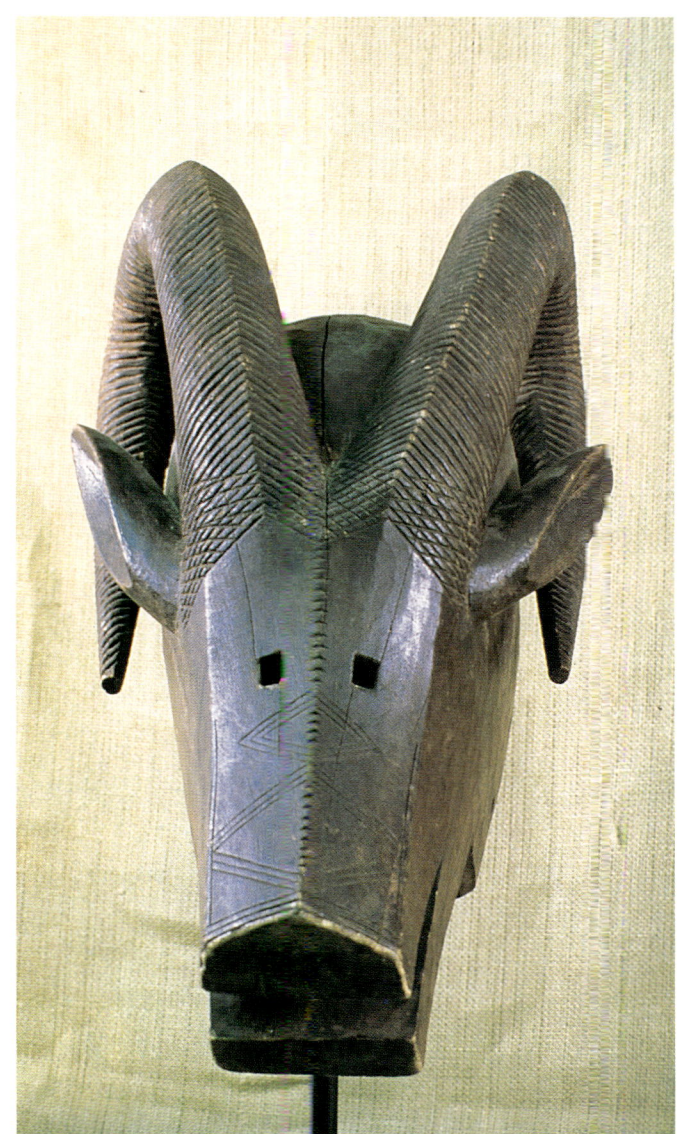

beast has prominent eyes and a long snout on which the painted detail employs the X motif. The effect of the heavily constructed head is ponderous; it conveys an impression of unlimited endurance.

An amusing buffalo mask, with a circular face that is said to represent the sun, is the product of Baule craftsmen. It is the *Kplekple* mask used in the *Won* dance of the Goli association (figure 83). Reduced to whimsical abstraction, the eyes are tear shaped and the mouth is a small rectangle. The horns enclose an oval space in contrast to the solid mass of the round face. The mask's utter simplicity has made it an object of admiration and popularity with western artists.

In the semiarid regions inhabited by the Dogon and the people of Mali and Burkina Faso, the antelope as subject plays an impressive role. In Cameroon, the bovine takes over the place of the antelope. The forest buffalo is one of the strongest and most dangerous animals (figure 84). In the carved masks, openings are rarely cut for the eyes. The masks are intended to be worn on the dancers' backs and attached to a raffia costume.[46]

Fig. 78
Detail of butterfly mask 77.

Fig. 81
Antelope mask, Ewa, Burkina Faso, wood, H. 33 in.

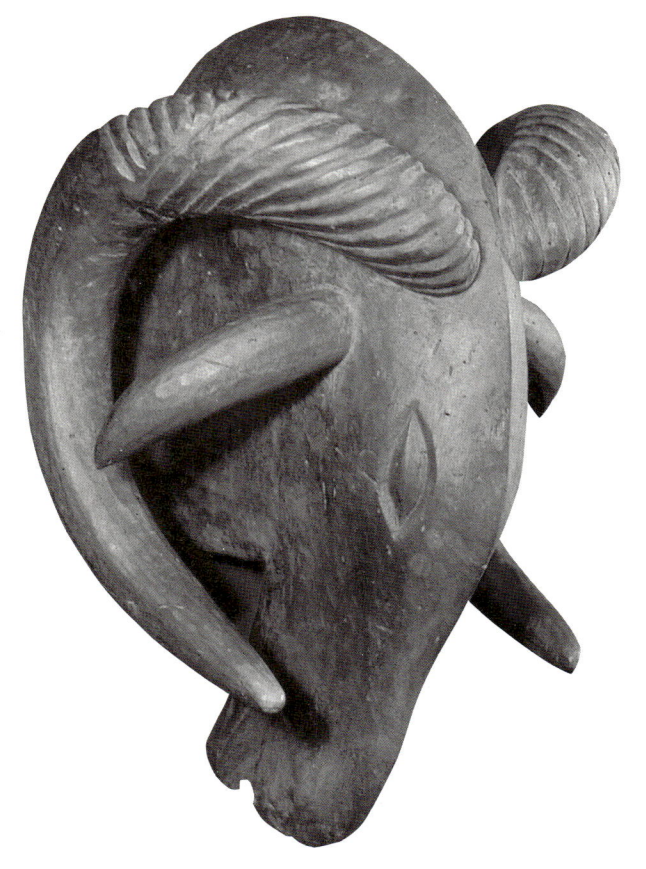

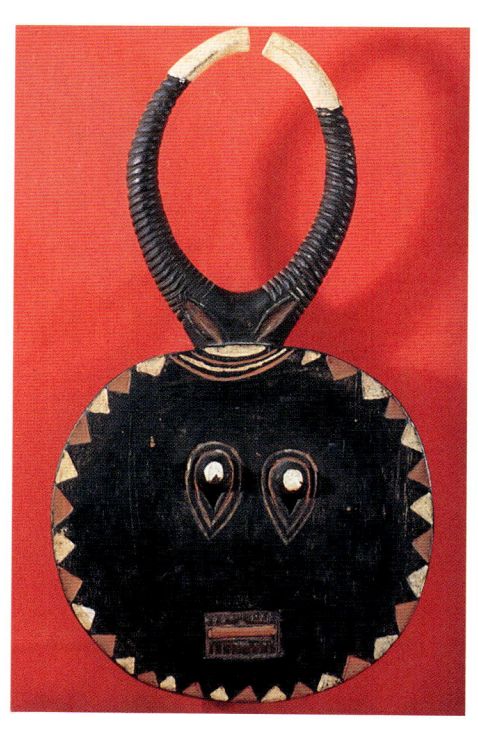

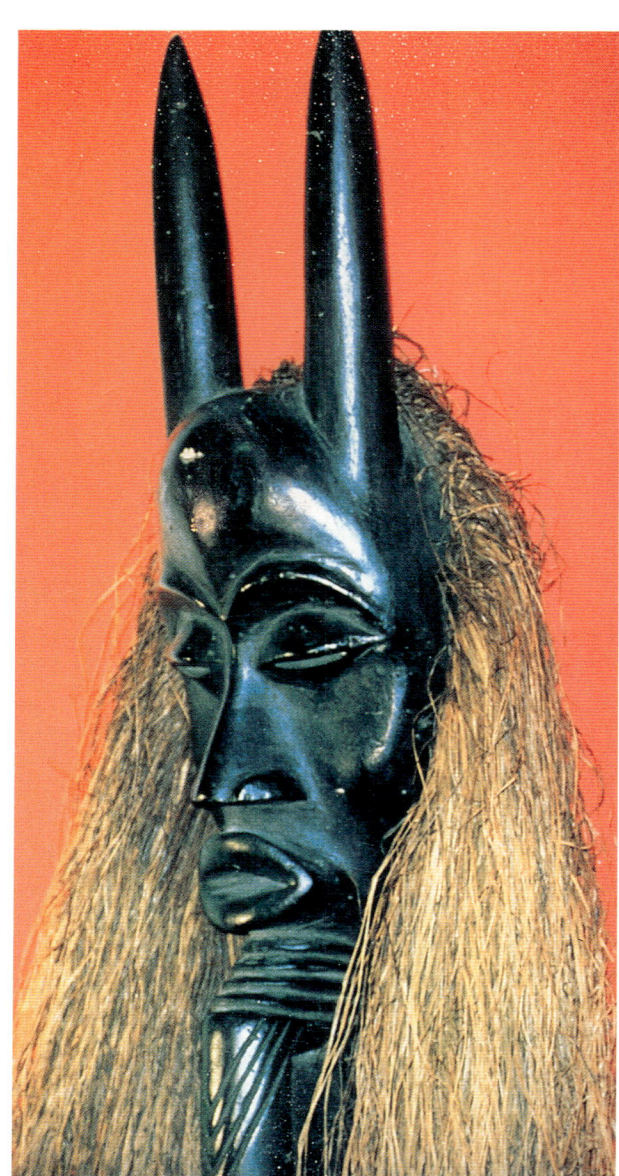

Fig. 85(Top left)
Ram mask, Yoruba, wood,
H. 14 in.

Fig. 86 (Top right)
Mask, Dan, Ivory
Coast/Liberia, wood,
raffia, H. 39 in.

Fig. 83 (Bottom)
Kplekple mask, Baule,
Ivory Coast, wood, paint,
H. 23 in.

Most of the animal masks discussed have horns as a common denominator. Horned animals were the most valuable and worthy of being offered as sacrifices to the supernaturals (figure 85). The Yoruba kept carved wooden rams' heads in their ancestral shrines at Owo.[47] The ram is sacred to Shango, and its horns are compared to the thrust and parry of the lightning bolt.[48] It was the ram whose blood was most frequently spilled on the sacrificial altars. A Bwa ram mask was worn by wood-carvers at burials as a sign of mourning.[49] Associated with prowess in the hunt, horns as trophies were worn or carried into battle. The symbolism conveyed was that of the macho youth, of masculinity, and, as Willett adds, the physical perfection and endurance of animals equated with the strength and vitality of the hunter (figure 86).[50] Horns are related to fertility, but they also symbolize the idea of nature's growth and the power of regeneration. Young animals' horns grow slowly, and as this process unfolds, there is an expansion of adult strength that provides the ability to gain mastery over foes.[51] Horns and their significance will appear again in the discussion of "power" figures.

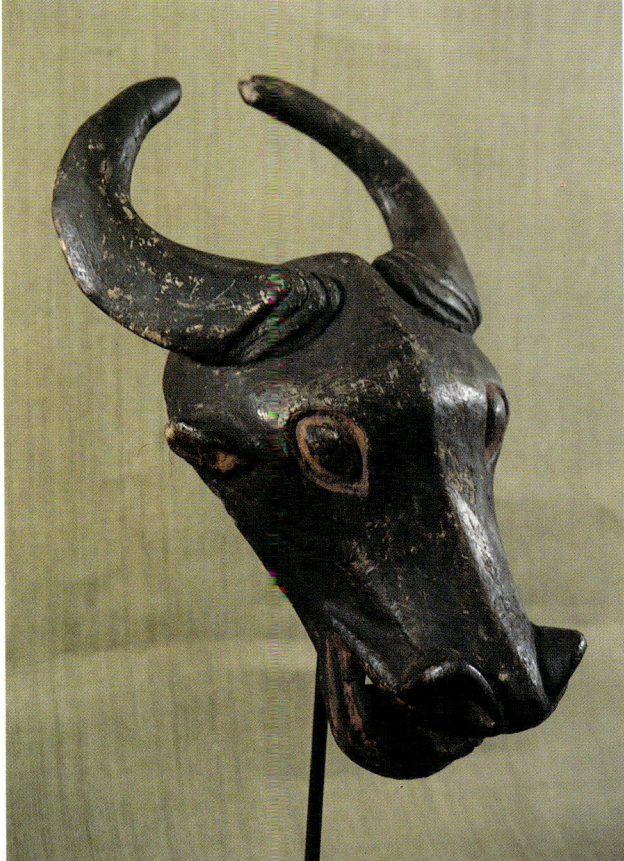

Fig. 84
Buffalo mask, possibly
Mileke, Cameroon, wood,
paint, H. 17 in.

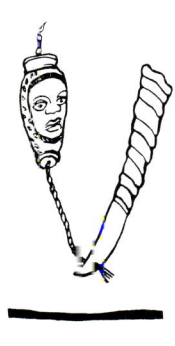

FIVE

Figures Carved in Wood

or Cast in Metal

They also praise those who know
how to shape images in wood or compose a song.

OLADIPO YEMITAN
quoting Ijala

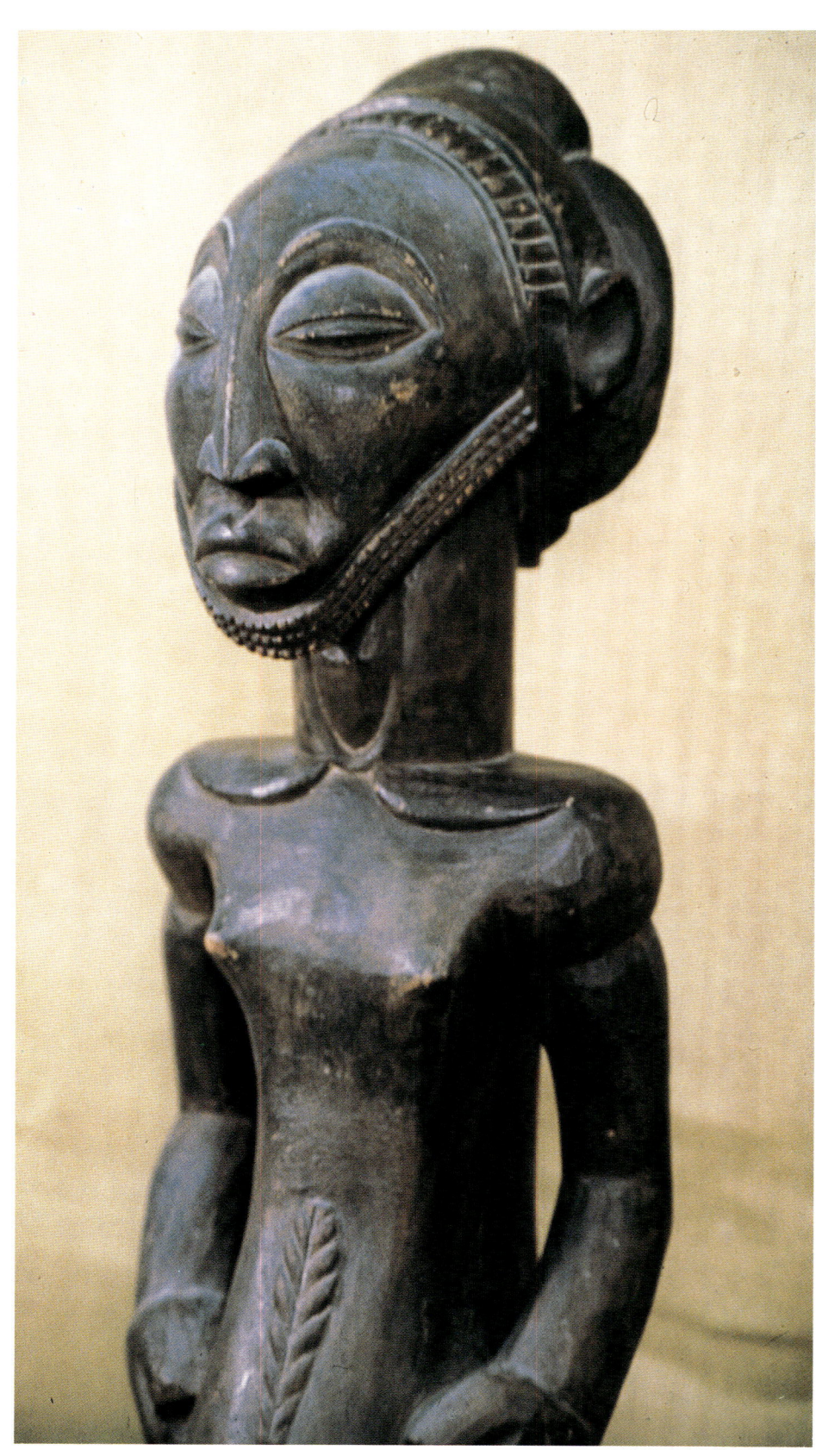

Fig. 87
Standing male figure,
Luba-Hemba, Zaire,
wood, H. 26 ¾ in.

I

Shrines

*A shrine is built
wherever the gods are likely to dwell
or call for sacrifices.*

HERBERT M COLE in
Icons: Ideals and Power in the Art of Africa

Figurative sculpture in western sub-Saharan Africa was not intended for museums or for display in a living room or gallery. Commissioned from a craftsman, a carving was intended to represent and honor deities, ancestors, and nature spirits, or to create a power figure whose function was thwarting evil and punishing mischievous bush spirits, witches, or enemies causing an illness, bringing misfortune to an individual or to a communal group. Such a carving might find a place at a family altar, where prayers and sacrifices were offered to ensure good health and good fortune, to appease a wrathful ancestor or supernatural.

Of greater importance to the inhabitants of a village as a whole were the shrine houses that varied in size, form, place, and purpose. Some shrines were associated with the gods and the elements and forces they controlled such as earth, water, thunder, the clang of iron, the fire at the forge. Other shrines honored founders of the family and heroes. There were shrines for warfare, for medicine, and for the use of diviners and oracles. In these shelters an assemblage of images and ritual paraphernalia were kept and sacrifices were made to be conveyed to the spirit world. The carvings housed in a shrine were ceremonially fed and periodically brightened with fresh paint, jewelry, and clothing. Sacred objects were recharged with magical bundles and potent charms.

The wooden figures were rarely displayed to large numbers of people except at ceremonies, initiation rites, and the funerals of important personages. When the carvings were brought out from a shrine they were washed and rubbed with oil. In some areas the village women would dress the sculptures in loincloths, add beads and head ties to renew their life and color.

Chinua Achebe in his powerful novel *Arrow of God* describes an occasion when the shrine figures were displayed in an Igbo village at the Festival of the New Yams. He writes:

> It was also the day for all the minor deities in the six villages who did not have their own special feasts. On that day each of these gods was brought by its custodian and stood in a line outside the shrine of Ulu so that any man or woman who had received a favour from it could make a small present in return. This was the one public appearance these smaller gods were allowed in the year. They rode into the market place on the heads or shoulders of the custodians, danced around and then stood side by side at the entrance to the shrine of Ulu. Some of them would be very old, nearing the time when their power would be transferred to new carvings and they would be cast aside; and some would have been made only the other day. The very old ones carried face marks like the men who made them . . . . At last year's festival only three of these ancients were left. Perhaps this year one or two more would disappear, following the men who made them in their own image and departed long ago.

ટ&

> The festival thus brought gods and men together in one crowd. It was the only assembly in Umaro in which a man might look to his right and find his neighbor and look to his left and see a god standing there.[1]

Anita Glaze mentions an occasion in a Senufo village when wooden figures are brought from a shrine and used in a dance; a performance that is generally associated exclusively with masks. In this case, the *tyekpa* funeral ritual gives to the Senufo carvings a "mysterious vitality in a multimedia theater of music, dance, and song. Raised above the heads of the members [of the society], the figures progress in a dignified manner, their movements large and measured; at intervals and in response to musical change, their restrained energy is released in a counterpoint of rapid, rhythmic twists."[2] African ceremonial art, as Cole has pointed out, "often exists to embody spirit forces, to augment the effectiveness and emotional impact of rituals, to remind people, through visual metaphor or allusion, that they are only in part responsible for their destiny."[3]

Carvings kept in particular shrines were usually covered with cloths and protected from curious eyes. It was dangerous for people to see them because of the spiritual power that they possessed. By the same token, when a ruler appeared to his people, he was wrapped in the clothing of office; so swathed that only his presence and royal symbols were evident. This was to keep people who could not withstand the power that he generated from becoming ill or overwrought. It was also believed that if figures and masks were viewed too frequently their magic would be diluted and no longer possess its original strength. The power inherent in certain masks was thought to be so uncontrolled and overwhelming that even the priests were endangered and after one wearing the mask was closed away in its shrine.[4]

Shrines differ widely in their sizes, building methods, and locations. Achebe mentions an Igbo shrine of the Oracle of the Hills and Caves in his novel *Things Fall Apart*. He writes, "The way into the shrine was a round hole at the side of a hill, just a little bigger than the round opening into a hen house. Worshipers and those who came to seek knowledge from the god crawled on their belly through the hole and found themselves in a dark, endless space in the presence of Agbala. No one had ever beheld Agbala, except his priestess. But no one who had ever crawled into this awful shrine had come out without the fear of his power."[5] This contrasts dramatically with Achebe's description in the same book of an Igbo family compound and its shrine. He wrote, the owner

> had a large compound enclosed by a thick wall of red earth. His own hut, or *obi*, stood immediately behind the only gate in the red walls. Each of his three wives had her own hut, which together formed a half moon behind the *obi*. The barn was built against one end of the red walls. . . . Near the barn was a house, the "medicine house" or shrine where Okonkwo kept the wooden symbols of his personal god and of his ancestral spirits. He worshipped them with sacrifices of kola nut, food and palm wine and offered prayers on behalf of himself, his three wives and eight children[6]

Achebe unintentionally touches upon the differences between African sculpture in its intended setting, for example, a shrine house that shelters an assembly of family carvings, and as it is viewed in most modern museums. Museum curators place African art in an ambiance of controlled and unchanging light totally unlike the changing path of the sun during the course of a day or the fires lighted at a plaza for dancing during the night. Exhibits are protected by glass cases; constant temperature and humidity are maintained throughout the year. Objects in a collection are placed against backgrounds that will emphasize their lines and contours, presenting the pieces to please a European or American audience. Visitors are encouraged to study each carving or mask through analysis, stylistic comparisons, and the aesthetics of the western world. Certainly this approach has merit, but it must be kept in mind that the original purpose of the objects was to serve the needs of a family or village, to take part in performances whose purposes were life-enhancing and a way of maintaining a link with the ancestors and the supernaturals. Shrines in the villages, and museum collections are caretakers of a rapidly disappearing heritage of traditional arts that becomes increasingly meaningful as it is thrust into the twenty-first century.

II

*Male and Female Figures,
Standing or Seated*

*Yoruba share a notion with Heraklitus:
a man's character is his fate. Yoruba sculptors
enlarge the human head to mark its importance
as the seat of character, the part conversant
with destiny.*

From "Yoruba Artistic Criticism"
by ROBERT FARRIS THOMPSON, in the
African Traditional Artist in African Societies

Single figures, standing or seated, are among the ceremonial objects that have a place in shrines. Many of the carvings, male or female, represent a god, a spirit associated with a natural force or an ancestor. In figure 87 it is likely that a distinguished ancestral figure is intended. A carving of this type may have been kept as a genealogical indicator in a personal shrine room in the living quarters of an important family or protected in the darkness of a funeral hut. The provenance is un-known—a problem imposed on many twentieth-century carvings by imprecise boundaries resulting from the rise of new countries and borders following the Second World War and from the migration and intermingling of ethnic groups. The seated ancestor in question shares characteristics with the Luba carvings of northern Zaire and related figures done by the Hemba from the Mbula Region. People living along

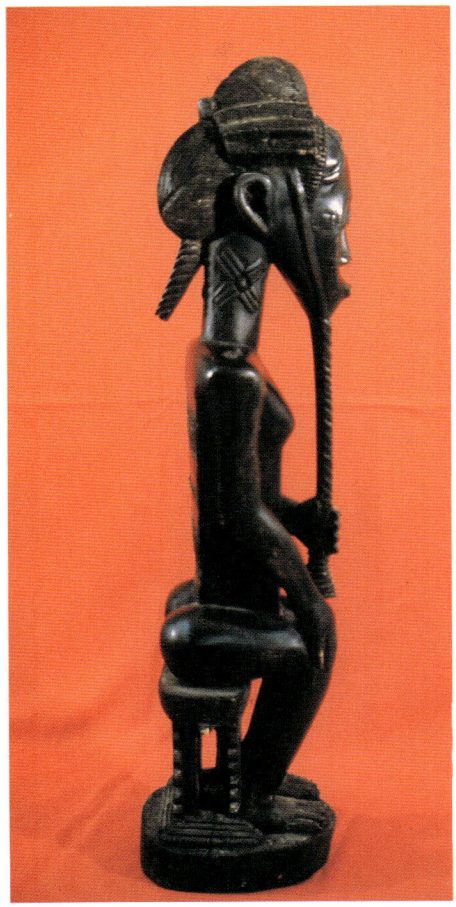
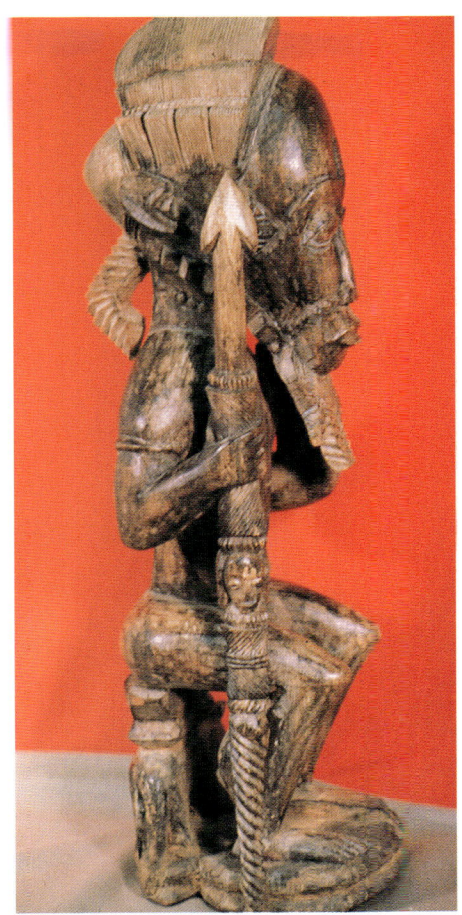

Fig. 88 (Left)
Seated male figure,
Baule, Ivory Coast,
wood, H. 32 in.

Fig. 89 (Right)
Seated male figure,
Baule, Ivory Coast,
wood, H. 22 1/2 in.

the northern Zaire River are known as Luba-Hemba. The male in figure 87 is represented with a typical hair arrangement—a circle divided into a cruciform at the back of the head. In this instance the horizontal lines are established by four rolls, carved in relief and fastened by two vertical pins. The figure's demeanor is dignified, a dignity that is enhanced by the static pose. Luba eyes are described as having the shape of coffee beans; the eyes of the seated man are half-closed upon the world, turned inward to "the invisible realities of the present and future." To some, this suggests death and the world beyond. Wide-open eyes are associated with attention focused on the present and are thought to be a sign of vitality. The ears of Luba carvings are amusingly spoken of as "small cats' ears."[7] The man's body has a cicatrix in a chevron pattern of leaflike designs from the chest to the navel. In some parts of Zaire, this is known as the "rising of the new moon," a lunar phase that refers to the difficult decisions that must be made in real life and their reflections "in the larger aspects of the world."[8] The arms are separated from the body, and the hands come to rest around the umbilical zone of a protruding belly. Such a gesture is a reminder that here the cord once tied an infant to its mother and in a broader sense it binds the African to the ancestors.[9]

A seated male possessing Baule characteristics (figure 88) resembles an ancestral figure in the collection of Pierre Verité in Paris. Made

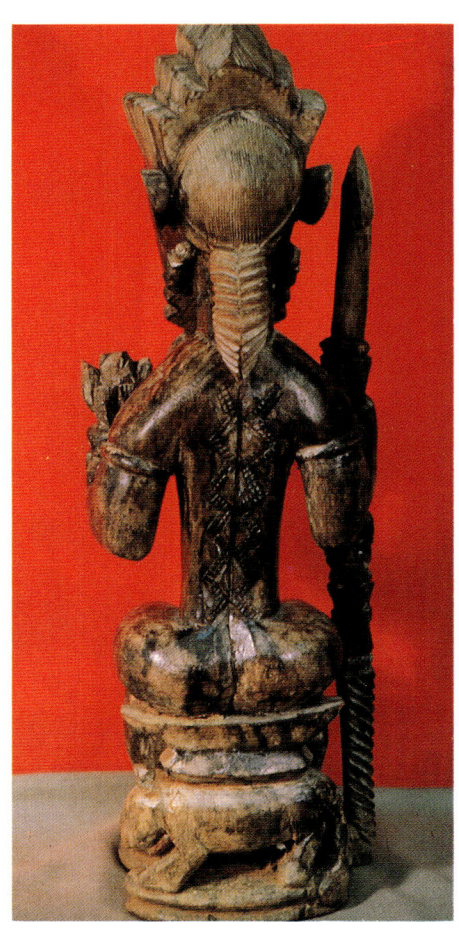

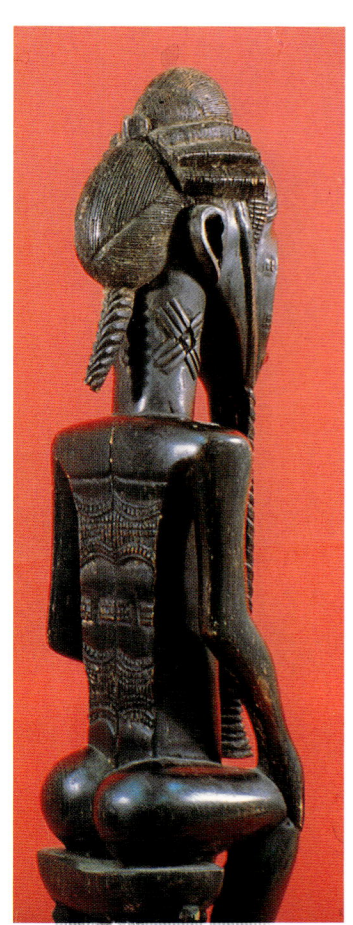

*Fig. 90 (Top left)
Detail (back) of seated
male 88.*

*Fig. 91 (Top right)
Detail (back) of seated
male 89.*

*Fig. 92 (Bottom left)
Detail of male figure,
Baule, Ivory Coast, wood,
H. 42 in.*

*Fig. 93 (Bottom right)
Seated female, Baule,
Ivory Coast, wood,
H. 32 in.*

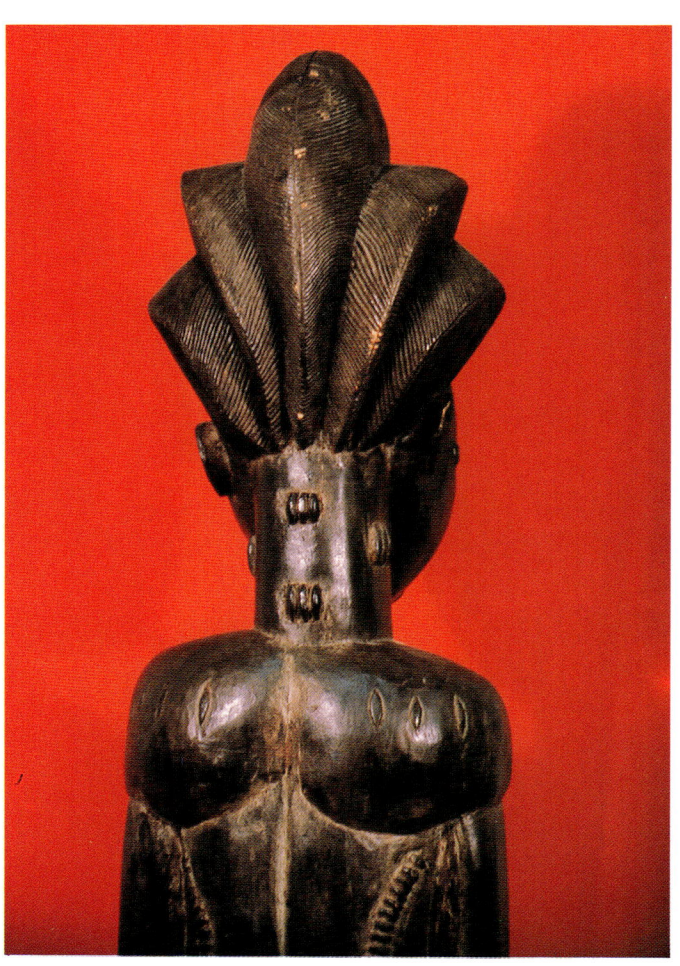

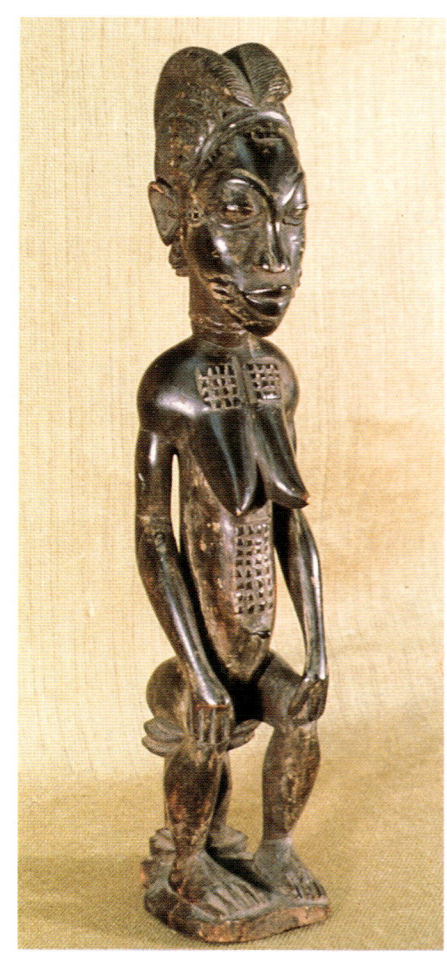

of blackened wood, the Verité piece has natural hair and a braided beard.[10] The carving at the Museum of Texas Tech University is also of blackened wood, but the three braided strands of the beard and the elaborately arranged hair are carved wood instead of fiber. Seated on a stool, the imposing personage rests one hand upon his knee. With the other hand he fingers his ceremonial beard, held in place by a strap around the chin. The patterns of scarification on neck and chin give a delicacy and richness to the skin surface (figure 90). A strong contrast exists between the attenuated, angular carving in figure 88 and the seated male shown in figure 89. The stocky, patriarchal man (figure 89) clasps a spear in his right hand. He sits on the back of an animal, similar to the carvings of leopards on the stools of royalty. The man's face with a cicatrix on the forehead—a square subdivided into smaller square—is framed by a beard and an architectonic hair arrangement. In back, the hair is pulled into a round lobe that ends with a looped twist. Without blackened wood or a highly polished sheen, the body is mottled, the color ranging from a brownish hue to light natural wood for the head and hair (figure 89).

Scarification covers the backs of both the men (figures 90 and 91). Until recently the cicatrix has played a significant role as an art form, for which the body acts as a fabric to be embellished with designs (figure 92). To produce the marks, irritants are rubbed into intricate incisions made on the skin; when healed the raised lines are permanent. Done ritually, this may be a part of initiation rites. The patterns provide information about group membership, rank, and status. In a carving of a living person or a dead ancestor, identification can often be established by a family member or friend because of a familiarity with the scarification (figure 93) or by a particular hair arrangement (figure 94).[11] An even more important purpose served by the cicatrix is an assurance of protection from evil powers.

Among the Yoruba the reason cheeks and bodies are adorned with lines has still another layer of meaning. To say, "This country has become civilized" means literally "This earth has lines upon its face." Civilization in Yoruba is *ilaju*—face with lined marks. The jungle is not tamed, there are few linear roads or carefully laid out towns. When man divides fields, puts down straight paths, and marks the squares of a village, civilization has a beginning. The basic verb to cicatrize (*la*) is associated with imposing human patterns upon the disorders of nature. The face and the forest, when they are "civilized," are "opened," like the human eye allowing the inner quality of the substance to shine forth (figure 95).[12]

The women in figures 94 and 95 have tall mounded coiffures with lines dividing the hair in strands or braids like the popular corn rows.

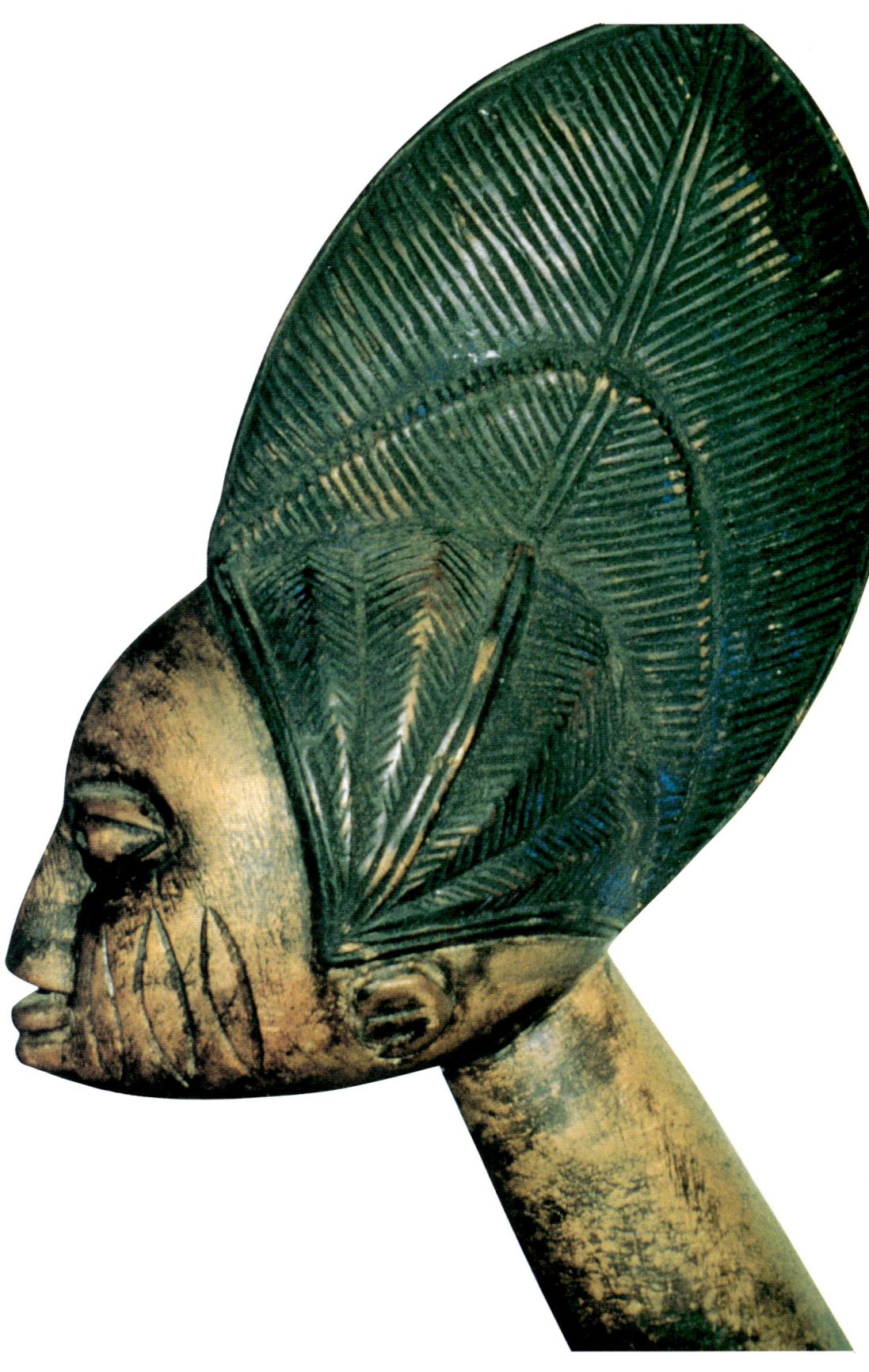

*Fig. 94
Woman holding a container (detail of head), Yoruba, Nigeria, wood, pigment, overall H. 25 1/2 in.*

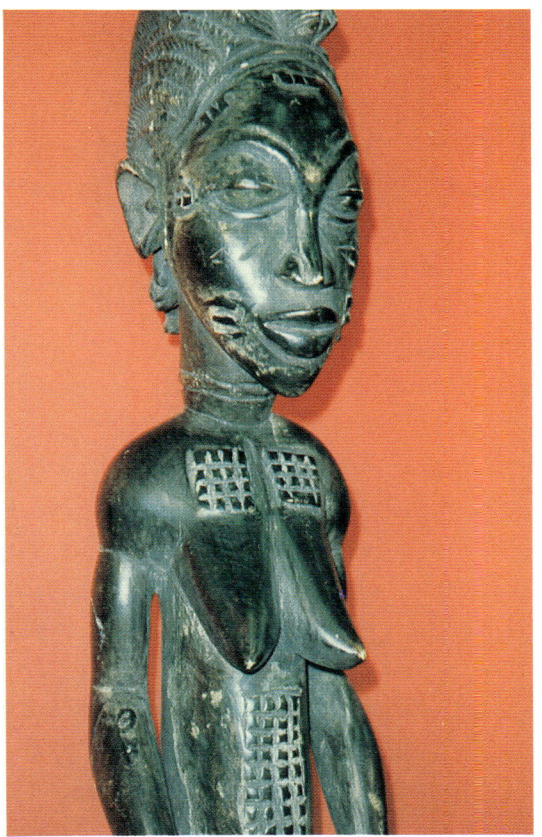

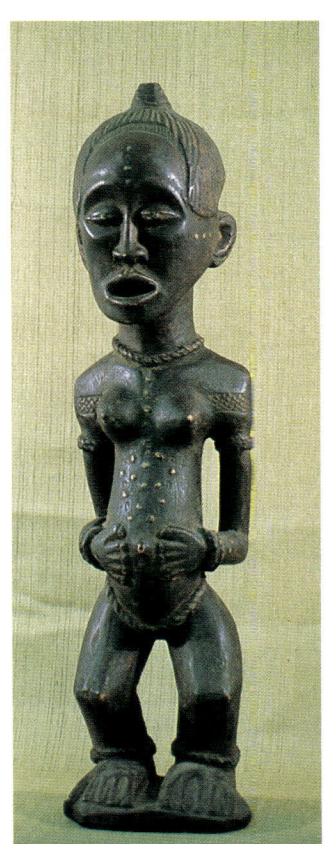

Fig. 95
Detail of seated female 93.

Fig. 96
Standing female, Songye,
Congo, wood, brass nail-
heads, H. 29 1/2 in.

These elaborate arrangements reveal social status. Such crested styles
are unsuitable for balancing heavy burdens on the head and indicate
that the ladies are the wives or daughters of prosperous families or
women of independent wealth. The seated woman (figure 95), with the
squared patterns of cicatrization on her abdomen and chest, has "long
flattened breasts—the breasts of a woman who has nourished many
infants," therefore, an indication of female power and maturity.[13]

A carving of a handsome young woman was sometimes commissioned by a male as his spirit spouse. The feminine entity was believed
to have been associated with the man before his birth. Such a surrogate
wife from the spirit world sometimes became jealous or envious and
caused disaster to an earthly marriage or brought about business losses.
To appease the troublesome supernatural being, an altar was set up in
a corner of the husband's sleeping room, and a carving was commissioned from the village craftsman to place on the shrine. Attention and
gifts to please the wrathful spirit lover were presented. The more
beautiful the carving of the unearthly companion, the better pleased
and mollified, it was hoped, the discontented "lover" would be and, of
course, less troublesome.[14]

The woman in figure 96 differs from the splendidly coiffured ladies
in the preceding illustrations. An example of a Songye carving from
Congo, the head is large, the eyes are elliptical and almost closed. The
mouth, a rimmed oval, is open. Out of normal proportion in relation

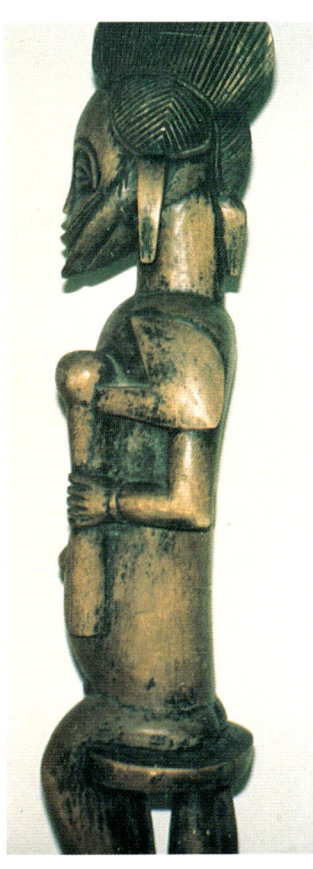

Fig. 99
*Seated male figure,
Senufo, Ivory Coast,
wood, H. 21 in.*

to the short legs, the long body stresses the place for the vital organs considered important to good health and a long life. The navel projects, possibly indicating pregnancy. Instead of scarification carved in the wood, the designs on the body are dots of inlaid metal. The use of additive materials is characteristic of Songye figurative carvings.

In contrast to the figures just discussed, the Dengese (Zaire) artist whose work is illustrated in figures 97 and 98, painted body designs on his wood carving. It is easy to recognize the Dengese style. Masculine carvings end at the hips and rest on a slightly elevated base (figure 97). A woman may stand like a slender column or sit with her legs crossed and a baby in her lap.

Figure 99 represents a seated man who belongs to the Senufo ethnic group. The short-handled hoe he holds marks him as a farmer. He sits on a two-legged stool with a precarious balance stabilized in front by his short rubbery legs. Senufo males have elongated torsos with little emphasis given to clearly defined musculature. In this carving, the shoulders bulge and flow in a tapering curve to the narrowing diameter of the upper arms and then to the sharp angle where the elbow bends. The face is stylized, with a jutting chin and a slightly concave plane where the eyes, nose, and mouth are located.

Also associated with the agricultural community, a Senufo woman (figure 100) positioned at the top of three ascending stools may have been intended for the apex of a "champion cultivator's" staff.[15] This coveted award is earned by a young man recognized for his hard work and productivity in the farming. The prize brings honor not only to the worker but also to his *katiolo,* the kinship group with whom the he lives and shares the cultivation of the fields. Hoeing competitions are important events celebrated with songs, dances, music, and the display of family staffs passed from one generation to another. The staffs were brought out at funerals of important persons, both male and female. The woman who is seated at the pinnacle of the triple stools is represented at the height of her attractiveness.[16] She is a symbol of the fertility of the fields and the promise of many children (figure 101). Her motionless dignity and serenity provide a sharp contrast to the efforts of the men bending over their hoes, striving to outdo their rivals. The uppermost stool on which the woman sits is supported at the middle level by two grazing creatures. Because they are horned, they may be interpreted as antelopes, symbols of success in farming and general good fortune (figure 102).[17] Among the Bambara, as noted in the chapter on wood carving, it is the legendary antelope, *Tyi wara,* who taught humans to cultivate the land with digging sticks.[18]

A detail in the carving of the woman is worth noting. The hands are small and sketchily crafted; the legs end in triangular shapes rather

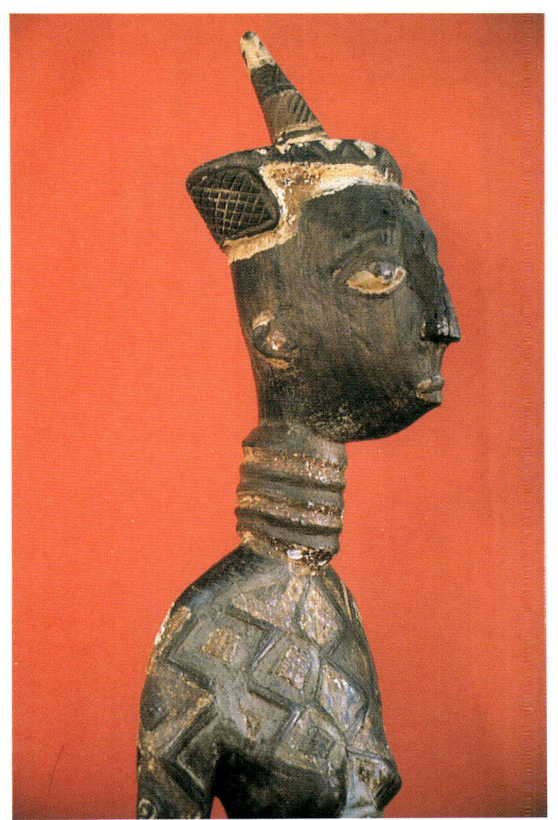

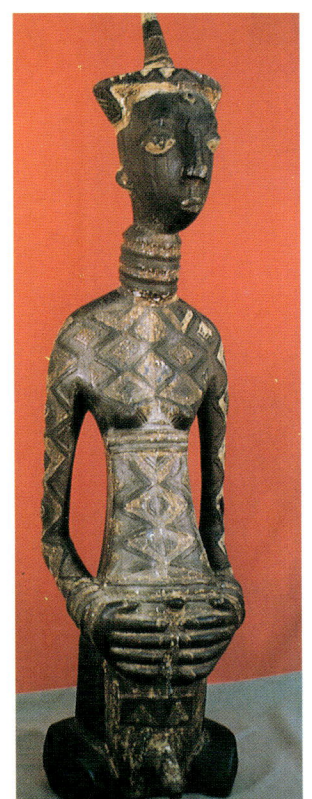

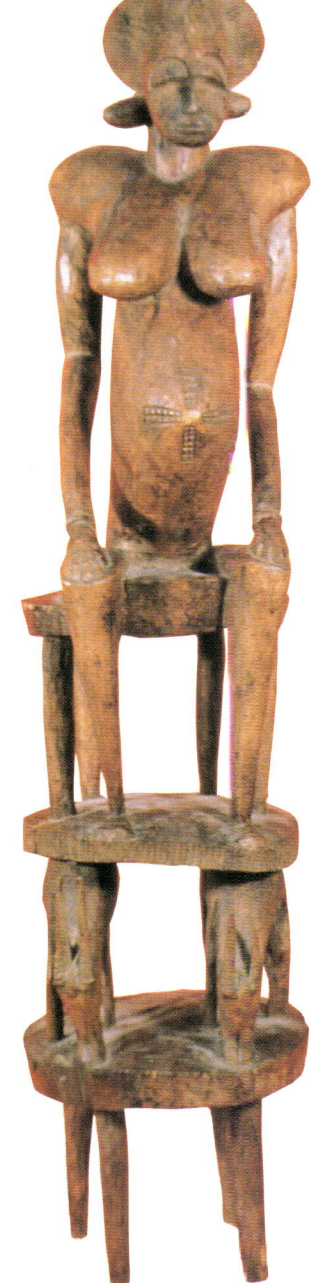

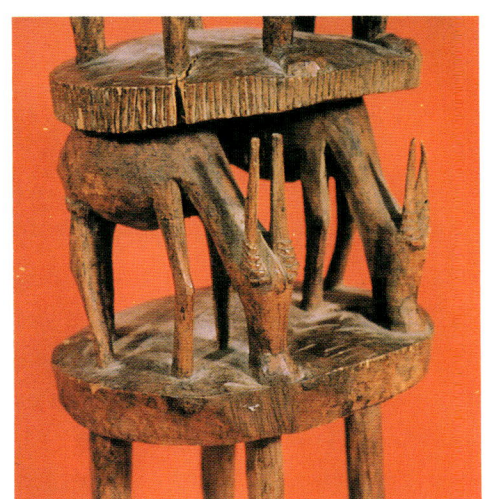

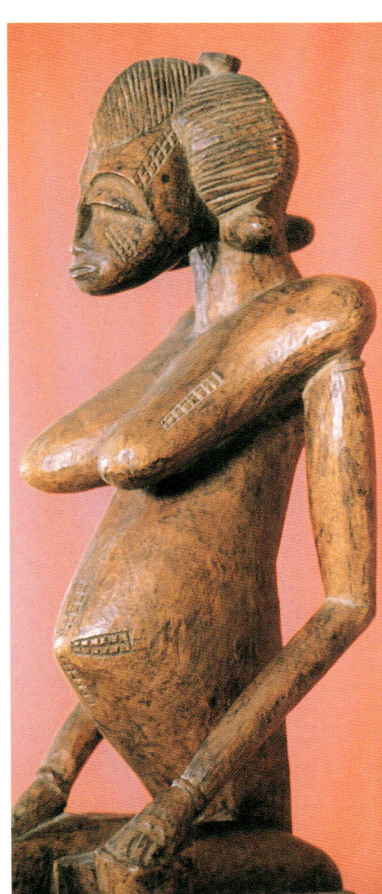

Clockwise from top left:

Fig. 98
Detail of male figure 97.

Fig. 97
*Male figure, Dengese, Zaire, wood, paint,
H. 42 in.*

Fig. 100
*Woman on high stool, Senufo, Ivory Coast, wood,
H. 36 1/2 in.*

Fig. 101
Detail of woman on high stool 100.

Fig. 102
Detail of woman on high stool 100.

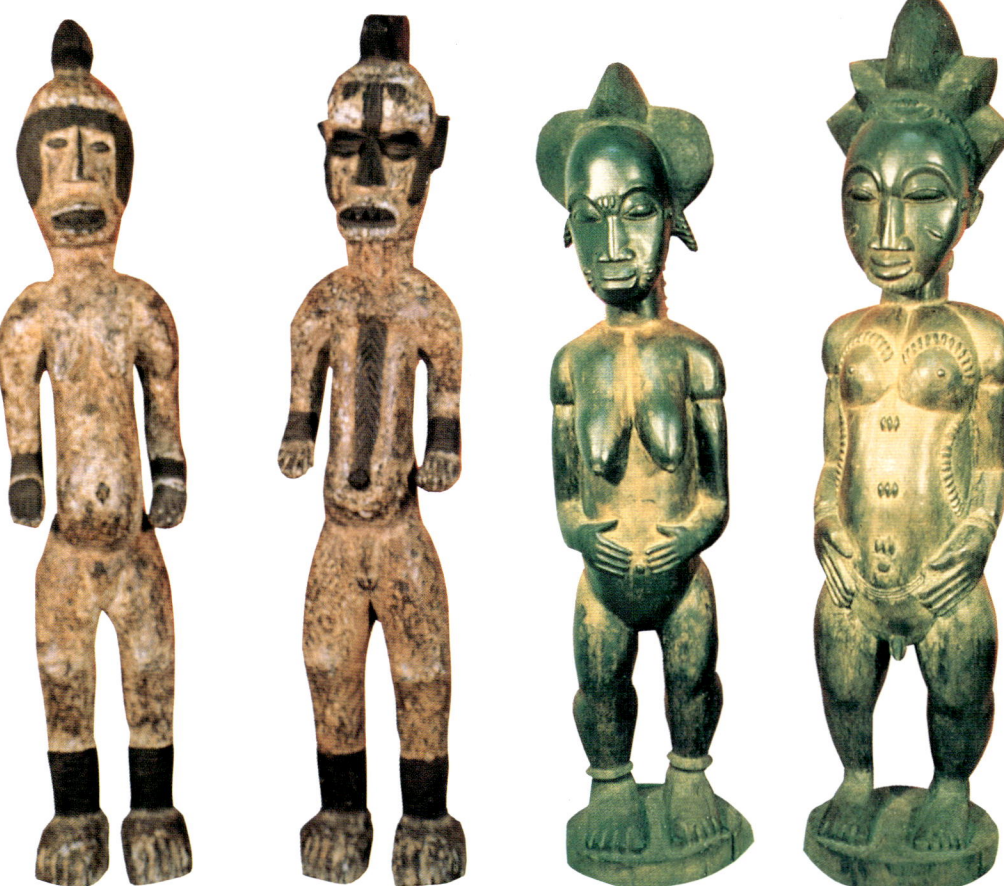

*Fig. 103 (Left)
Standing female and
male figures, Igbo, Ni-
geria, wood, paint:
woman, H. 33 in.;
man, H. 32 ½ in.*

*Fig. 104 (Right)
Standing female and
male figures, Baule,
Ivory Coast, wood:
woman, H. 40 in.;
man, H. 42 in.*

than carefully delineated feet. Wood carving was not only practiced by those trained as specialists, but also by the blacksmiths. Blacksmiths, perhaps because they were required to make the wooden handles for the metal tools wrought at their forges, also became proficient at figure carving. There was a difference, however, that distinguished the pieces made by the smiths: they did not carve the feet or the hands in detail. Hands were barely separated from the lower arms and had only a hint of fingers; feet were spatulate and without toes.[19] It is appropriate that a blacksmith may have carved a decoration intended to top a farmer's staff, a prize won with the help of metal tools forged in the smithy.

Male and female couples were frequently placed in shrines (figures 103 and 104). The man and woman might represent a married couple, otherworld lovers, twins, ancestors, gods, or spirits. The size of the sculptures ranges from small to over six feet. Regardless of scale, the sculptures usually possess a quality of monumentality and dignity. Anita Glaze observes that the couple symbolizes the civilized state of mature adults.[20] These guardians are brought out for funerals of esteemed persons. They represent a harmonious relationship and prompt reverence for the ancestors. The carvings differ in styles and techniques.

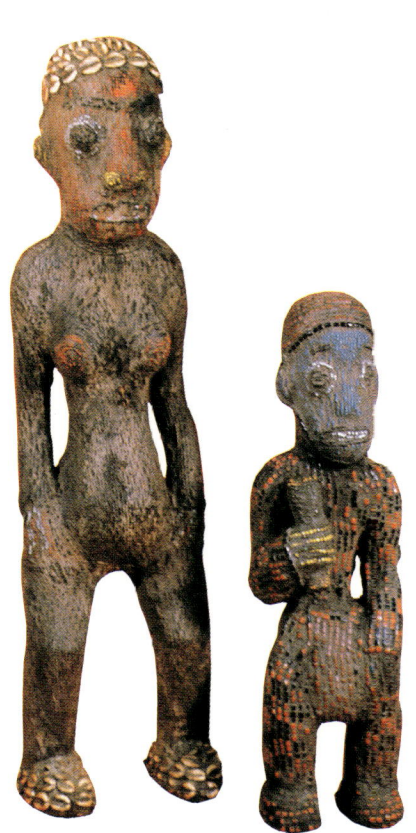
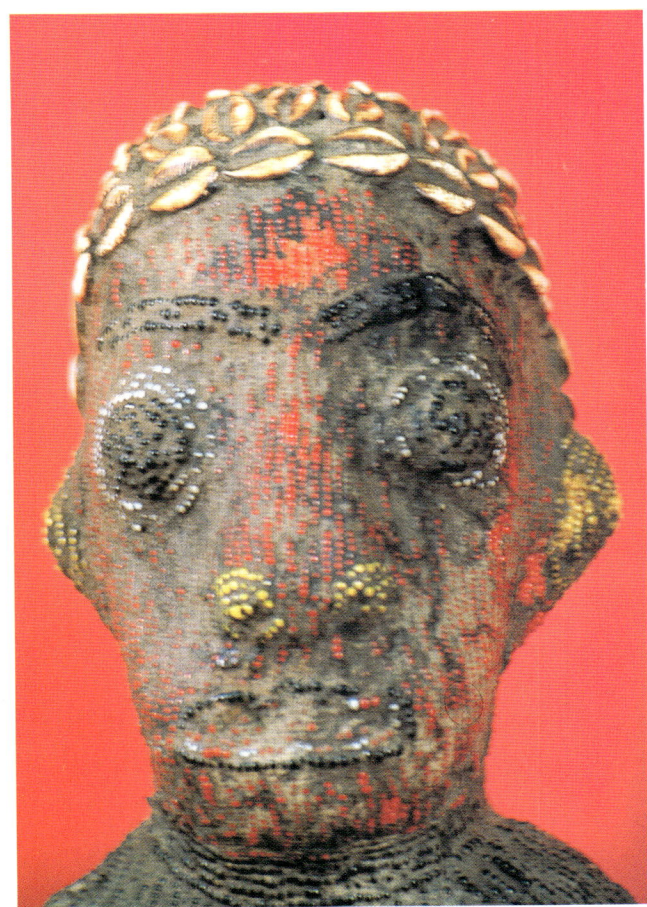

Figure 103 may have been done by an Igbo craftsman. The painted bodies, the dark wrist and leg bands, and the vigorous features present a strong contrast to the subtle and refined carving of the man and woman associated with the Baule style (figure 104). A male figure may be dominant in size, but not always. For example, in figure 105, the woman (left) is considerably larger than her male companion. The man and woman in figure 105 present a completely different approach to figurative representation. Their bodies and faces are covered with beads (figure 106), a practice common among the Mileke (Cameroon) craftsmen.

The larger size given the woman is found in many Senufo carvings. It is "a sculptural convention [that] seems to express by means of proportion . . . the importance of the female" in a matrilineal environment. The creator deity in its feminine aspect is known as "Ancient Mother" and is acknowledged by the Senufo men's Poro Society with a formal greeting that includes the phrase "at our Mother's work."[21] The sustaining power of deity interacting with human women stresses the importance of the feminine role as earthly

*Fig. 105
Standing female and male figures, Bamileke, Cameroon, wood, glass beads, cowrie shells inlaid on woman's head and feet: woman, H. 30 in.; man, H. 21 in.*

*Fig. 106
Detail of woman's head 105.*

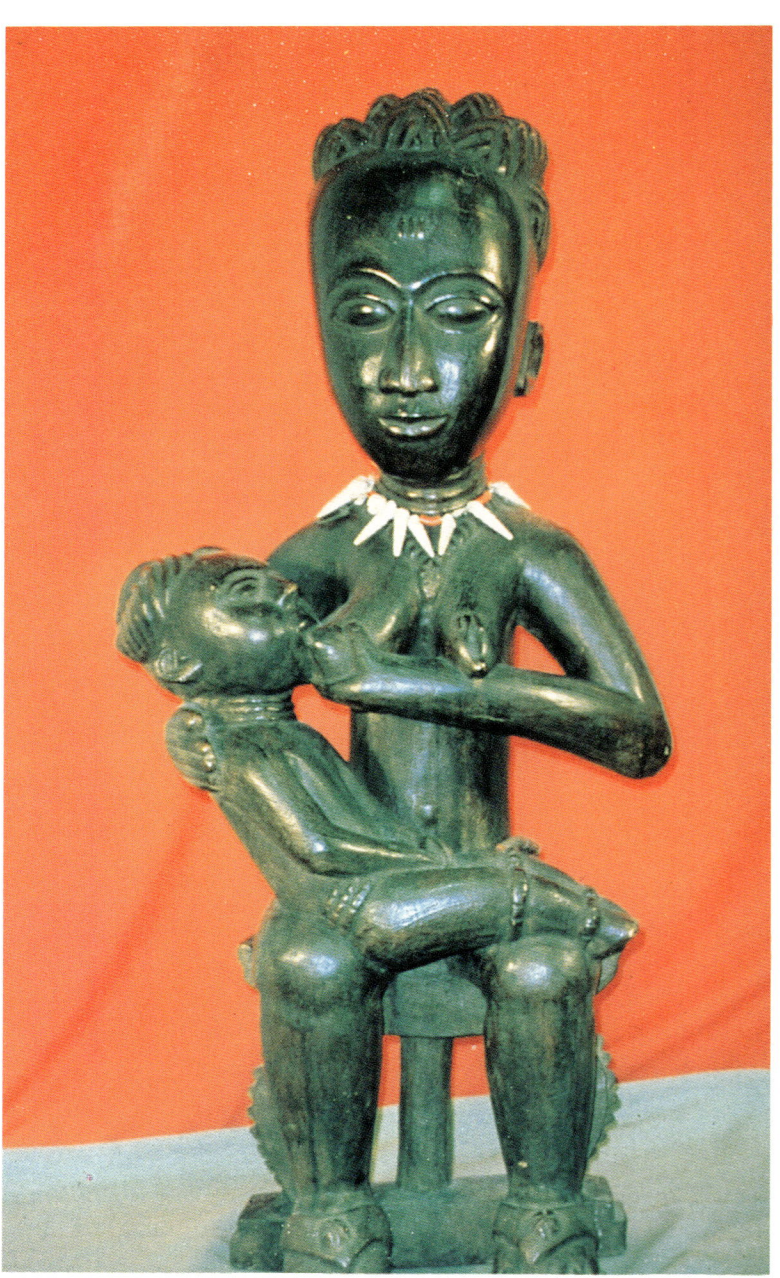

*Fig. 107
Mother and child,
Asante, Ghana, wood,
necklace of beads and
shells, H. 37 in.*

procreator and as one who intercedes in the world of the supernaturals for the good of the people.

A few Senufo women of the Sandogo Society become diviners and are known as Sando. They communicate with the spirit world to give advice and council to people who come to them with problems and difficulties. The objects used in the divination ritual are kept in a large lidded basket. The words designating the basket and its lid are "mother and child" respectively.[22] The subjects of nursing infants and their mothers or mothers with older children clinging to them are themes frequently chosen by African carvers (figure 107).

III

Mothers, Children, and Twins

My mother you are beautiful, very beautiful.
Your eyes sparkle like brass.
Your skin is soft and smooth.
You are black like velvet.

Translated by ULLI BEIER from
The Yoruba Speaks

Children are the reward of life.
Zaire proverb

Although the position of women within ethnic groups of western sub-Saharan Africa differs, the sculptural theme of mother and child expresses the age-old concern for the continuity of the family and the woman's ability to bear the children who bind together the past, present, and future. Oshun, the feminine deity of the Yoruba; Katyeleeo, the female aspect of deity among the Senufo; and the maternal presence known by many names and revered throughout western sub-Saharan Africa—all symbolically represent the mother of the people and of the cultures. The mother is generally regarded as the preserver of the morality and health of the villagers. She is the one who nurtures the crops, thus preventing famine. She presides over birth, death, and rebirth.[23]

The importance of children in sub-Saharan Africa is sensitively expressed in the lines from a Yoruba poem translated by Ulli Beuer:

A child is like a rare bird,
A child is precious like coral.
A child is precious like brass.
You cannot buy a child on the market.
The child you can buy is a slave.

One's child is one's child.

On the day of our death, our hand cannot
hold a single cowrie,
We need a child to inherit our belongings.[24]

The woman who bears no children, no matter what excellent qualities she may possess, is an object of humiliation; she is considered irreparably scarred in the eyes of her relatives and the village. On the other hand, when their childbearing days are over, women who have given birth to sons and daughters are honored and considered at the height of their powers.

Many of the carvings of a woman holding a baby or a woman with several children are placed in shrines where the representations of babies and nursing mothers reassure those who wish to become pregnant and others who ask for aid in the delivery of healthy babies. Expressing this desire, the words of a song repeat, "Plump, plump children, I carry plump children on my back."[25]

Children not only ensured that the family lineage and time-honored customs would continue, but they were economically necessary to help grow food, to carry on the family crafts, to act as herdsmen, and to care for younger brothers and sisters. This explains why several wives helped to increase the chances for prosperity and a good life, if a man could afford the care of each wife and her young ones.

The subject of mother and child to Western eyes recalls the legacy of an adoring Mother interacting with the Christ child. It would be a mistake, however, to allow this familiar treatment of a Christian theme to foster an erroneous interpretation of African mothers with their children. In African carvings, the mother does not represent a loving parent snuggling a cuddly infant. She is the generative force that perpetuates the race and brings renewal to crops and animals. The children that cluster around the mother or sit on her lap, while a younger child is supported in a carrying cloth on her back, are not given strong individual characteristics. They are extensions of their mother's personality.[26] Explaining the idea more fully, Susan Vogel writes:

> Because children are not fully "civilized" (or socialized), productive members of society, their depiction in art makes little sense. Infants . . . [represent] the productivity of the mother. To cite a parallel from life, one often sees a woman dressed up and carrying a child (not necessarily her own) as sort of a costume accessory. A woman looks better with a baby.[27]

In carvings, the attitude of mothers toward their children is ambivalent. A ceremonial rigidity is present in the Bena Lulua mother and child from Zaire (figure 108). The slender female figure is forty-three inches in height; without demarcations for legs the carving tapers to a small base. (In other contexts similar canelike shapes are placed as guardian figures in homes or implanted in fields.) The Lulua mother holding her

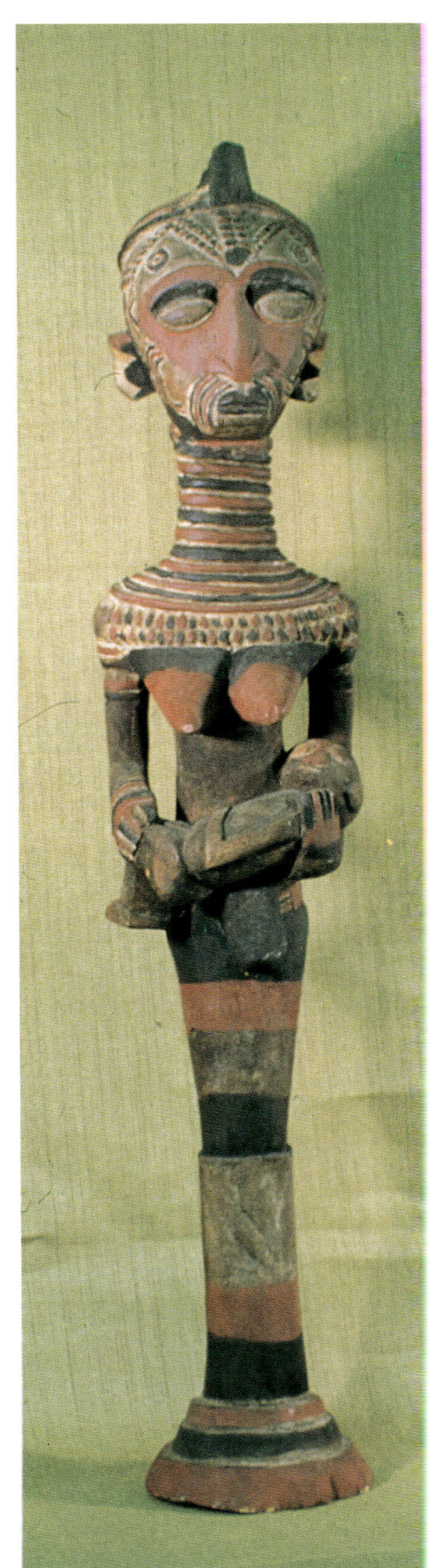

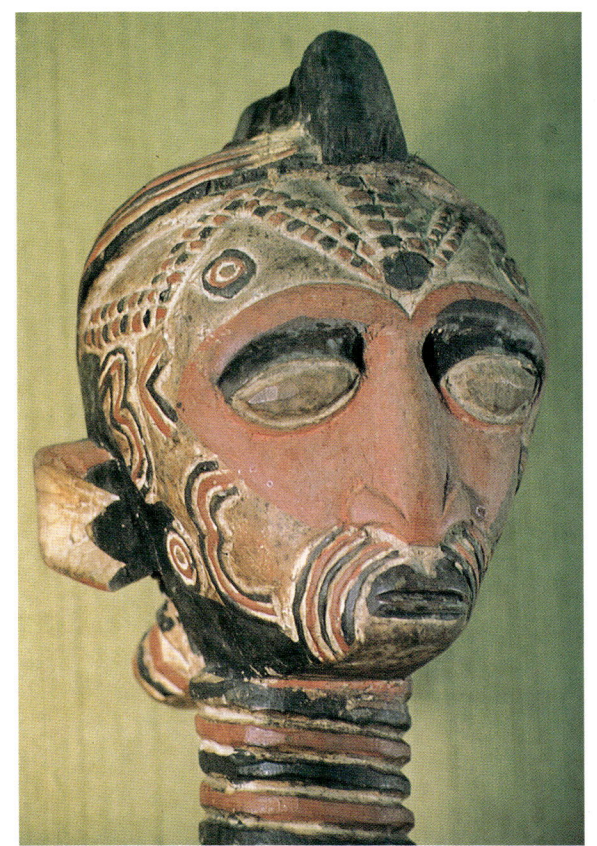

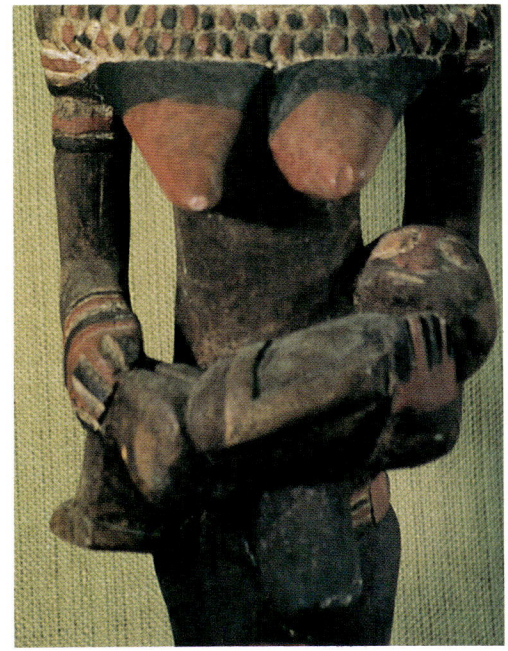

Fig. 108 (Left)
Mother and child, Bena
Lulua, Zaire, wood, paint.
H. 43 in.

Fig. 110 (Top right)
Detail of mother 108.

Fig. 109 (Bottom)
Detail of mother and child
108.

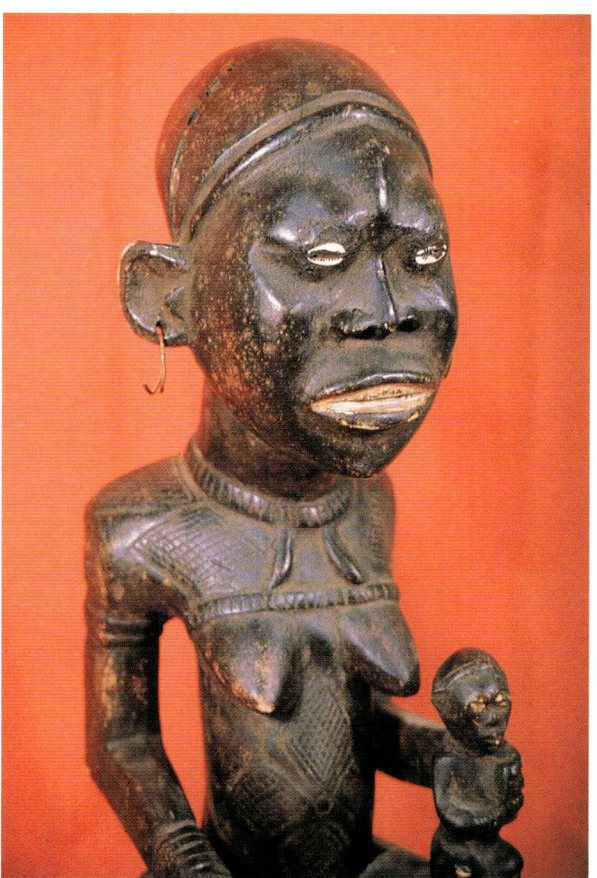

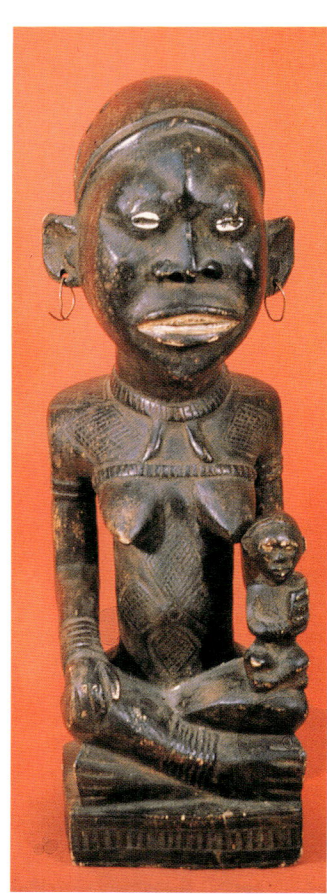

Fig. 112
Detail of mother and
child 111.

Fig. 111
Mother and child,
Yombe, Congo, wood,
metal, cowrie shells,
H. 19 ¾ in.

small baby (figure 109) has an elegantly painted cicatrix design over her body, around the forehead and cheeks, and framing the mouth and chin. The eyes are shaded by heavy half-closed lids. Alternating bands of red and black form concentric circles about the elongated neck (figure 110). Just below the almost formless infant in the Lulua mother's arms, the navel pushes forward representing the mystic center.[28] The figure becomes a symbol of the creative female principle, rather than an expression of empathy between mother and child.

A carving of motherhood associated with the Yombe from Congo is represented in figure 111. The woman assumes a seated position like that of Kongo dignitaries. She wears a woven pineapple fiber cap, a sign of authority. The bracelets, multiple anklets, necklace, and brass hoop earrings indicate wealth and a high social rank. Her head is enlarged, a sign of intelligence and important status (figure 112). A breast-binding cord is worn, and her torso is ornamented with refined scarification. The small infant on its mother's knee assumes a grown-up pose, seated upright with legs crossed. Cowrie shells are implanted in the woman's eye sockets, and her mouth is open showing white teeth.

The aristocratic attitude of the Yombe mother is represented by a mother and nursing child in the Asante style of Ghana (figures 113 and

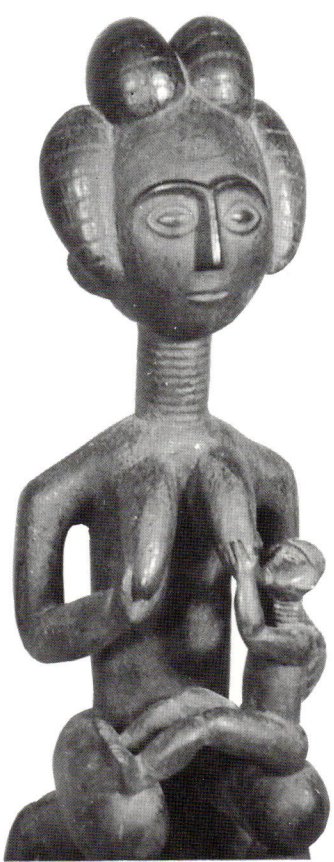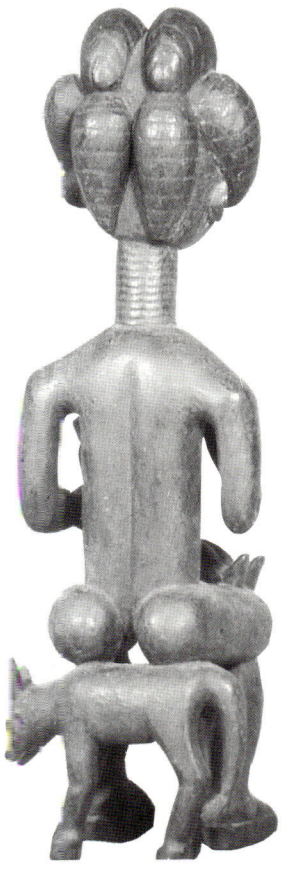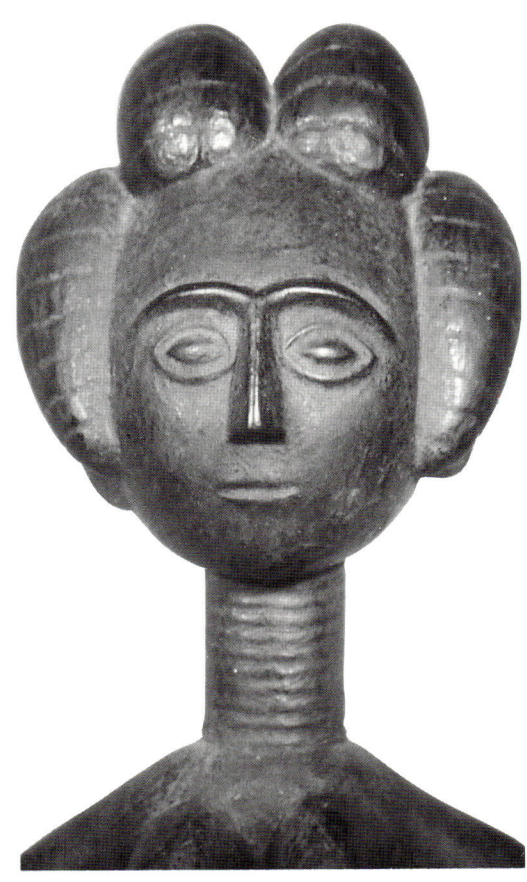

114). The carving is blackened wood. The woman's firm breasts are reflected in her hairstyle that comes to points on each side of the head and at the back. A straight spine ends in the geometric circles of the buttocks (figure 115). The place of the lady among her peers is made clear by her sandals that prevent her feet from touching the ground. Her stool is carved in the form of an animal, apparently domesticated because it stands peacefully instead of adopting a menacing glare like the royal leopard that supports the seated woman in figure 120.

A familiar and often repeated Asante subject is another treatment of the mother and infant theme (figure 116). The carving is known as *akua'ba*. These popular subjects are intended to bring about pregnancy and to ensure a healthy and handsome offspring. Unlike the mother with a child in figure 116, a woman (figure 117) stretches out her arms at right angles to her body; the arms end in rounded points instead of hands. The legs are cylindrical and taper to a round base. The body with its cruciform shape is crowned by a large, round, and flattened head, decorated on the back with an incised design. If such a carving is commissioned, when it is finished, it is blessed by a priest of the fertility deity and then carried about and cared for like a real infant by the woman for whom it was made. After a baby is successfully delivered,

Fig. 114
Mother and child
(front) Asante, Ghana,
wood, H. 23 1/2 in.

Fig. 115
Mother and child (back).

Fig. 113
Mother and child
(detail, head).

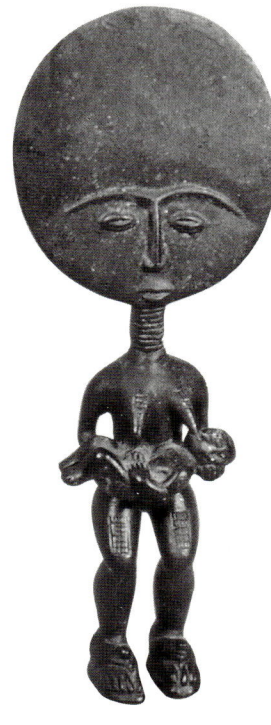

the *akua'ba* may be kept for a daughter to play with and as a means of teaching proper parental skills.

The *akua'ba* carvings capture the qualities associated with feminine beauty among the Asante. The round head with features in the lower portion of the circle indicates the admiration given a high forehead; this is a mark of feminine beauty and may be cultivated in a baby girl by massaging her soft skull. The arched eyebrows, delicate nose, and small mouth are desirable, as is the long neck with "rings to depict creases caused by subcutaneous fat, indicating . . . good health."[29]

Like the *akua'ba,* the "doll" is a popular subject of carvings among the Mossi of Burkina Faso (figure 118). Christopher Roy, who has done extensive research on this subject, explains that one of the doll's functions is to train little girls for their future roles as mothers. The toys are fed, washed, and dressed in bits of cloth and carried about on small backs just like the babies that are bundled on the backs of their mothers.[30] The wooden figures are made in the blacksmiths' compound by smiths in their spare time.[31] The "dolls" can hardly be called a substitute for Barbie with her constantly changing wardrobe for the fast lane. The Mossi figures have neither legs nor arms to break off from the cylindrically shaped bodies. The heads are centered by a semicircular shape, with the edge of the half circle facing the front. Roy suggests that this unusual form is related to the "female coiffure extending from the front of the head to the back." The smaller masses on each side are inspired by braided hair sometimes indicated by incised lines.[32]

The affection of the young owners for the figures is suggested by Roy's comment, "When searching for firewood in the bush, the girls bring back wildflowers for their dolls, and when they go to the market they carry the dolls in their skirts, showing them to vendors who give them small gifts."[33]

The function of the Mossi doll becomes more serious as a girl attains womanhood. It is hoped that the doll will encourage an early pregnancy and a vigorous baby. After a successful birth, the doll is kept for the female child it may have helped usher into this world.

At the Museum of Texas Tech University, among the carvings of mothers and their children that probably date from the 1950s and 1960s, one particularly handsome carving is of a woman who holds a nursing child in her lap (figure 3, 107). The youngster, who is not a newborn infant, serves as a reminder that children often are nursed by their mothers and carried about until they are two or three years of age. The mother's necklace of real shells and beads is an indication of wealth. Her social position is further confirmed by the sandals that protect her feet from touching the ground, and by the stool on which she sits. The design of the stool suggests a link to an Akan ethnic group. Any Akan

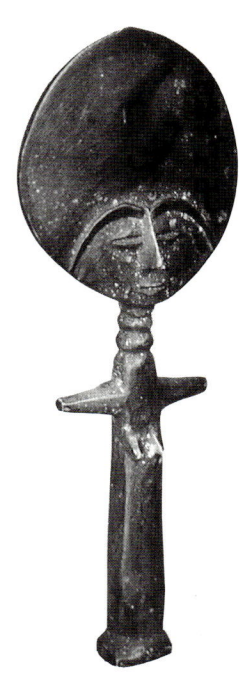

Fig. 116
Akuaba *figure, Akan,
Ghana, wood, H. 17 in.*

Fig. 117
Akuaba *figure, Akan,
Ghana, wood, H. 14 in.*

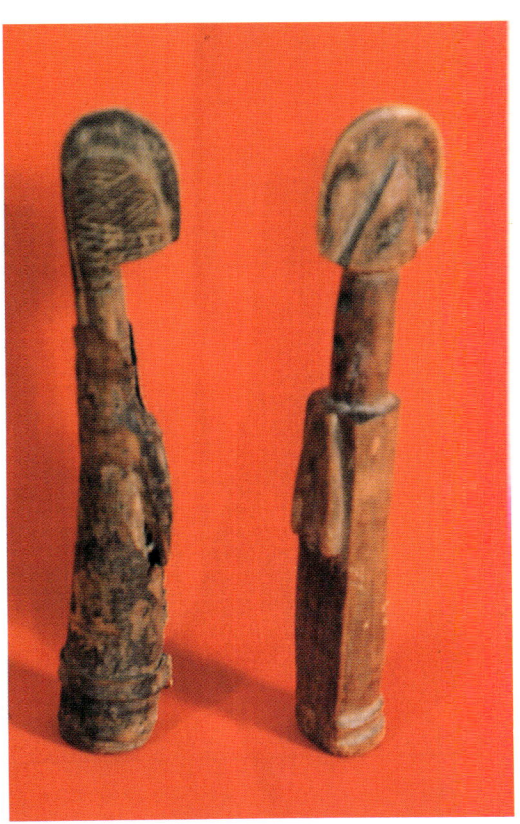

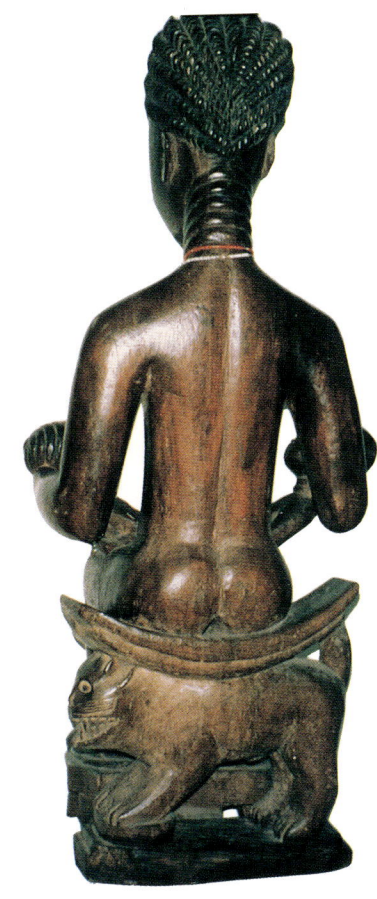

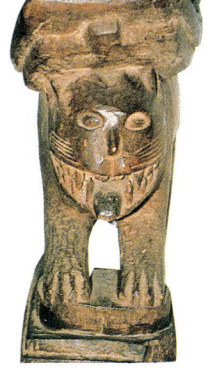

*Fig. 118
Dolls, Mossi, Burkina
Faso, wood, figure on
left, H. 9 ½ in; figure
on right, H. 9 in.
(Gift of Ambassador
and Mrs. Julius Walker
to ICASALS; now on
permanent loan from
ICASALS to the Mu-
seum of Texas Tech Uni-
versity.)*

*Fig. 119
Mother with twins, As-
ante, Ghana, wood, neck-
lace of glass beads, H. 18
in.*

*Fig. 120
Detail (leopard stool) of
mother with twins 119.*

person may own a stool and there are usually a number of stools in a
household. The design of the stool is determined by the rank of the
buyer. Stools similar to the one on which the woman is seated, but
overlaid with silver decoration, are called *asantehene* and are possessions
of a queen mother.[34]

Certain stools, whose importance is recognized by the design and
elaboration of the carving, are regarded as prerogatives of royal office
and embody the symbols valued by a culture. For example, the mother
with twin children in figure 119 is firmly placed on a saddle-shaped seat
that is mounted on the back of an unpainted toothy feline with tongue
lolling out (figure 120). The leopard is associated with royalty and
admired for its ability to survive, its cunning, and its swiftness to pounce
on its prey. "King of the bush," it was a symbol of the Oba in the
Kingdom of Benin, expressing the ferociousness and aggression considered virtues appropriate for rulers and for their survival in the social
jungle.[35]

A Yoruba mother (figures 121, 122) is also positioned on a leopard
whose identity is clarified beyond a shadow of a doubt by painted spots.
A boy and girl sit on their mother's lap producing a pleasingly balanced
composition. The woman represents the type of ideal beauty that is

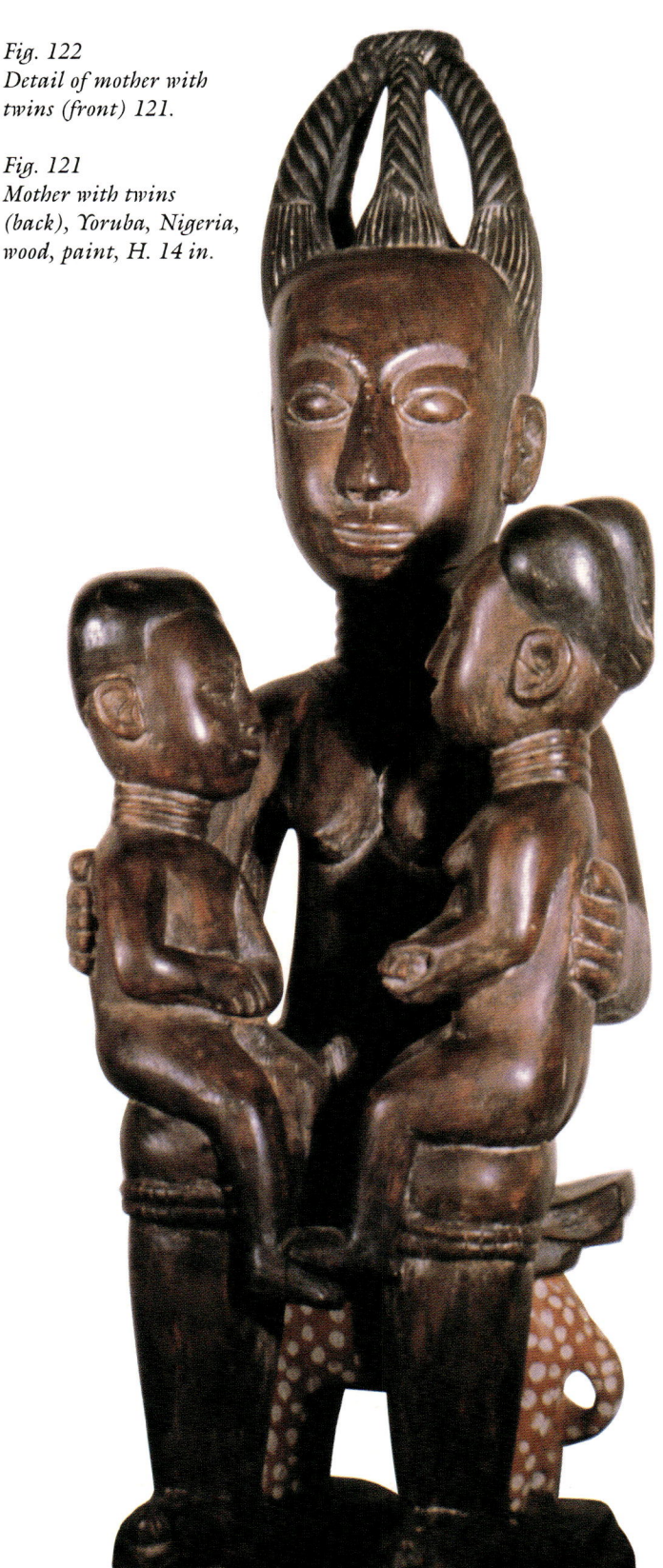
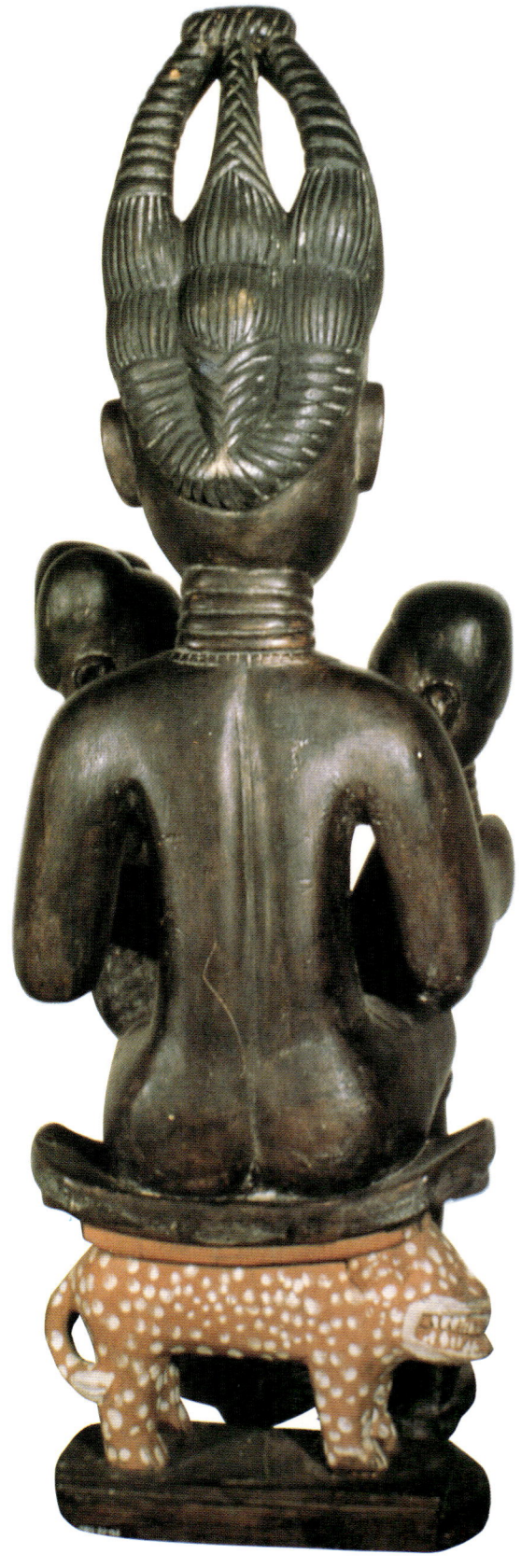

Fig. 122
Detail of mother with
twins (front) 121.

Fig. 121
Mother with twins
(back), Yoruba, Nigeria,
wood, paint, H. 14 in.

admired in a young female. The gleaming smoothness of skin is addressed by a Yoruba priest of Erinle at Oke-Iho with the words, "The cheek . . . is beautiful; it is not swollen but rather shining."[36] The hair to be complimented should be intricately arranged, and the woman should possess symmetry and straightness in her carriage.[37] For a man, straightness is equated with the need during a masquerade to maneuver without faltering while supporting a heavy ceremonial headdress. It is just as necessary for women to hold themselves erect without tilting to balance containers on their heads, while holding children in their arms and a younger one on a strong back. The young ones in figure 122, held by their Yoruba mother, are as elegant as their parent. Both the boy and girl have hair that is shiny black. The dark blue-black is made from the leaves of indigo or from the indigo vine. To be colored with the midnight hue *(dudu)* means to possess "deep wisdom." This is appropriate, because it is said that the "wisdom of Sango [a Yoruba deity] is like looking into an indigo dye pot."[38]

Twins represent a blessing sought for and valued by many western sub-Saharan African cultures. Twins are believed to be powerful spirits who are capable of bringing good fortune to their family. Carefully nurtured, the affection and regard with which they are held is apparent in a few lines of a song whose subject is the twin children of well-to-do parents:

> Taiwo and Kehinde are rich children.
> They give me pleasure as does a crown,
> As does one with a long, graceful neck,
> As does one whom it is good to see in the morning,
> As one who attracts attention,
> As one with beautiful eyes.[39]

Among the Yoruba, if a twin should die, a carver is asked to make an *ere ibeji* figure. This requires a careful ritual, which includes giving an offering to the tree from whose wood the figure will be shaped. When the parents have been notified that the carving is ready, they travel to the carver's compound, bringing food for him and his family. The bereaved mother, after making the proper sacrifices, will receive the wooden figure. Placing it in a carrying wrapper as she would a living child, she performs the songs and dances that honor twins. The twin figure is treated exactly as a living child. It is bathed, fed, and cared for; eventually it is dressed and given cowrie shell bracelets, brass rings, or a bead necklace. It is no longer considered a memorial but assumes the spirit of the dead twin through the rite of transformation. In this way the carved image is regarded as an affirmation of life. If both twins die, they are each represented by a carving (figure 123) that is placed in a

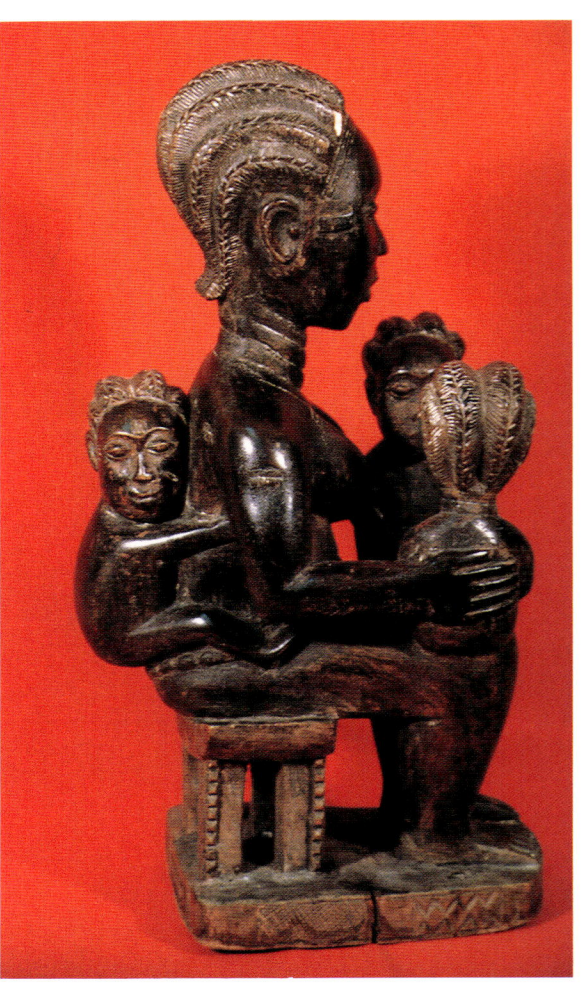

Fig. 125
Mother with three children, Asante, Ghana, wood, H. 21 ½ in.

shrine dedicated to Sango.[40] The small wooden figures pictured in figure 124 wear the conical headdress of the Yoruba and are dressed in robes to which cowrie shells are sewn. Such shells often appear on belts and jewelry and are sometimes inserted in wood carvings to represent eyes or as lines indicating patterns of scarification. Cowries were first brought to western sub-Saharan Africa centuries ago from islands in the Indian Ocean. They were transported across the Sahara in camel caravans. In some parts of Mali, the cowrie was used as currency as late as the 1940s.

Three children are represented close to their mothers in figures 125–126. In each carving, two youngsters sit on the mother's lap while an infant clings to her back, recalling the saying, "A mother's back is the baby's medicine."[41] The gentle realism expressed in figure 126 differs from the formality in figure 127. In the latter, ceremonialism seems to bind the present to the ancestors of past ages and to invoke ancient maternal deities. In contrast to the short, stylishly arranged hair of the woman in figure 126, the matriarch's hair is dressed in three parts divided by precisely combed strands. A heavy coil descends from each of the three divisions. The face, breasts, and torso reveal complex scarification. Half-closed eyes turn attention inward. Twins, one on each

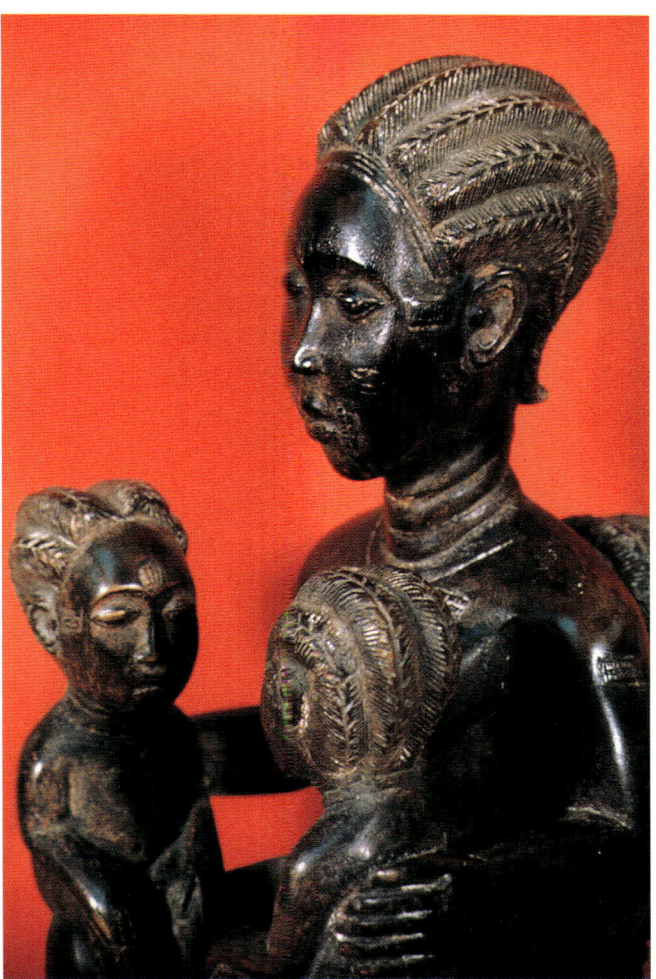

*Fig. 126
Detail of mother with
three children 125.*

knee, sit upright; they are small and show little expression (figure 128).
A baby holds to its mother's back with arms and legs spread; turning
its head, it looks like a small frog (figure 129).

Diametrically opposed to calm introspection and quiescence, a
brass casting churns with energy (figure 130). The woman and her
young ones are an example of the grotesque work of craftsman associated with Fumban, the capital under Sultan Njoya of the Bamun people
living on the Cameroon grasslands. The Sultan, who reigned at the
beginning of the twentieth century, was a distinguished monarch and
a patron of the arts. The royal workshops produced remarkable brass
pieces.[42] The use of metal makes possible the exaggerated gestures and
animated expressions present in the lively figures of the mother with
her unruly brood. One child is sprawled on its mother's hip, half
slipping in a precarious fashion; the other balances on one foot with a
hand behind the mother's knee. The woman's slender arms are snake-
like and her smile sinister. The children have the faces of adults (figure
131). Technically exquisite, the casting of the cicatrices on the woman's
back produces an intricate and lacelike fleshy "fabric"(figure 132).

The explosive sense of movement in the brass sculpture provides a
dramatic foil for the tallest carving in the collection of the Museum of

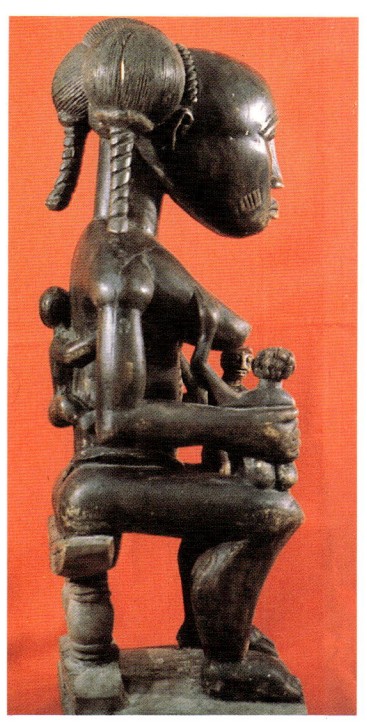

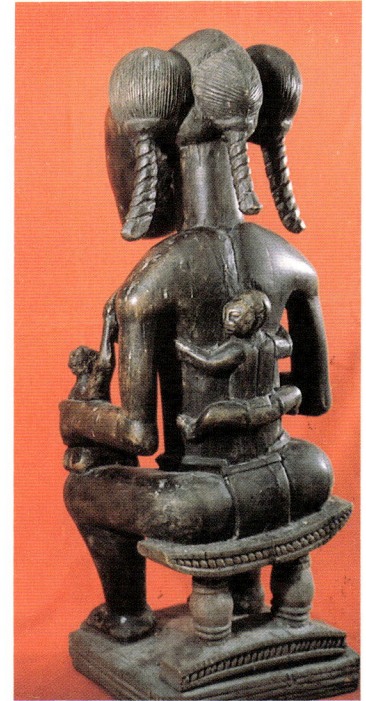

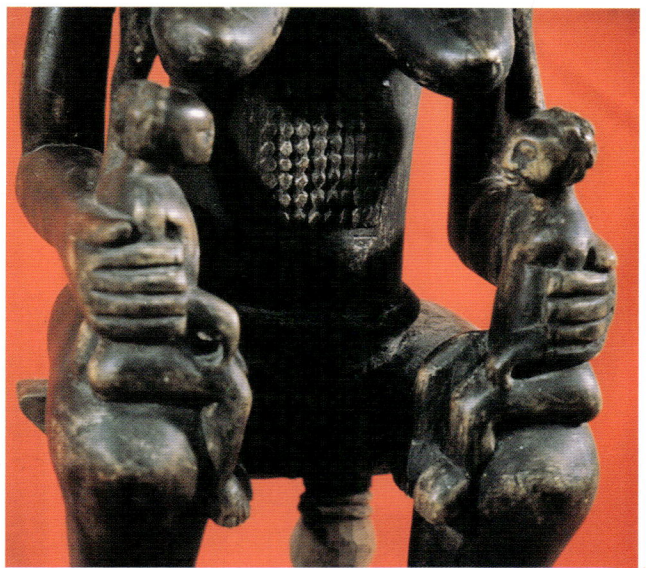

Clockwise from top left:

Fig. 127
Mother with three children,
Bamana, Mali, wood,
H. 34 1/4 in.

Fig. 129
Detail of mother with three
children 127.

Fig. 128
Detail of mother with three
children 127.

Fig. 124
Twins, Yoruba, Nigeria,
wood, paint, fabric, cowrie
shells: woman, H. 12 1/2 in.;
man, H. 11 1/4 in.

Fig. 130
Mother with two children,
Fumban, Cameroon, brass,
H. 33 1/2 in.

Fig. 131
Detail of mother with two
children 130.

Fig. 123
Twins, Yoruba, Nigeria,
wood, paint, H. approx. 11
in. (Courtesy of John O.
Evans III)

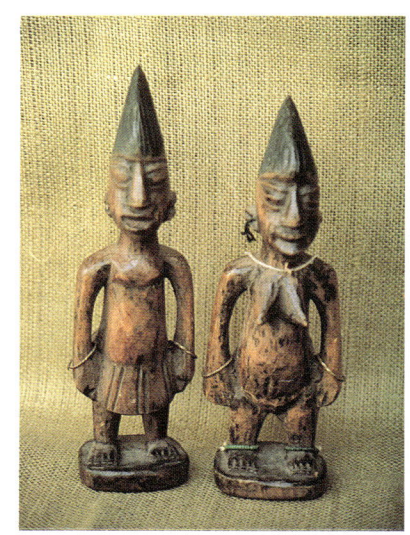

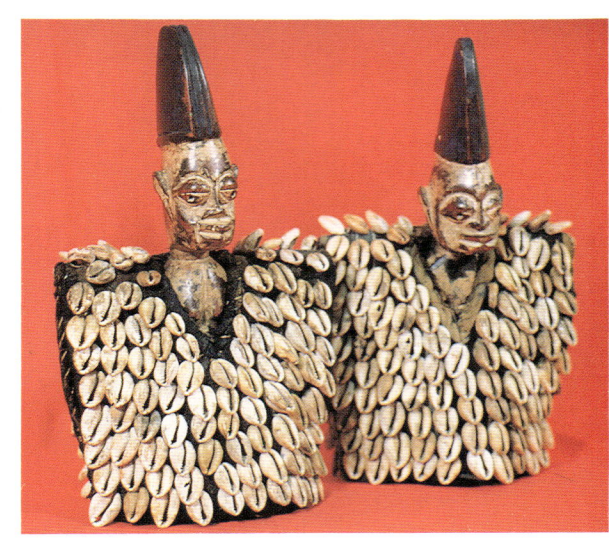

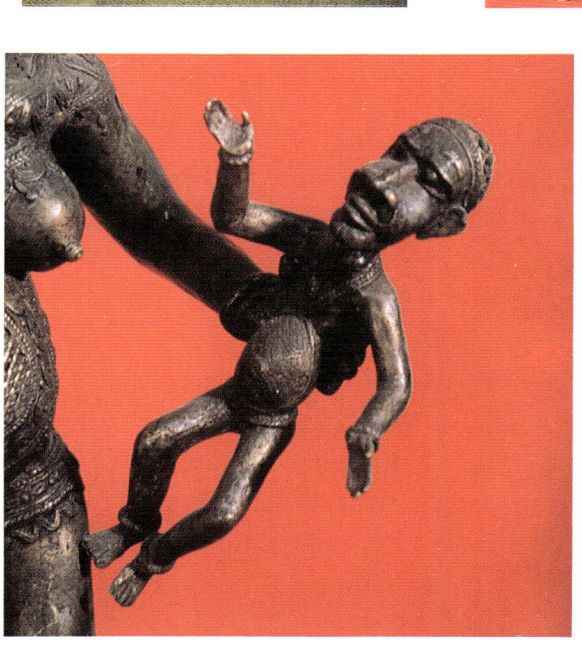

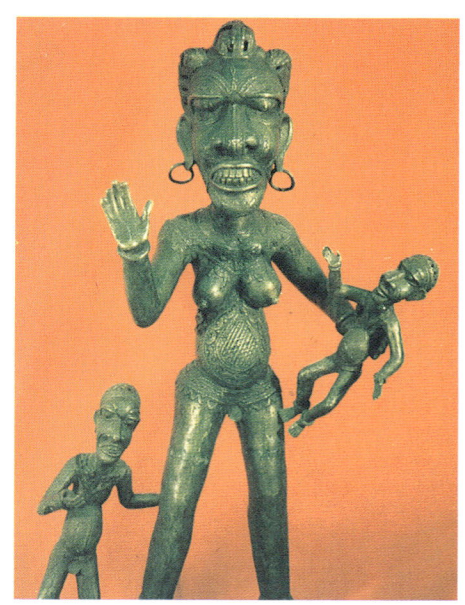

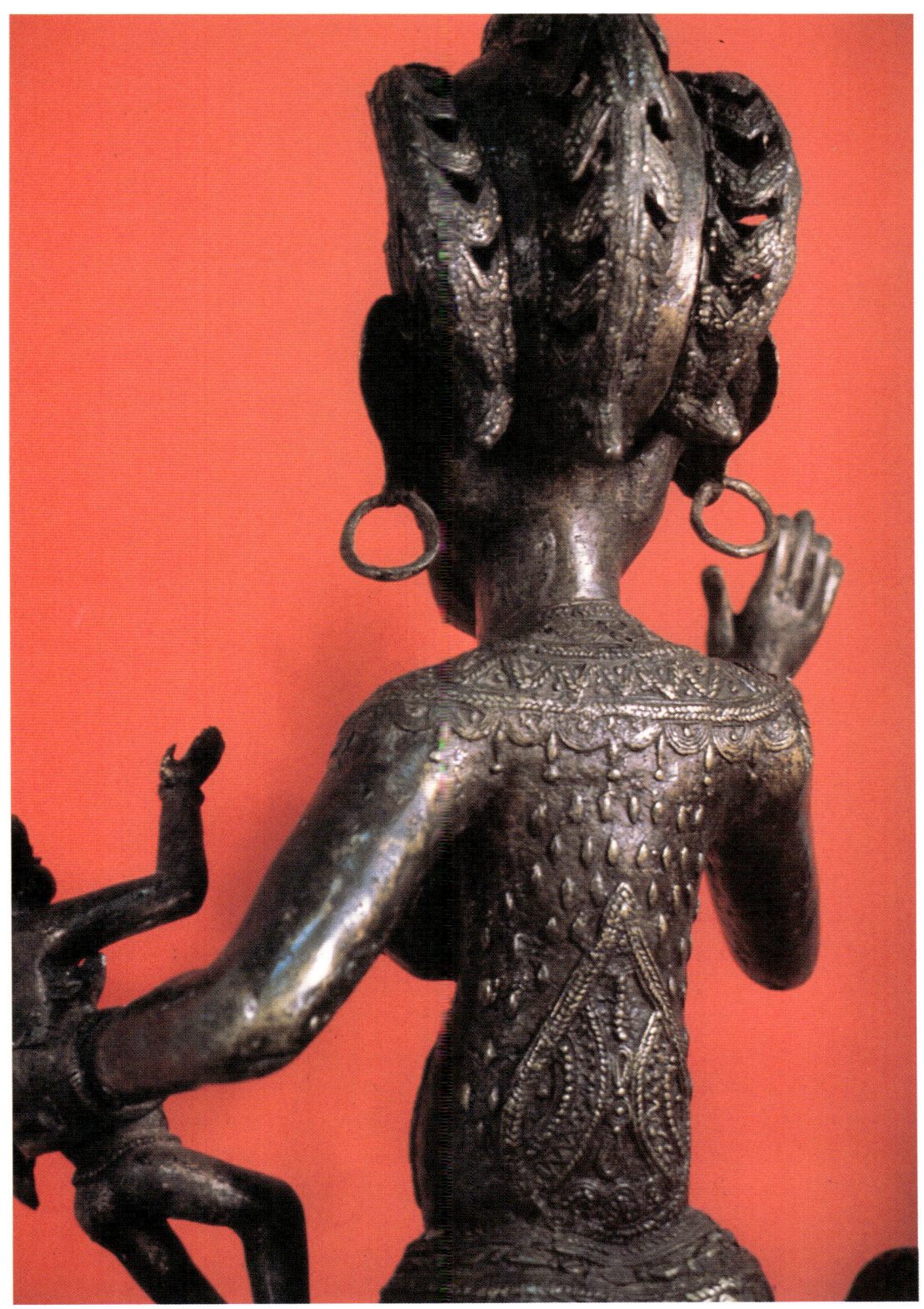

Fig. 132
Detail of mother with
two children 130.

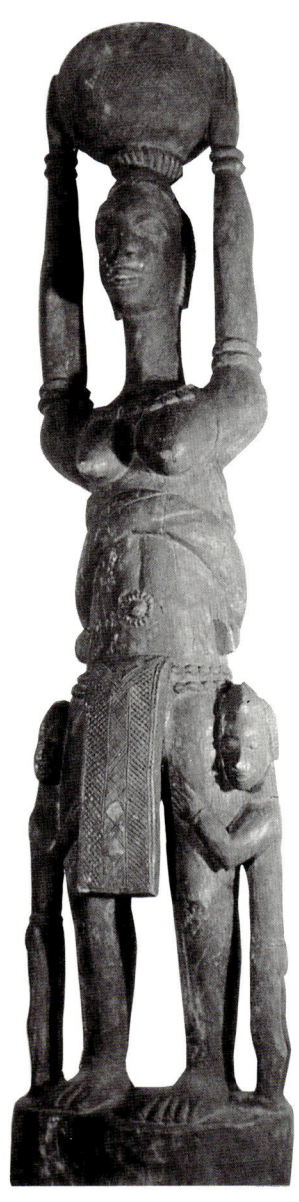

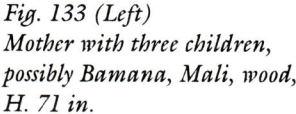

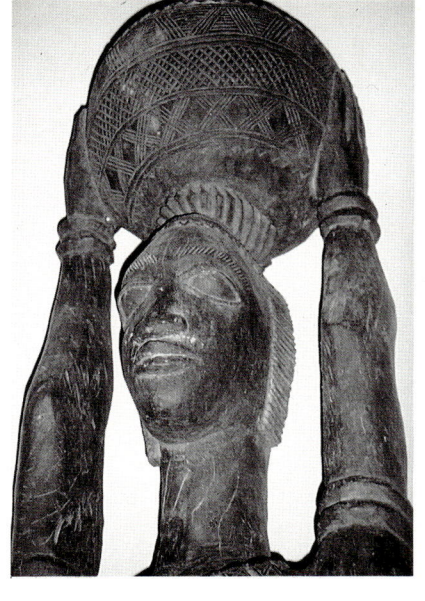

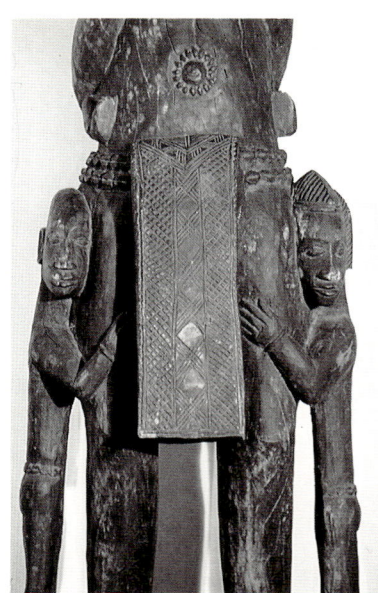

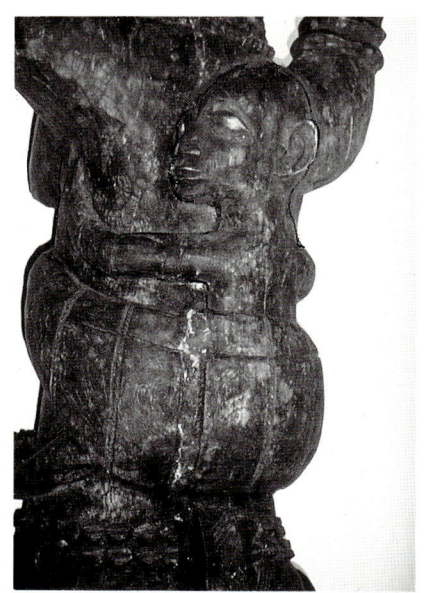

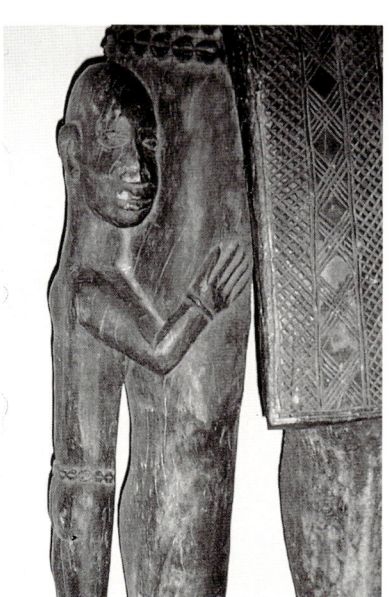

Fig. 133 (Left)
Mother with three children,
possibly Bamana, Mali, wood,
H. 71 in.

Fig. 134 (Top middle)
Detail of mother with three
children 133.

Fig. 135 (Top right)
Detail of mother with three
children 133.

Fig. 137 (Bottom middle)
Detail of mother with three
children 133.

Fig. 136 (Bottom right)
Detail of mother with three
children 133.

Texas Tech University. A monumental figure of a woman stands seventy-one inches in height. She dominates the space she commands (figure 133). With eyes wide-open she concentrates upon this world. Her features are strong and purposeful. The long column of her neck is a mark of beauty. Her arms are spearlike in their strength as they are uplifted to balance a bowl resting on her head (figure 134). The woman's importance is evident from the double bracelets worn on her wrists and upper arms and the double strand of cowrie shells carved to form a belt around her waist. Even though her arms are not free, the viewer senses that this woman has the protective strength of a sturdy tree, sheltering the children who hold on to her skirt (figures 135, 136). Supported on its mother's back, a baby is wrapped in a cloth that crosses gracefully beneath the woman's breasts (figure 137). The sculpture is an apt illustration for the African proverb that observes, "It is a hard working woman who carries her child and a load at the same time."

IV

The Hunter

*It's better not to shoot at the leopard at
all than to shoot and miss.*

Asante Proverb

While women remained in the village or nearby fields, caring for the young, keeping order at home, and performing women's rituals, men left the safety of the compound to confront the dangerous wild creatures lurking in the bush or forest and, when necessary, to make war. The hunter and warrior are related; both meet danger and attempt to successfully overcome obstacles and unknown terrors. Taking command and triumphing over a wild beast or an enemy is the mark of a leader symbolized by the hunter image.

The hunter, represented in figures 138 and 139, wears a round, domed head covering and carries a gun; his quarry, with feet bound, rests across his shoulders. Among the Yoruba, the hunter's metal weapons establish a tie with Ogun, the god of iron and war. A hunter also owes his success to Osanyin, the god of herbal medicine. Entering the bush, those in search of game wear clothing that through magic has been made resistant to poisonous plants and insects and offers protection against the unexpected attack of fierce animals. A knowledge of the powerful herbs growing in the forest and where to gather them was a part of the hunter's education. The Yoruba were aware of the spiritual dimensions of the hunt. Henry John Drewal explains:

Forests are not only the abode of animals, but also of spirits. Hunters therefore have to arm themselves with guns, arrows, traps, and knives as well as with spiritual armaments—amulets, incantations to protect themselves and charm their prey into agreeing to be caught . . . . Some of the hunters' magical medicines allow them to transform themselves, to make themselves invisible at moments of danger, or to stop a charging animal in its tracks. Other stories tell of a mythic time when animals and humans spoke the same language and changed their outer appearance, humans into animals, animals into humans. . . . In addition, hunters' lore records an ancient agreement with animals. Humans could kill them, but only

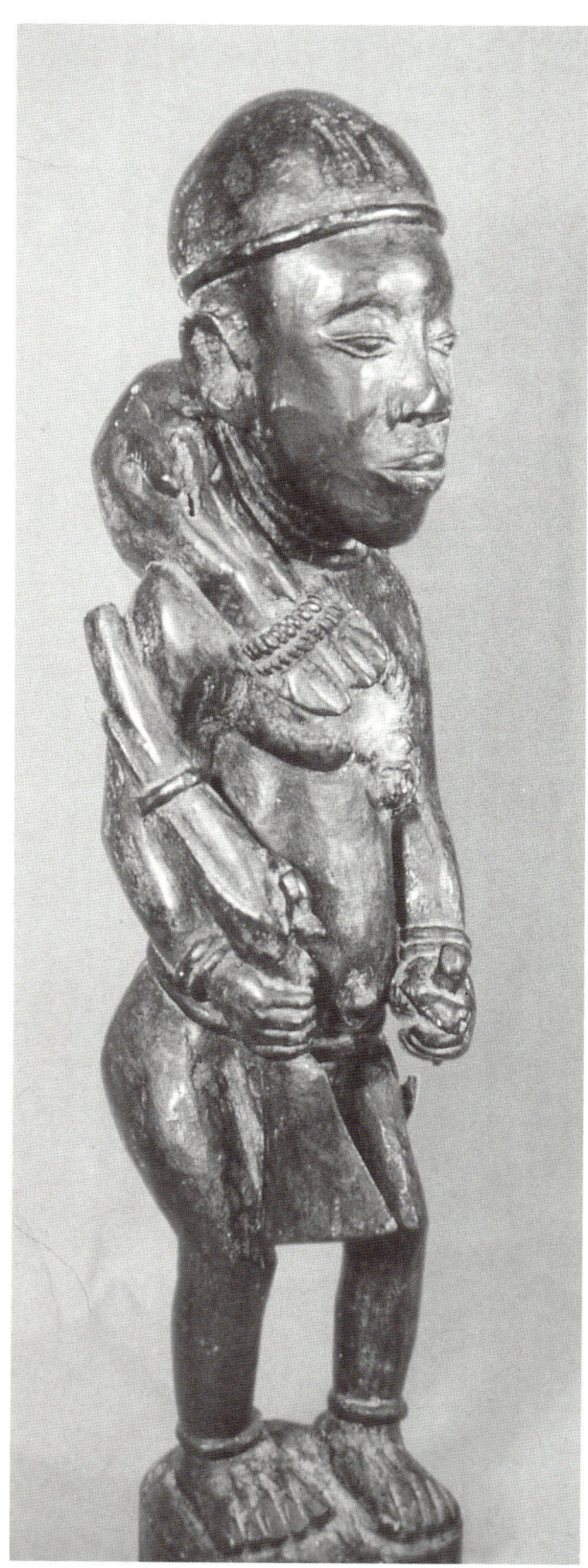

Fig. 138
Hunter, Yoruba, Nigeria, wood. H. 26 ¾ in.

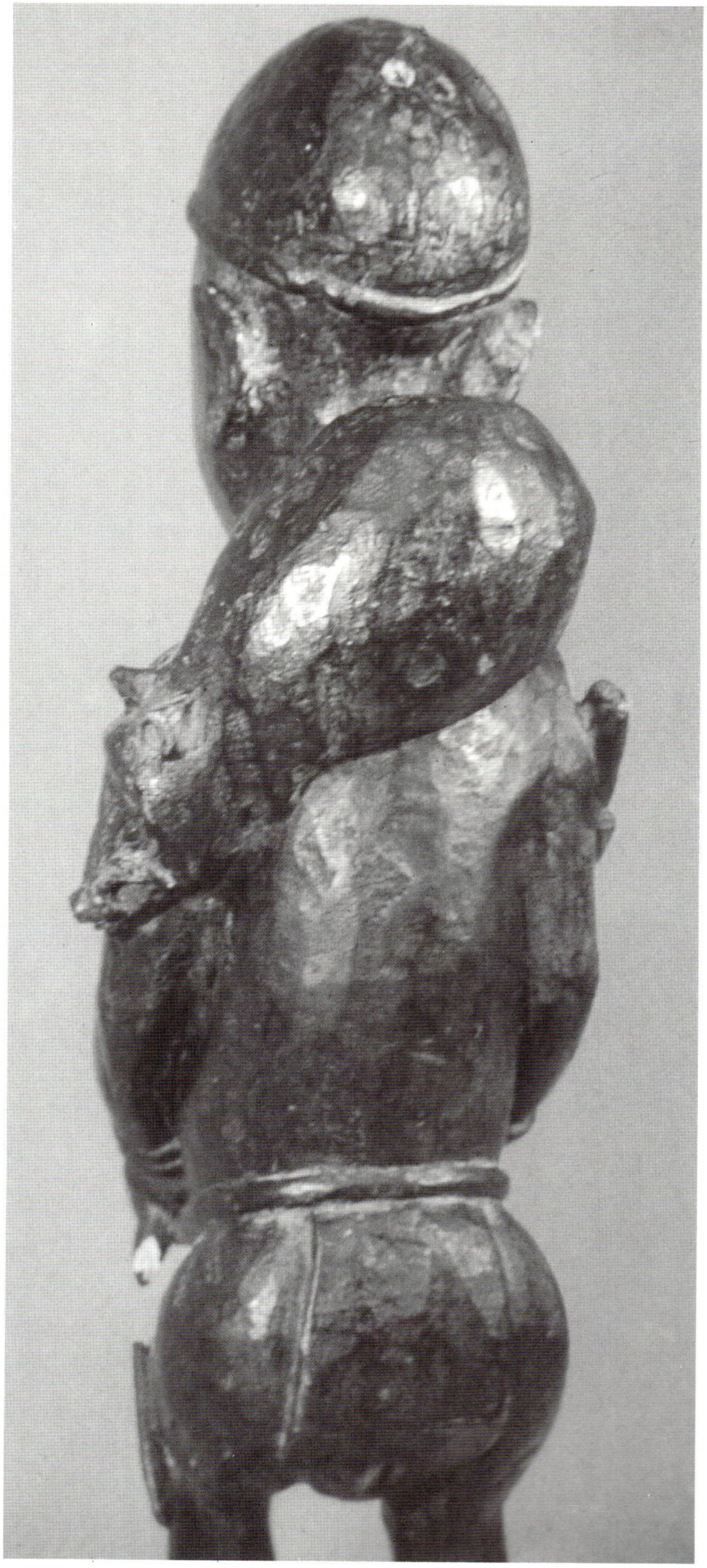

Fig. 139
Detail of hunter 138.

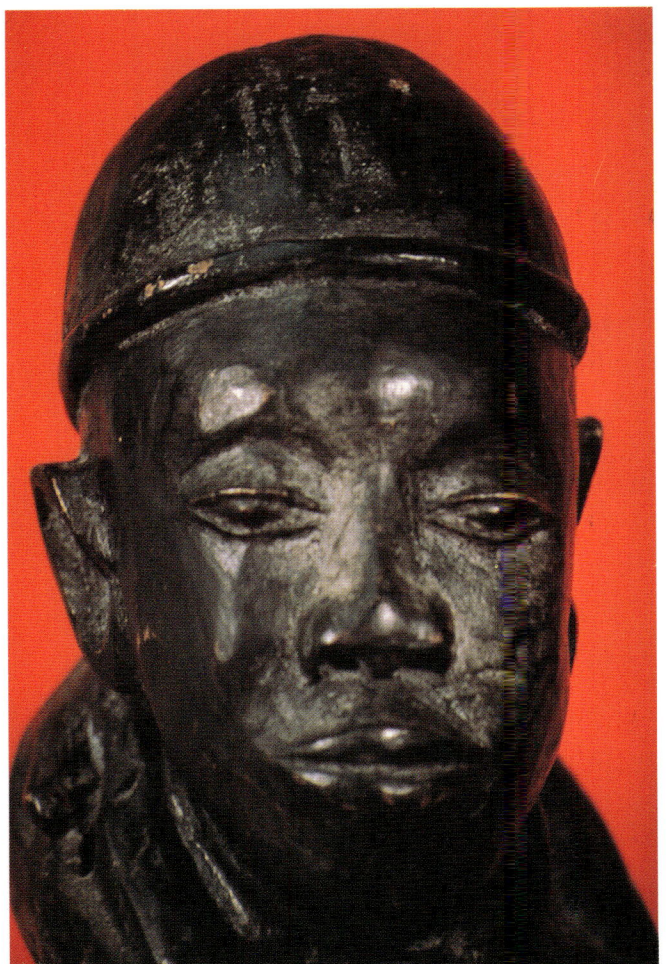

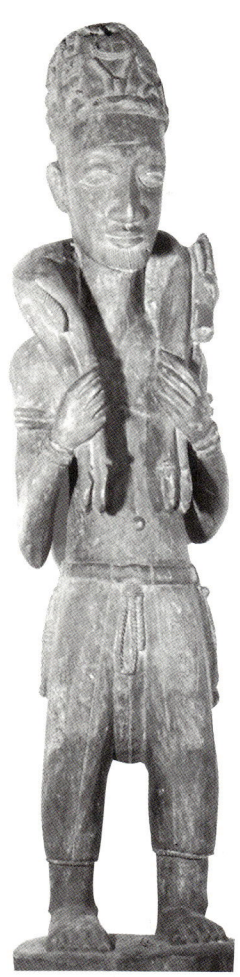

Fig. 140 (Left)
Detail of hunter 138.

Fig. 141 (Right)
Hunter, origin un-
known, wood,
H. 69 in.

Fig. 142 (Below)
Detail of hunter 141.

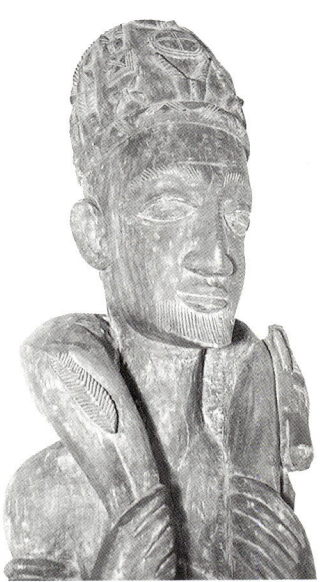

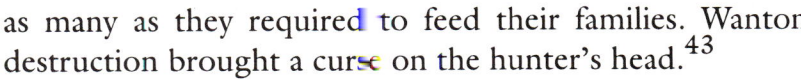

as many as they required to feed their families. Wanton destruction brought a curse on the hunter's head.[43]

A detail of the hunter's face (figure 140) seems to portray a retreat into a meditative state. Realism is present in the artist's keen observation and anatomical interests. The faceted surface of the skin, created skillfully by the adz blade, reproduces the quality of living flesh. The expressive features appear haunted by the need to live in two worlds—that of everyday reality and the realm of the spirits.

A nearly life-sized carving of a huntsman (figures 141, 142) displays a style that suggests the sculpture may have come from a Baule or Bamana workshop. The man is bearded, a characteristic associated with wisdom. He carries an antelope or deer over his shoulders. His simple trousers are held in place by a rope belt to which a knife is attached; a pouch is secured at the waist. Barefooted, the man stands on large feet implying the endurance and physical stamina needed to survive the hardships encountered in the pursuit of game. The hunter's head is covered by a cap to which significant insignia associated with the hunt are attached. These charms include small hoofs, intended to magically attract game, and horns, a sign that the wearer knows how to invoke supernaturals powers.[44]

V

Equestrian Figures

to dance carrying a baby on the right arm,
sling another on the back with the left one
and ride on horseback

Divination wish from
Yoruba: Nine Centuries of African Art and Thought

Equestrian figures share with hunters and warriors qualities of power and prestige. Raised from the ground, towering over those who move on foot, the mounted man personifies wealth, without which he could not own his horse or attain that high visibility associated with leadership. The rider mounted on a standing horse possesses a regal dignity (figure 143). Set in motion in figure 144, the meshing of human and animal strength is charged with a demonic force. Strength is held at bay waiting to be released in figure 145. This is the opposite of the frenzied charge that activates the brass casting in figure 144.

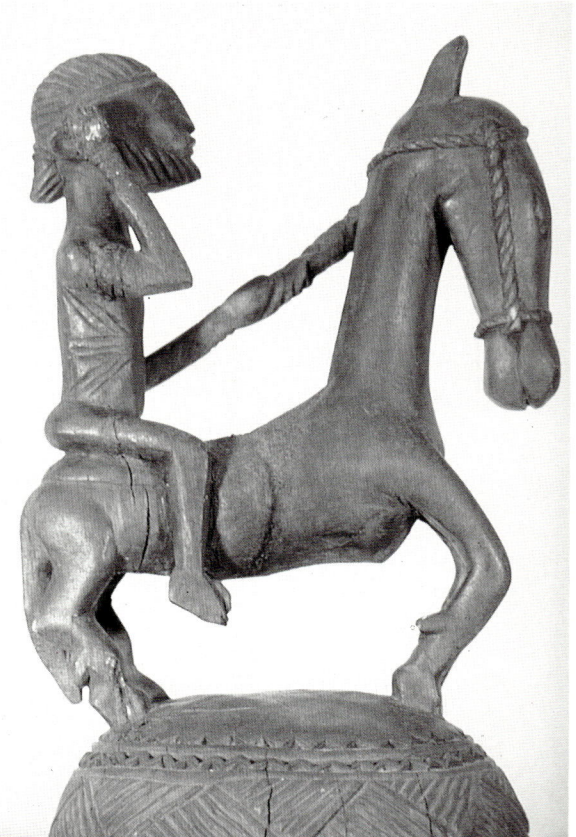

Fig. 143
Equestrian, Dogon,
Mali, wood, H. 10 in.

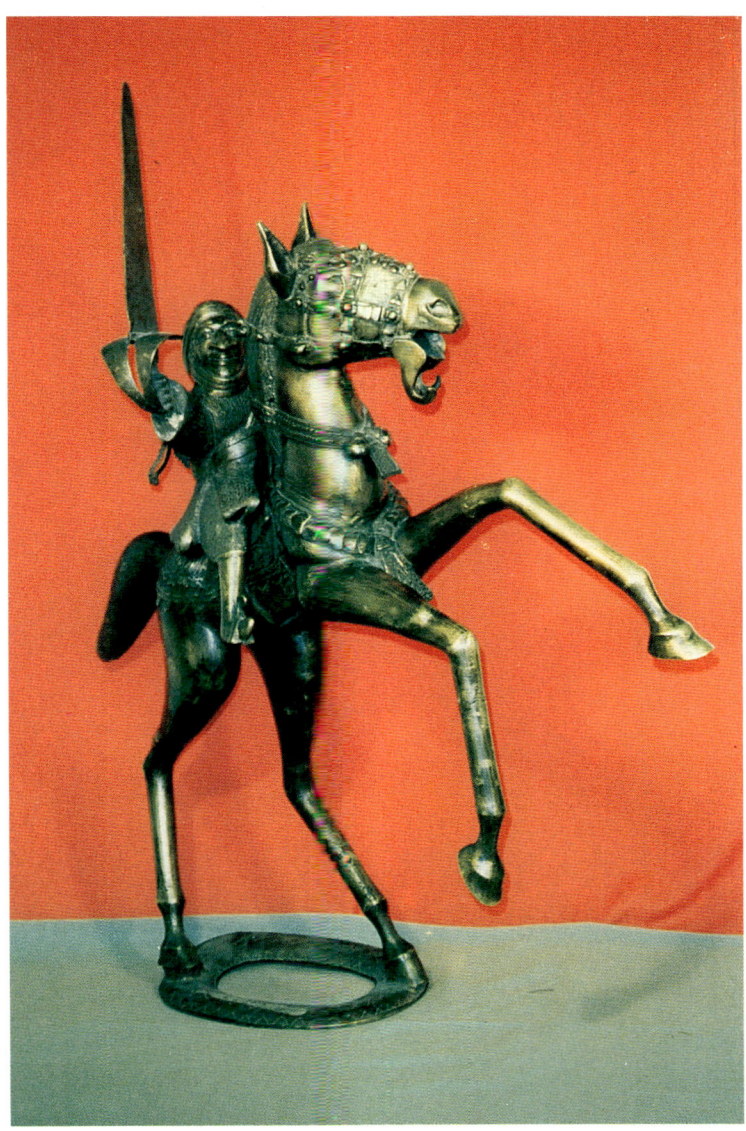

Fig. 144
Equestrian, origin
unknown, brass in two
separate pieces, overall
H. 37 1/2 in.

Evidence of the presence of horse and rider appear in early rock engravings on African cave walls. Mythic heroes also have been pictured riding on the backs of crocodiles, leopards, tortoises, and other unlikely mounts associated with the spirit world. A man lifted above his fellows, condemned to plod along on foot, gets respect. In the modern world, this deference goes to the one who rides a bicycle or preferably a motorcycle with its accompaniment of loud roars and puffing exhaust plumes—prerogatives once the exclusive rights of dragons.

The equestrian theme is especially popular among the Dogon who make their homes on the fringes of the Sahara. A controversy exists about the type of Dogon settlement in which the horse was first bred. Was it the cliff villages or the flatlands? The preferred answer seems obvious and points to the flat plains. Why were the Dogons successful in breeding horses when many other sub-Saharan Africans failed? In the

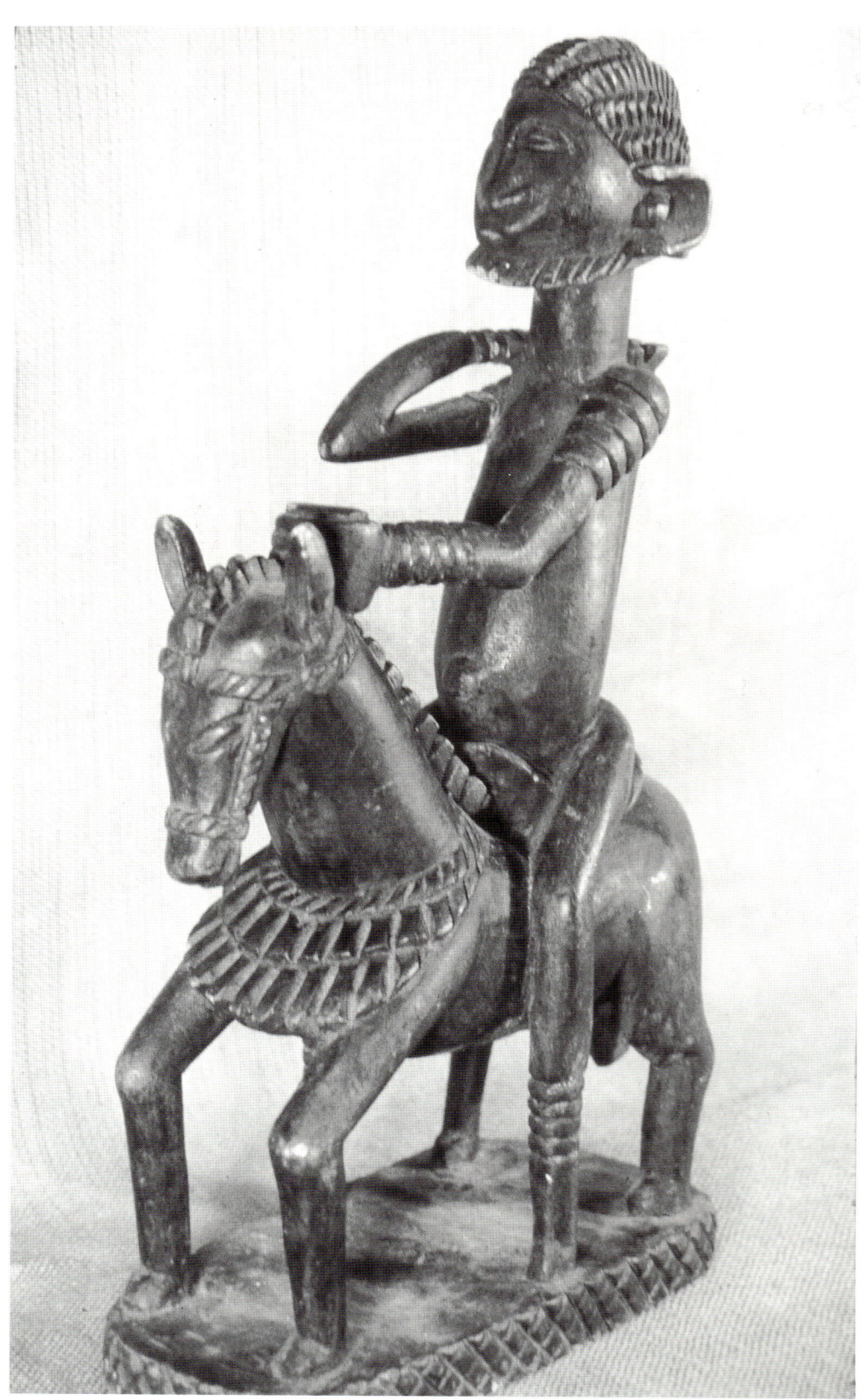

*Fig. 145
Equestrian, Dogon,
Mali, wood,
H. 19 ½ in.*

dry climate horses were not exposed to the fatal sleeping sickness carried by the tsetse flies of the forests. Horses also were able to survive on the savannas and flood plains of the Niger River. As early as the fourteenth or fifteenth centuries A.D., horses were bred and sold in this region. The best breeding stock to improve an equine line was obtained from the Arabs and frequently paid for in slaves.[45] In the arts, Herbert Cole cites an archaeological find near Djenne in Mali, of small mounted figures molded in terra cotta.[46] These early pieces project an imagery that may have served as a prototype for the later wood carvings of their neighbors.

The interpretation of the Dogon carvings of equestrian figures has been a subject for speculation. It is likely that the intention was to commemorate a hero or deceased leader. An honored ancestor might also have been the intended subject. There is, however, little doubt that a man on horseback was associated with leadership, honor, and status.

In the early twentieth century, Desplagnes described the funeral of a *hogon,* the spiritual leader of the Dogon village. The ritual included the binding of the *hogon's* corpse in an upright position on the back of a horse so he might make a farewell promenade through the narrow paths between the family complexes.[47] The relation of *hogon* and horse has its origin in Dogon mythology. Lebe, often represented on horseback, was revered as the oldest man and the first *hogon,* whereas the horse was honored as the first creature to emerge from the ark dropped by the *nummo* at the end of the rainbow bridge. Thus, the horse's priority as a symbol of preeminence made it a companion worthy of enhancing Lebe's image.[48]

Figure 145 is an equestrian carving that bears a relation to the early Dogon treatment of the theme as it occurs in a statuette from the Barbier-Mueller Collection in Geneva.[49] In both representations the riders' necks are long and the bodies erect. The refined features of the faces end in short beards; the hair is arched over the ears in ridges. In figure 145, the rider's legs touch the ground, ending with only a vestige of feet; by this device, six supports—four equine legs plus two human ones—give stability to the carving. The left hand of the rider holds a rein. The arm is adorned with four bracelets (a masculine number) placed near the shoulder and four more worn close to the wrist. The right arm reaches around to touch a quiver carried on the rider's back. The gesture forms a graceful oval, repeating the curve of the horse's front legs. The horse wears an elaborate collar; its mane is groomed in a scalloped pattern and its hindquarters are rounded and firm. The carving projects a particularly pleasing relation between the solid positive form and the negative space. The absence of color contrasts with two Yoruba equestrians, both of whom are painted.

In figures 146 and 147, the riders are similar except for differences in scale. The taller rider (figure 146) measures about thirty-four inches, whereas the smaller one is twenty-seven inches tall (figure 147). The techniques, compositions, and details suggest that they may have come from the hands of the same carver. Both men are mounted on horses that are diminutive when contrasted with the height of the riders. As a part of each carving, there are three small men who walk beside the horse, two on the rider's left and one on the right. The foremost figures in both instances hold guns. The subordinate position of the attendants is indicated by their scale and simple garments. The riders wear hats, asserting a superiority to the bareheaded followers. Their importance is further underscored by their large heads in proportion to their bodies. The heads and hats equal the dimensions of the upper bodies from shoulders to seat in the saddle. The legs are short, implying that it does little harm to neglect those body parts not associated with the vital organs. Each man holds a long rein in his right hand and touches the short rein with his left. The riders' features are not mirror images; each exhibits individuality. The taller figure has prominent eyes with black pupils that convey an alert and piercing glance (figure 148). The shorter man's face has heavier contours and the expression is relaxed (figure 149). The clothing of each is detailed with paint. A black band is painted around the neck of the tallest rider; from it an amulet is suspended.

In contrast to the small sculptures just described, one of the most striking pieces in the collection of the Museum of Texas Tech University is an unusually large horse and hunter (figure 150). The carving possesses a grandeur, enhanced by scale, that explains why the Yoruba consider the horse and rider an appropriate subject for bestowing praise on the gods.[50] In this monumental carving, the artist has displayed keen observation. He omits the exaggerated head and torso of the man in contrast to a small token horse intended to underscore the wealth that permits such a prestigious means of transportation. Symbolic indicators are not needed to communicate the purposefulness and beauty of this rider and his mount; they exist in a unity that needs no explanation. The impression is of grave decorum and unshakable dignity.

The collector, Elliot Howard, identified the piece as Dogon. It has, however, Yoruba characteristics. The horseman's finely chiseled features reinforces the Yoruba ideal of the head as the site of man's essential nature and his spiritual essence.[51] The conical headpiece, which often contains power substances, is a symbol associated with the internal qualities "calm, self control, and patience."[52] Ideally, the physical appearance should reflect the inner essentiality, the sought after "nobility of mind and dignity."[53] The cone is also a form that is related to the first men and women and their settlement on the earth. A Yoruba

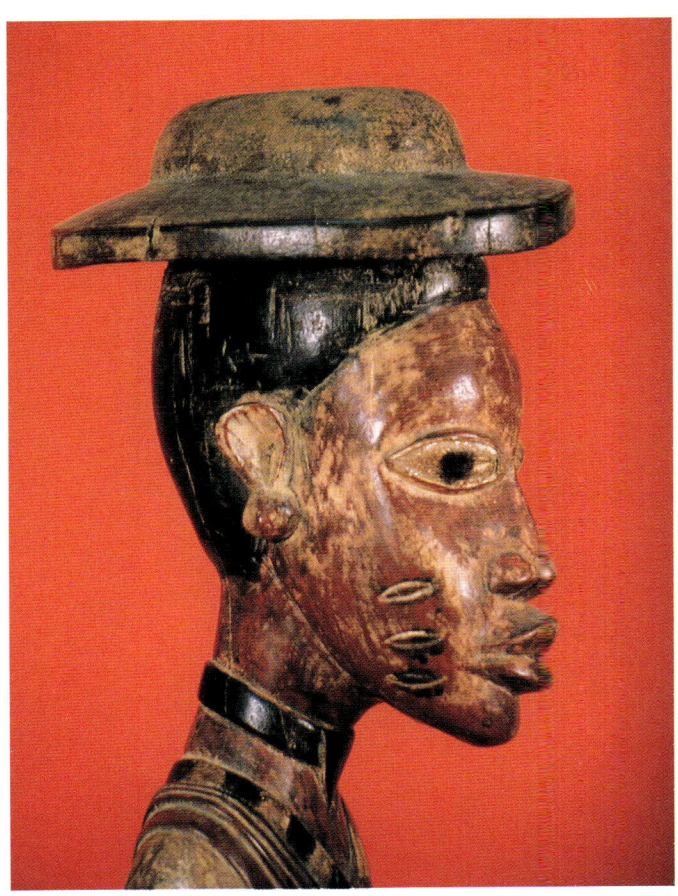

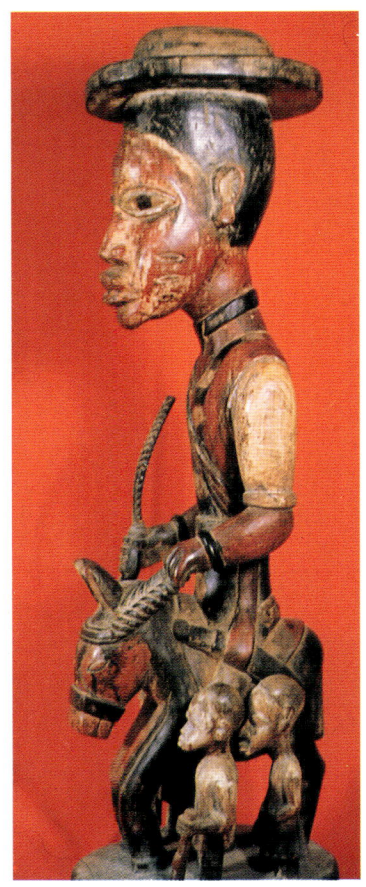

Fig. 148
Detail of equestrian 146.

Fig. 146
Equestrian, Yoruba, Nigeria, wood, paint, H. 34 ¾ in.

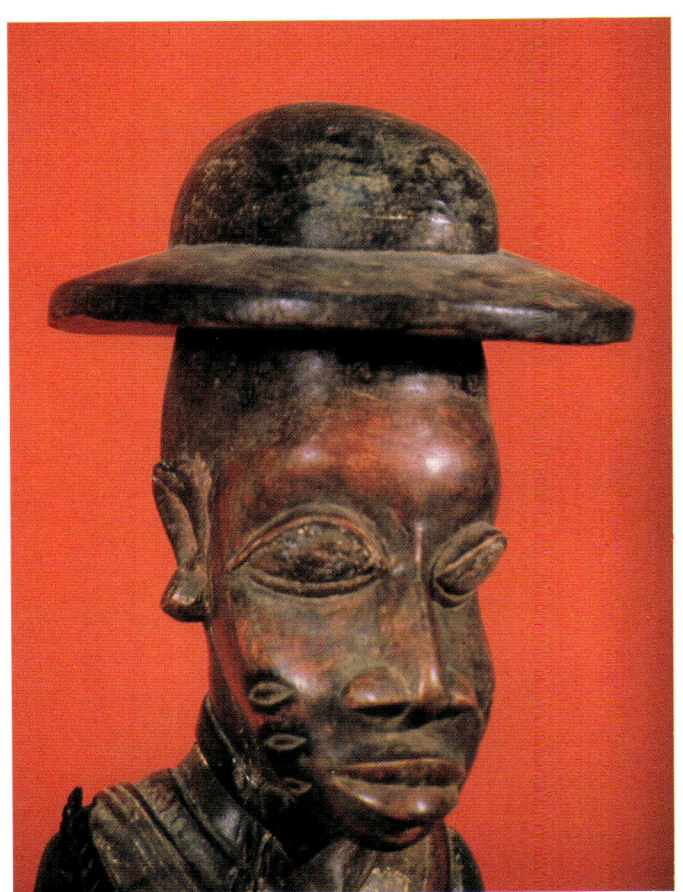

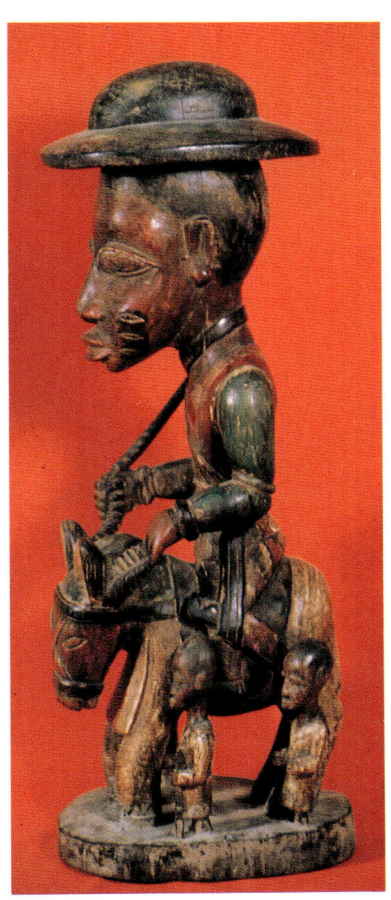

Fig. 149
Detail of equestrian 147.

Fig. 147
Equestrian, Yoruba, Nigeria, wood, paint, H. 27 in.

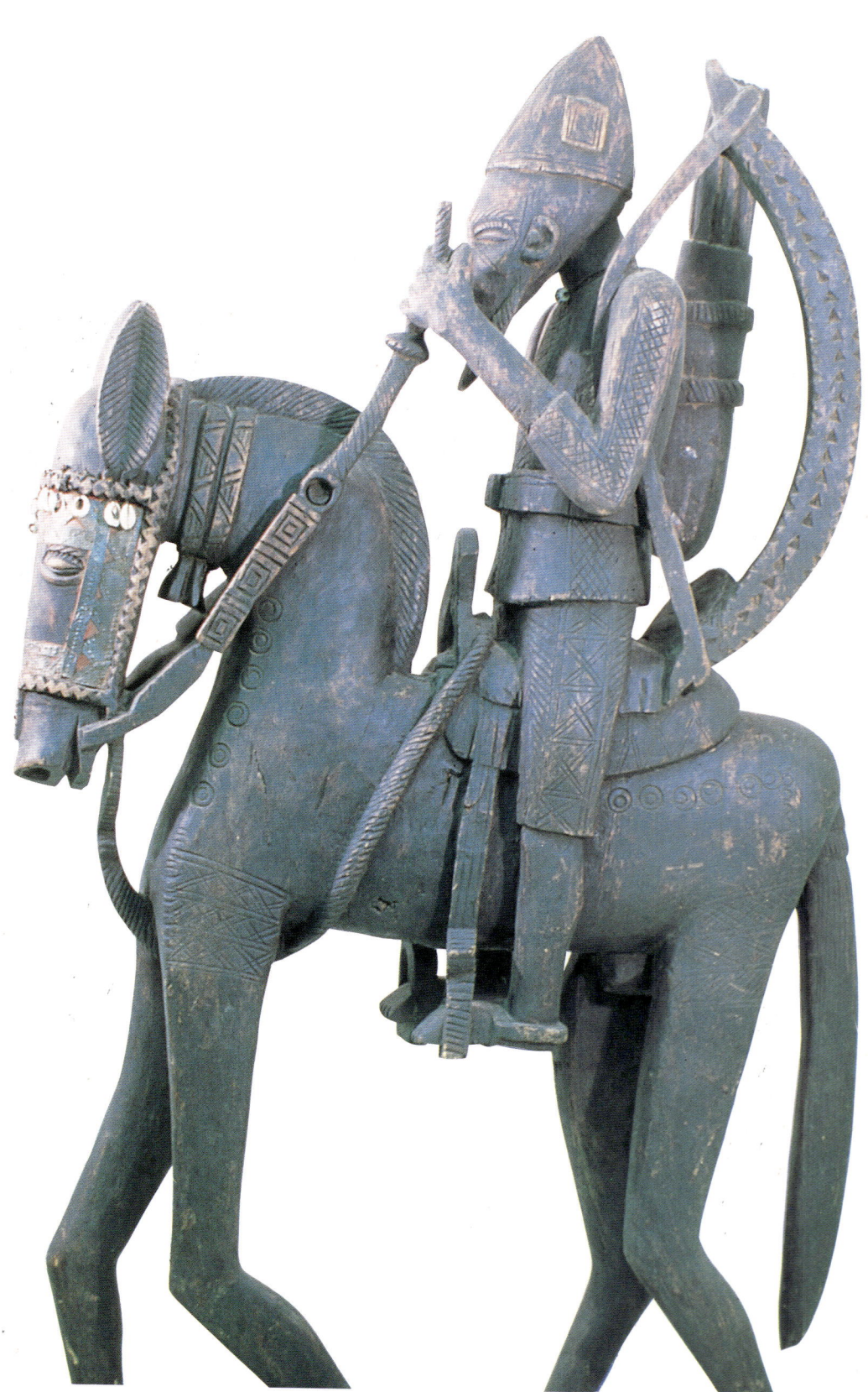

*Fig. 150
Equestrian, Dogon (?),
Yoruba (?), wood,
H. 68 in.*

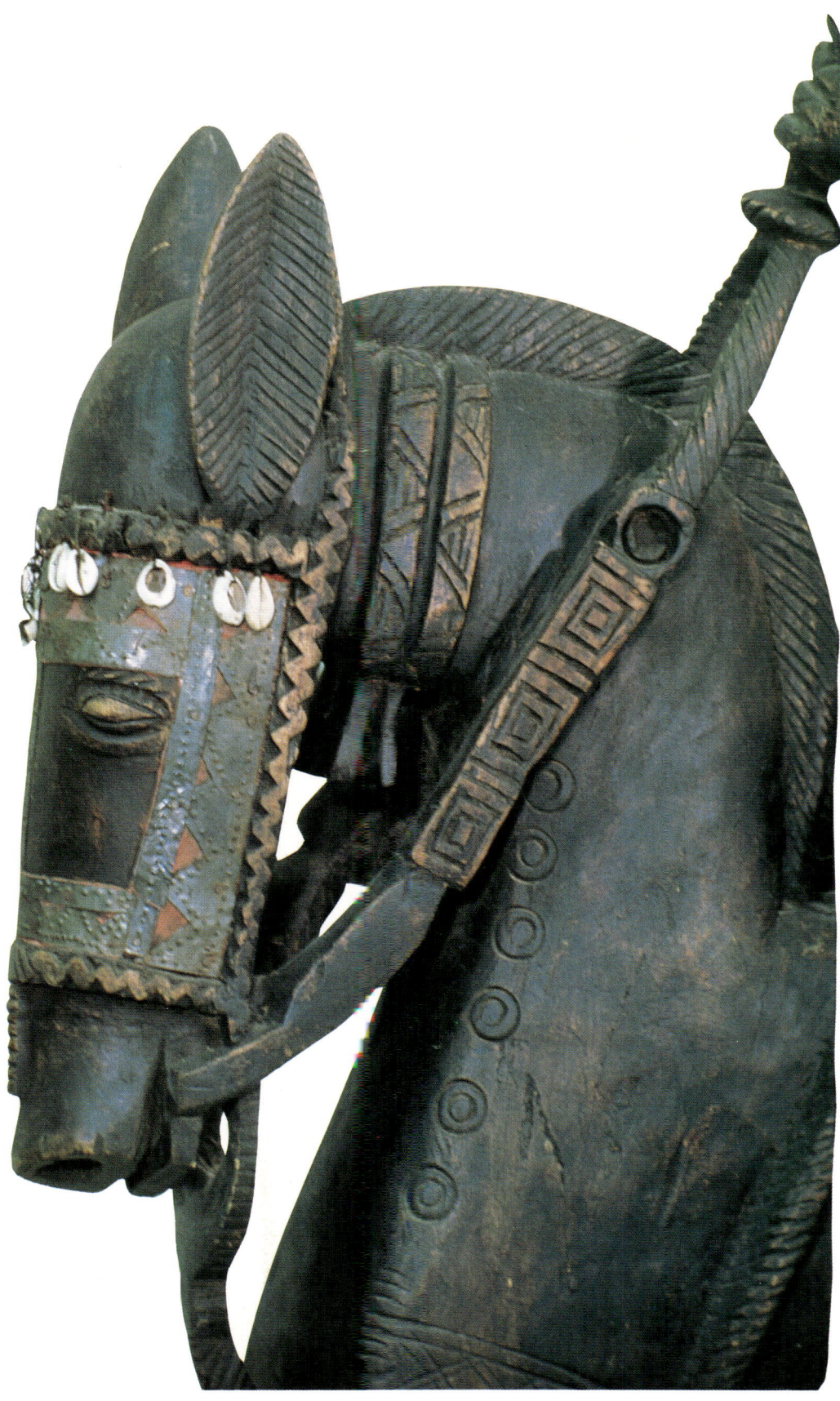

Fig. 151
Detail of equestrian
150.

creation myth says a conical mass of land was first raised above the water's surface.[54] Today, the cloth cones of umbrellas, which can be unfurled like the sky dome, continue to add to the colorful pageantry accompanying kings and rulers on ceremonial occasions.[55] (The umbrella of rulers and dignitaries is carried by the wrought iron horseman in figure 14.)

Like all great three-dimensional sculptures, the equestrian figure and the fine horse on which he is mounted (figures 150, 151) need to be viewed from every angle to make the discoveries that wait to be revealed. In silhouette, the mass and the spaces are handsomely defined. The term *mass* is misleading, the overall effect is linear. This is established by the curve of the hunter's bow, by the reins held high and fastened with a ring held in the rider's left hand, by the movement of the horse's legs, and the graceful tail separated from the body. The carving is freed from blockiness. The arch of the horse's neck and the refined delineation of the head are an assurance that this is no ungainly nag, but a prince among horses (figure 151). The craftsman carved the headstall to resemble tooled leather; he also cut from the wood a fringe of cowrie shells decorating the forehead. The saddle is the result of careful craftsmanship and a desire for authenticity. The rider's legs and feet are separated from the horse's body and rest firmly in the stirrups. The vivid realism and spirit suggest a picaresque hero.

Among the Senufo, who live to the south of the Dogon and Bamana, the equestrian figure assumed a different role. The Senufo cultivate their crops in the moist savannas; they live close to the bush and forest lands, which hold the elements of uncertainty, danger, and the intervention for good or evil by supernaturals in the affairs of humans. Anita Glaze, in her studies of the Senufo, describes the horse and rider as a portrayal of a "bush spirit."[56] She says that "to place a figure, especially an armed figure, on a horse is to express" the status and aggressive power associated with the spirits, or *madebele,* who inhabit the thick underbrush and who require horses for night journeys.[57] In the Senufo representations, as in those of many other ethnic groups, the rider wears a hat believed to possess magical properties. This may be either fedora-shaped or conical and is often covered with a wildcat skin or leather amulets.[58] Because the intentions of the *madebele* towards humans are uncertain, they are feared as much as the witches that prowl in the night. The fearsomeness of the *madebele* is increased because they prefer to travel on horseback, thus increasing both their speed and strength. For these reasons, equestrian subjects are often included among the Senufo diviner's possessions cared for in the shrine.[59]

To curb the aggressiveness of enemies—human, animal and those from the spirit realm—"power figures" offered a means of protection. The following section investigates those carvings that are intended to counter the dangers threatened by known or unknown sources.

VI

Power Figures

The purpose of secrecy sometimes is to keep the magic power from the hands of unbelievers or of enemies who may use it for sorcery.

BRUNO BETTELHEIM

The dangers encountered by those going into the bush or journeying through the forests are described in the nightmare phantasmagoria constructed in the novels and stories of the contemporary Nigerian writer, Amos Tutuola. An account in *The Palm-Wine Drinkard* explains that the bush through which it was necessary to move was so thick "that a snake could not pass . . . without hurt."[60] When night came, there was no light, so the travelers slept in the horrifying tangle until about two o'clock. Suddenly they were awakened by a hideous sight. A harmful creature was near; he "was white as if painted with white paint, he was white from foot to the topmost of his body, but he had no head or feet and hands like human-beings and he got one large eye on his topmost. He was long about 1/4 of a mile and his diameter was about six feet, he resembled a white pillar."[61]

Rampant with a folklore of such misadventures, the bush required a knowledge of strong spells and magic to protect the hunters who went into the overwhelming plant growth for game and those who faced unknown dangers to collect herbs for healing or wood for cooking. The bush was, however, only one of the threats. There were ill-intentioned people among the living and the dead, jealous spirit-lovers, angry ancestors who resented neglect or improperly performed ceremonies, supernaturals ruffled over slights or too few sacrifices. As a result of

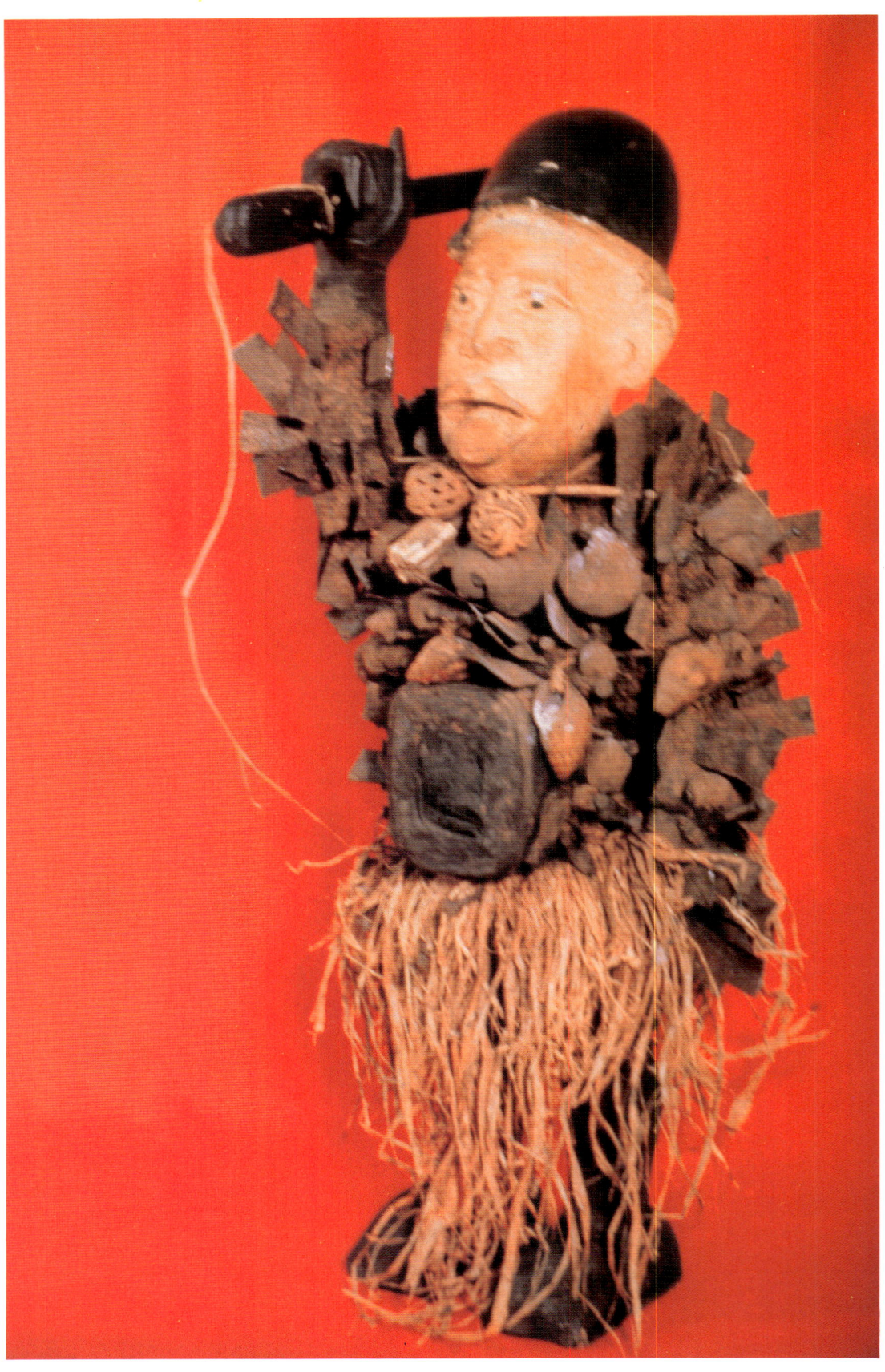

Fig. 152
*Power figure, Kongo, Congo, wood, paint, raffia, shells, vines, woven wicker balls, metal blades,
H. 29 1/2 in.*

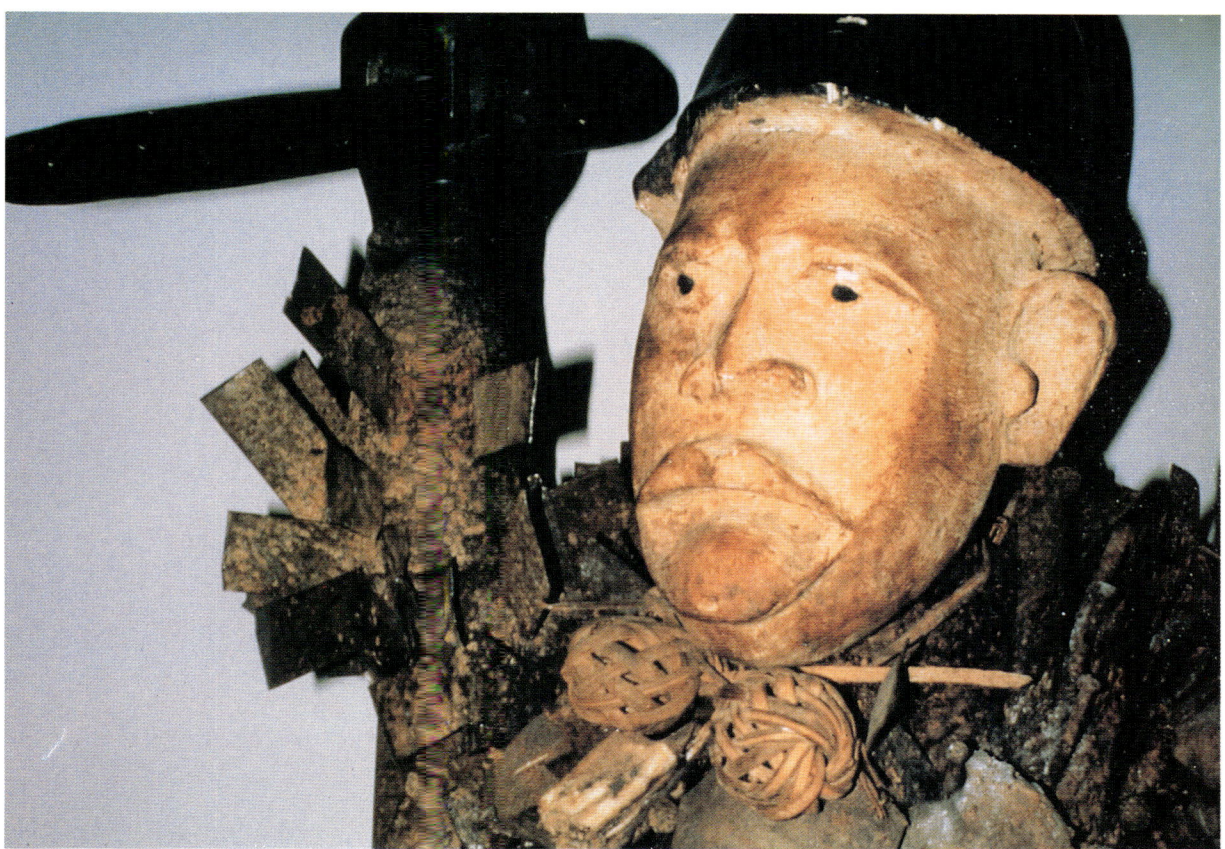

*Fig. 153
Detail of power figure
152.*

known or unknown transgressions, people needed the powers of the shaman to counteract the unruly forces concealed about them. The shaman when consulted could subdue enemies, deflect evil, and heal psychic injuries. Results were often sought by the construction of a "power figure," bristling with nails and blades driven into the wood. Earlier, such a piece was referred to as a nail fetish, despite the fact that objects in addition to nails were utilized in activating the potency of the carving (see figures 152–157). The native terms—nkondi, associated with the spirit that is animated by *bilongo* (medicines) or alerted by the insertion of sharp blades and sharp points and *nkisi*, which means a charm or a medicine of god—are used singly or in combination.[62] Two individuals are necessary in the preparation of the *nkondi:* one is the worker in wood who creates the carving and the second is the sorcerer who by the use of appropriate rituals animates its power.[63] It is the investiture of the figure with the appropriate magical substances together with the spines of metal that release the forces summoning the spirit *(nkondi)* to moral duty that produces the power necessary for countering evil and restoring a state of harmony to a community, a family, or an individual.

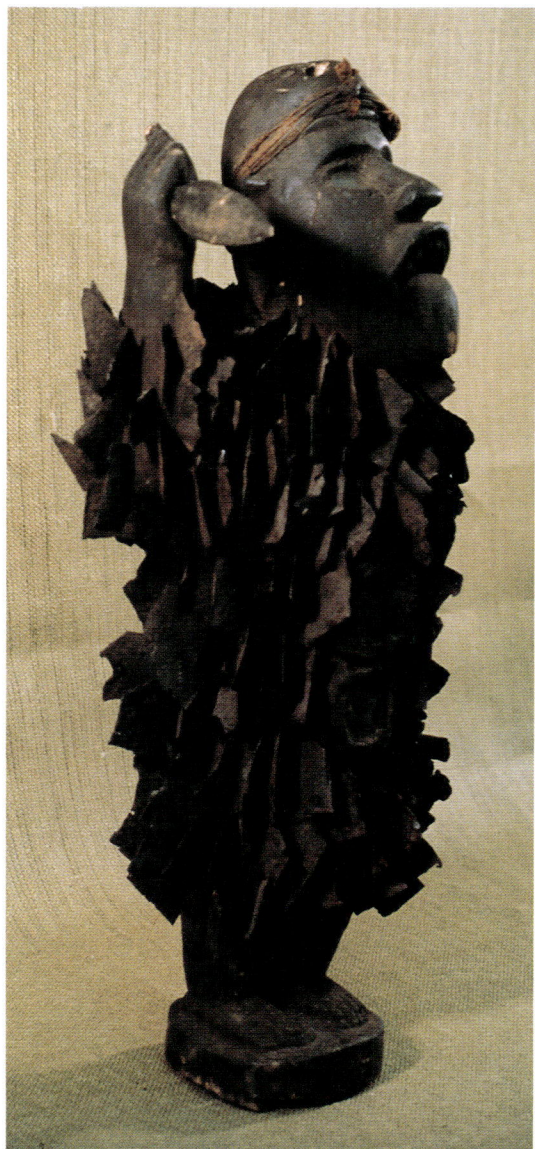 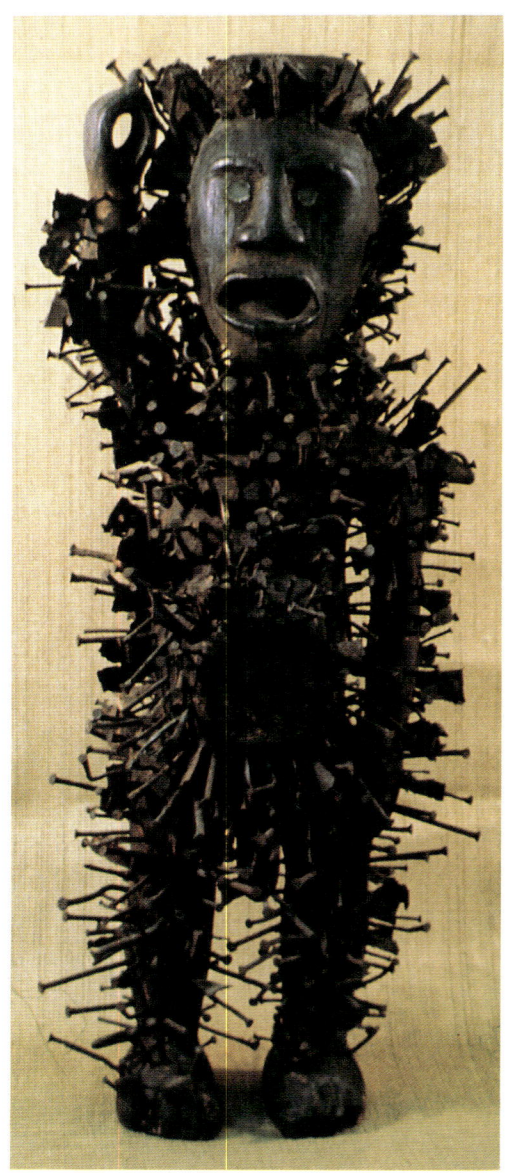

Fig. 154 (Left)
Power figure, Kongo,
Congo, wood, metal
blades, H. 28 in.

Fig. 155 (Right)
Power figure, Kongo,
Congo, wood, metal
blades, nails, glass,
H. 30 in.

In spite of the assemblage of nails, jagged metal, and knife blades, the faces of the carvings do not differ greatly from the calm expressions of other gentler subjects (figure 157). This may be a reminder that power figures are intended to protect those who are innocent and ensure that justice is done. The open mouths of the carving, disclosing teeth and tongues, indicate the role of mediator and the need to speak out in defense of those wronged (figures 154, 155). An open mouth also indicates communication (figure 158) and a mouthpiece for messages between the living and the deceased ancestors or between mortals and supernaturals.[64]

Many *nkisi nkondi* are made by the Kongo carvers (figures 152, 154, 155, 157). In all of the figures, cavities have been hollowed in the abdomen to be filled with *bilongo* (medicines) chosen by the shaman to accomplish the desired purposes. Similar cavities may be constructed in the head or back to contain the concoctions made from varied ingredi-

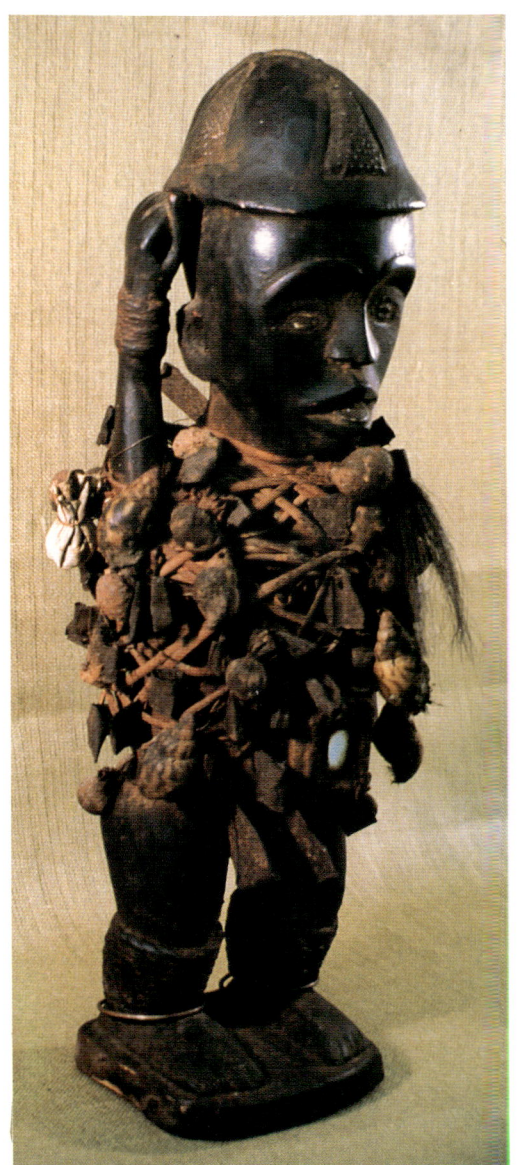

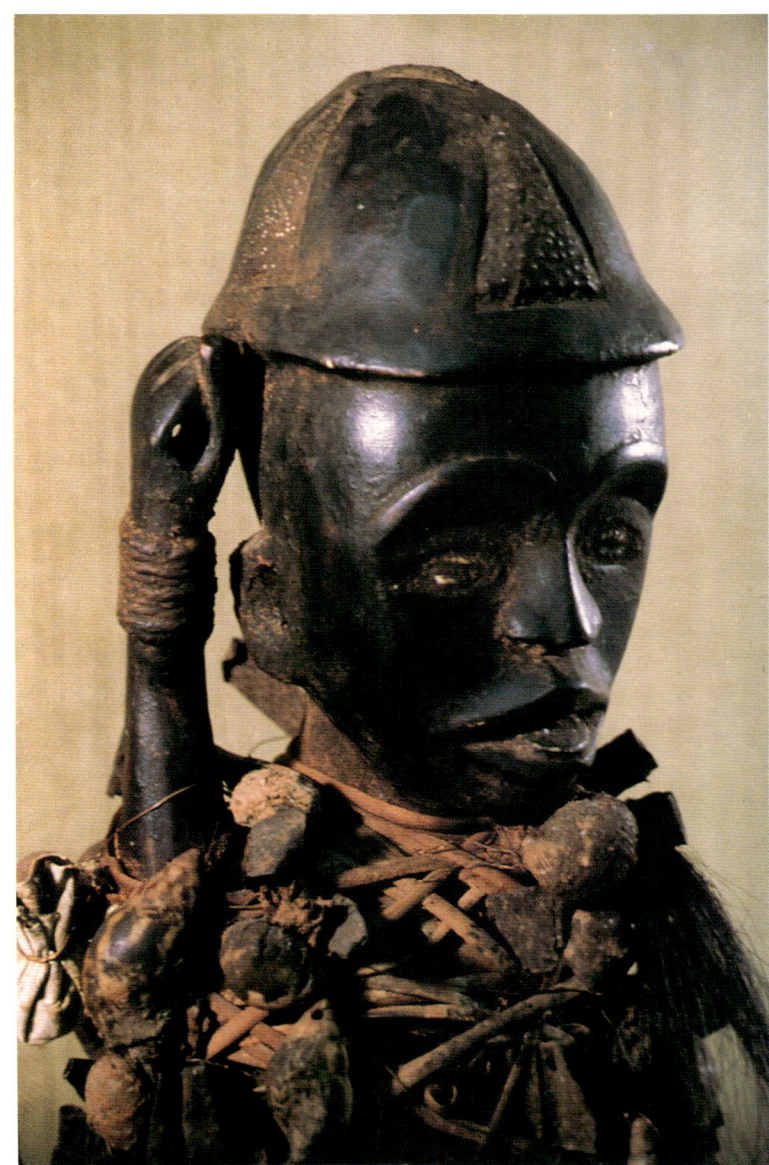

ents: plants, grasses, teeth of a feared beast, fingernails, hair, dead insects. This "medicine" is introduced into the opening to the accompaniment of traditional incantations and spells. The cavity is then sealed frequently by a mirror, the meaning of which is subject to a number of interpretations. Because mirrors reflect the sun's radiating heat and blinding brilliance, they are believed to repel evil spirits that cannot withstand bright light. A mirrored surface may capture the reflection of the one who is responsible for the disruptive physical or psychological damage directed against an intended victim.[65] The eyes are also frequently of glass, possibly for the purpose of intensifying the vision and increasing their reflective power. In figure 152, the eyes of the figure are painted a penetrating black.

Typically, each of the four carvings have their right arms upraised in a menacing gesture. Two hold knives in clenched fists; in the hands of the other carvings, there are openings where knives must once have

Fig. 156
Power figure, Kongo,
Congo, wood, vines,
wicker work,
H. 29 1/2 in.

Fig. 157
Detail of power figure
156.

been inserted. Spikes, blades, and nails have been driven into the bodies of each. The surfaces of the face, head, and feet rarely have metal blades inserted. This is not true in the case of figure 155; in this carving there is a crown of nails around the forehead, and nails project from the ankles and feet. In some instances, metal pieces are accompanied by shells, whisks, fur, hair, and vines. When shells and vines are twined about the man in figure 152, it may be for decorative purposes or to harness the magic of the bush and the water forces. Kongo power carvings usually represent areas with which people are associated, that is, land, sea, and sky. The primary purpose of the attached shells is to receive protection from the domain of the *basimbi* water spirits.[66]

The action of adding magical properties or embedding the nails and potent objects in a carving was thought to intensify the sorcerer's strength and to channel energy toward the accomplishment of a particular goal. This goal was not always to overcome witchcraft or to ward off mischievous schemes. The swearing of oaths might take place in the presence of the power figure or an *nkondi* might be invoked to settle military or territorial disputes.

The pieces of metal projecting from the wood are cumulative; the addition of a nail indicates a new request for help. After a request is fulfilled, an illness cured, or danger checked, the sorcerer is expected to remove the particular nail or nails. To avoid the consequences of withdrawing the wrong blade, it is obligatory to remember the reason for which each piece of metal was pounded into the carving.[67]

Many figures were too dangerous to be guarded by an individual or a family; these were placed under the protection of a priest or shaman and kept in a specially prepared place. An *nkondi* was benevolent and protective to those under its care but it could be deadly if directed against enemies. Precautions are taken before a power figure is sold to a museum or shown in an exhibition to make sure it has been ritually divested of all dangerous substances and freed from its original purposes.

Not all *nkondi* are fashioned in the shape of humans. Wood carvings of animals may also be conveyers of supernatural energy. Crocodiles, leopards, and dogs are often found stuck with as many nails as a porcupine has quills. The dog is valued primarily as a hunting companion, or as the proverb says, "The dog is great among dogs, yet he serves man."[68] A carving of a dog, when covered with nails, has all of the capacities of the dog in a hunting society, greatly magnified by the magic incantations pronounced by the shaman. Just as the dog accompanying a hunter smells game and does not lose his way in the bush, the Kongo believe that the dog as a power figure hunts spirits in the night and can sniff out those bent on mischief. Dogs are sometimes carved with heads and open mouths located at either end of the body. Their tongues

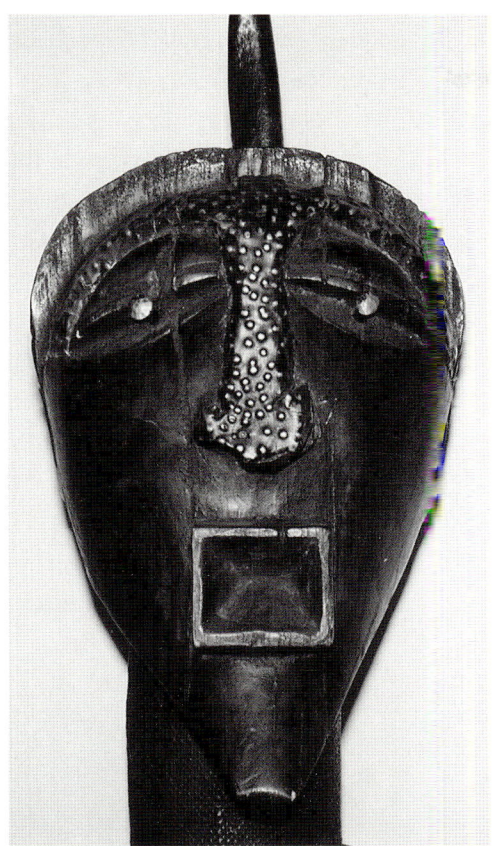

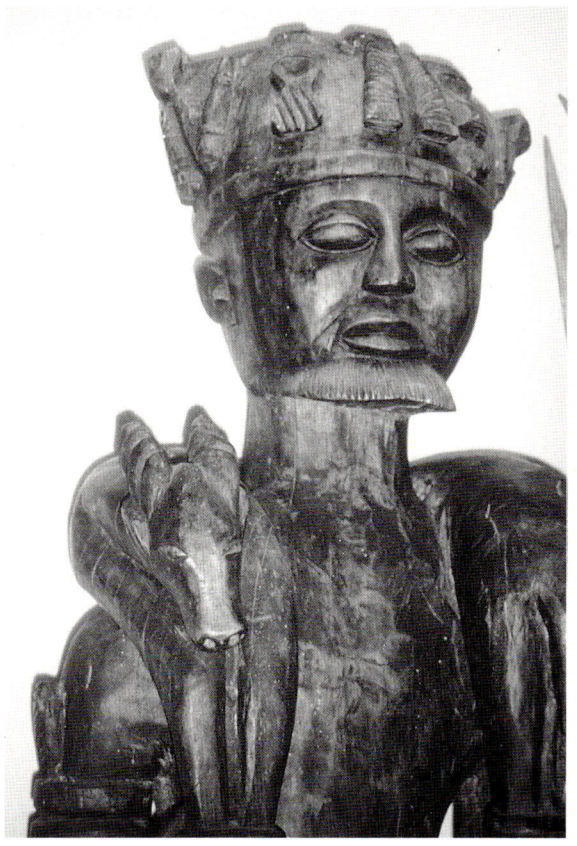

project like those of their human counterparts. The menacing mouths threaten aggressive attacks. The dog that protects the house of its owner can be trusted to detect the approach of supernatural danger and put an end to it before damage can be inflicted.

The Songye, inhabitants of a large area in southeastern Congo between the territories of the Kuba and Luba people, have distinctive power figures. Such carvings may have large heads, long necks, short bent legs, and bulging navels regarded as primary receptacles for cosmic forces. It is in the navel that the potent substances are usually enclosed. A curving horn, a container for energized ingredients, is often located on top of the head.[69] The detail of the head in figure 158 is characterized by a pointed chin held on a thick, extended neck. The mouth projects like a square box, suggesting the amplification of sound. The eyes are large with a round copper piece sunk in each. Bits of copper are studded along the eyebrows and the flattened nose. The markings, which may cover the entire face, are not only associated with the patterns of scarification but, in some cases, they may refer to the scars left by smallpox. The horn that rises from the top of the head usually holds potent charms and herbs.

Fig. 158 (Left)
Power figure, Songye,
Zaire, wood, nail heads,
H. 33 ½ in.

Fig. 159 (Right)
Hunter, Bamana, Mali,
wood, H. approx. 58 in.

The horn motif, as a meaningful ornament and magical container, has been mentioned as a device worn by hunters on their caps (figure 159); the horn shape is also similar to some of the complex hair arrangements. Frank Willett discounts the popular concept that the horn is primarily a fertility symbol. Instead, he calls attention to the fact that horned animals are highly valued and are offered as sacrifices to the gods.[70] For this reason, horns are a proper attachment and symbol to associate with power figures. The horn, Willett writes, shares its importance with the shells of edible snails. Both horn and shell are natural containers for the "medicines" carefully prepared to guard against the evil schemes of witches or spirits. Rams' horns filled with the shamans' potions were once fastened to the heads of warriors for protection in battles. If they survived combat, the horns were worn as a mark of bravery. Real horns were sometimes incorporated in masks (figure 64) or carved to give the performer in the masquerade the endurance, swiftness, and grace of the animal

VII

Figurative Objects

*If you are rich, you do not laugh at the poor—
Little people can become grand.
When you come into the world
You own neither a wife, nor a car, nor a bike
Nothing you have brought and
No one knows the future.*

Excerpt from *Nukoromahan* of Dahomean origin,
quoted by ROBERT FARRIS THOMPSON
in *Flash of the Spirit*

One of the most graceful Yoruba carvings in the collection of the Museum of Texas Tech University is a kneeling woman who holds a bowl covered by a lid. The bowl is partly supported by five female figures, who also kneel (figure 160). The design is influenced by a masterpiece carved about 1925 by the early twentieth-century artist, Olowe of Ise. Olowe's bowl is now in a private collection. In this ambitious composition, the carving is enhanced by a liberal use of color.

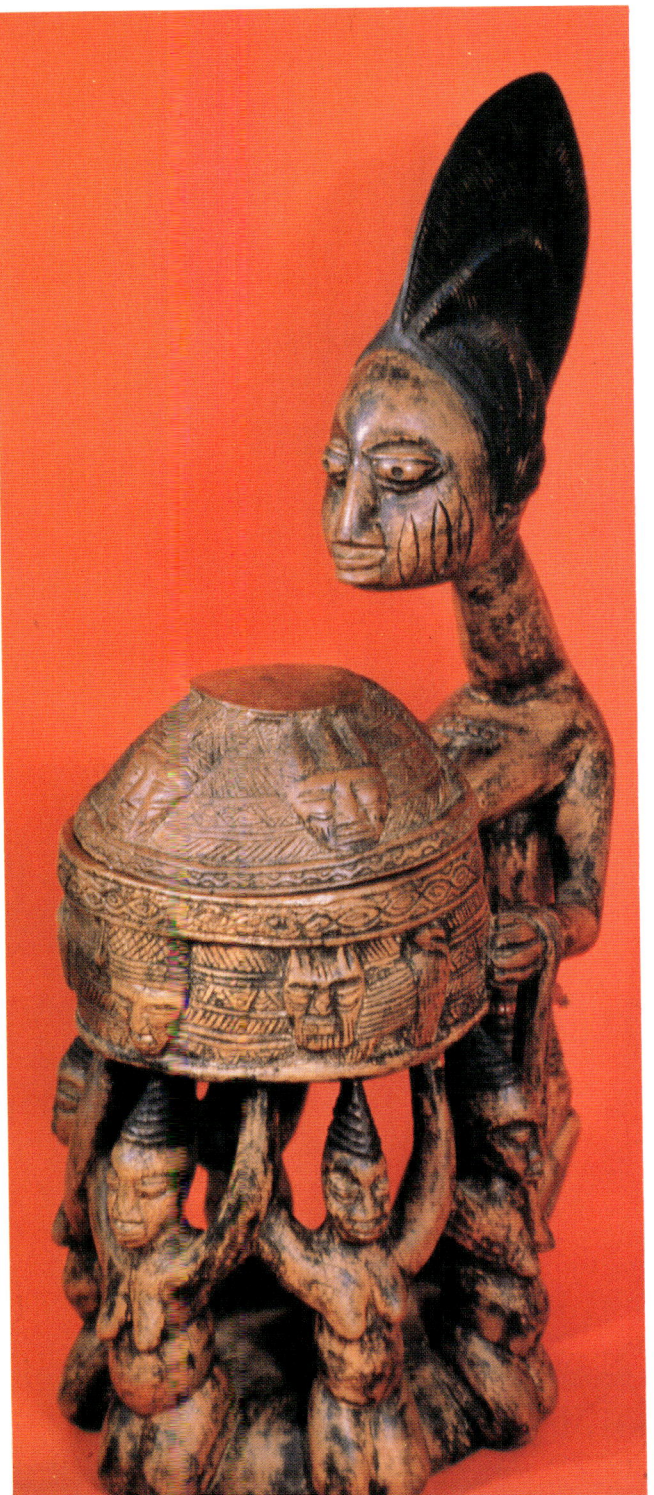

*Fig. 160
Container, Yoruba, Nige-
ria, wood, pigment, H.
25 1/2 in.*

The primary figure, a woman, with a child in a "baby tie" on her back, supports the bowl. She is aided by male and female helpers represented at a smaller scale. Interestingly, the arms upholding the container form a cage for a bearded head that moves freely within the confined area but cannot be removed from the space. On the lid of the bowl, there are four standing women, their arms resting on the shoulders of those closest to them. Each has an elaborate hair arrangement painted with

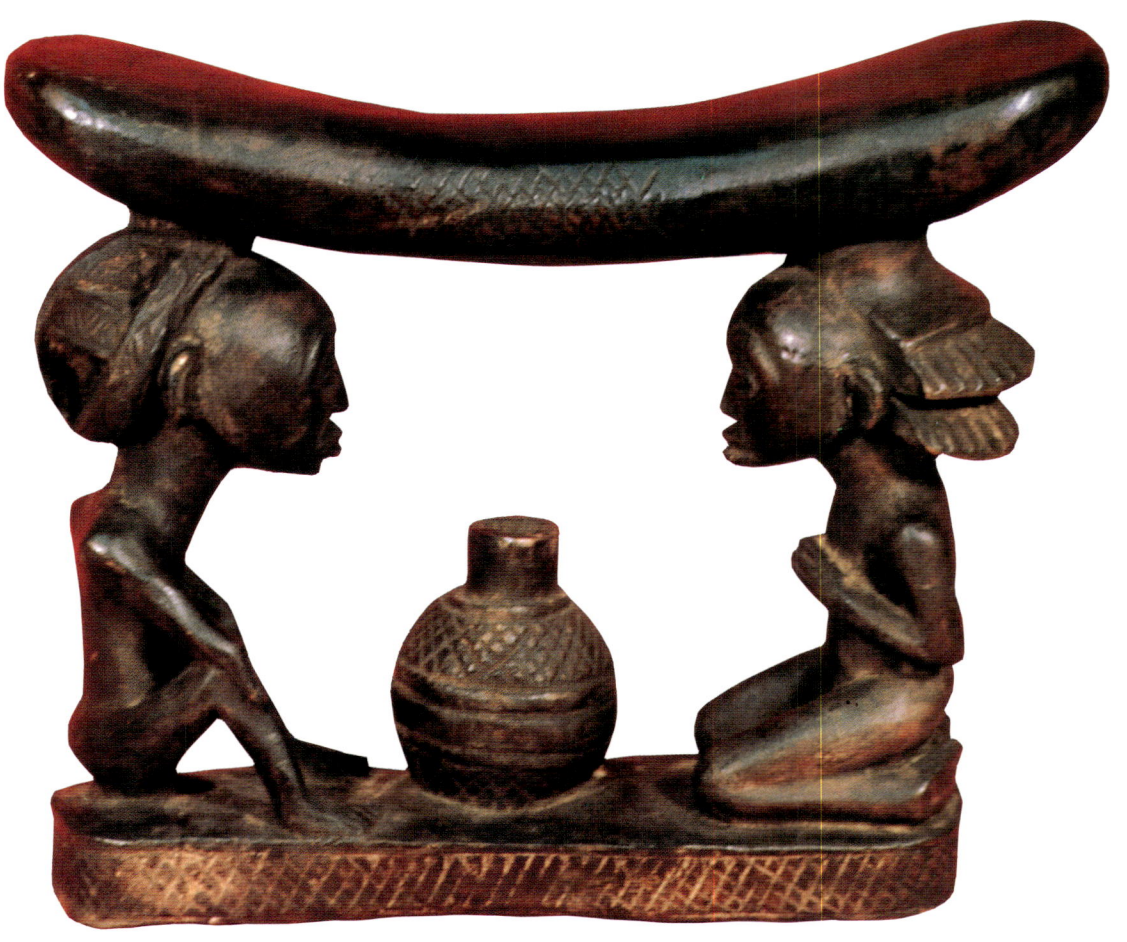

*Fig. 161
Headrest, Luba, Zaire,
wood, H. 13 in.*

black pigment. In the University Museum's carving, the kneeling woman, who supports a container, is sleek and sophisticated. Her neck is almost too slender to hold and balance her head with its tall coiffure (figure 94). There is a typical Yoruba cicatrix of three ovals on the woman's cheeks; the eyes are wide-open. The lid and rounded sides of the bowl are decorated with human heads, or masks, alternating with faces of animals, some feline and others with rams' horns. Five women with high, pointed hair arrangements kneel and lift their arms up to help sustain the weight of the container. There is no head imprisoned in the area framed by the figures.

Among the Yoruba people, a carving of this type is known as a prestige bowl.[71] It might serve as a place for storing valuable possessions, or as a suitable place for the divination articles of a priest. It could be used for presenting gifts of food or kola nuts, a sign of welcome and peaceful intentions offered to important guests. Generosity is the highest form of morality in traditional Yoruba beliefs; this is evidenced visibly by an offering made to a distinguished person by one who falls to his or her knees.[72] Quoting a senior priest, Robert Farris Thompson writes:

> If you wish to talk to an elder, you do not stand, you kneel. When presenting a plate of food to someone important, *kneel* as you make the presentation. Kneel and give with hands, the left with the right, the "mother hand" and the "father hand," the hand-which-keeps and the hand-which-acts. Giving with both hands, in a gesture of submission, emphasizes in traditional terms the act of giving as an embodiment of character and perfect composure, a point given further focus, in both art and life, by the firmness of the facial expression that accompanies the noble act.[73]

Another handsome and useful object with figures is a headrest (figure 161) carved in the Luba manner. There are two figures. A naked woman kneels, cupping her breasts in her hands in a gesture of giving; opposite her a man is seated.[74] Between the couple there is a carved bottle with a short neck shaped like a snuff container. The man's hair is bound up in the characteristic cross shape associated with the Luba-Hemba; the woman's fashionably styled hair is built up in three tiers described by Westerners as a "cascade" and worn in the Luba-Shankadi area until the late 1920s.[75] A hair design of this kind was constructed over a frame of canework. To complete, it might occupy several persons for fifty hours or more. A headrest preserved this handiwork for as much as two or three months.[76] Beautifully arranged hair was said to give a woman's face an added radiance. No wonder headrests were prize possessions. If at the death of an important person, the body was destroyed, the headrest of the deceased was buried instead.[77]

Little is known about the wooden staff pictured in figures 162 and 163, but throughout western sub-Saharan Africa, staffs, as well as chairs and stools, are symbols of authority and status. At the top of the staff, a man holding an ornate pipe sits on a stool. In Africa, tobacco, after its introduction from the New World, was either smoked or taken as snuff. The pipe helps to affirm that the staff was intended for a person of means.

A man smoking a pipe is present among a throng of figures carved in relief on a door of Yoruba origin displayed at the Museum of Texas Tech University (figures 164, 165). The participants in the five bands that divide the door panel alternate between peaceful activities and the violence of warriors who wave swords and pistols or hold shotguns—one man is armed with a crossbow (center of figure 166)! Beside him, two women, with infants tied on their backs, face each other and tend

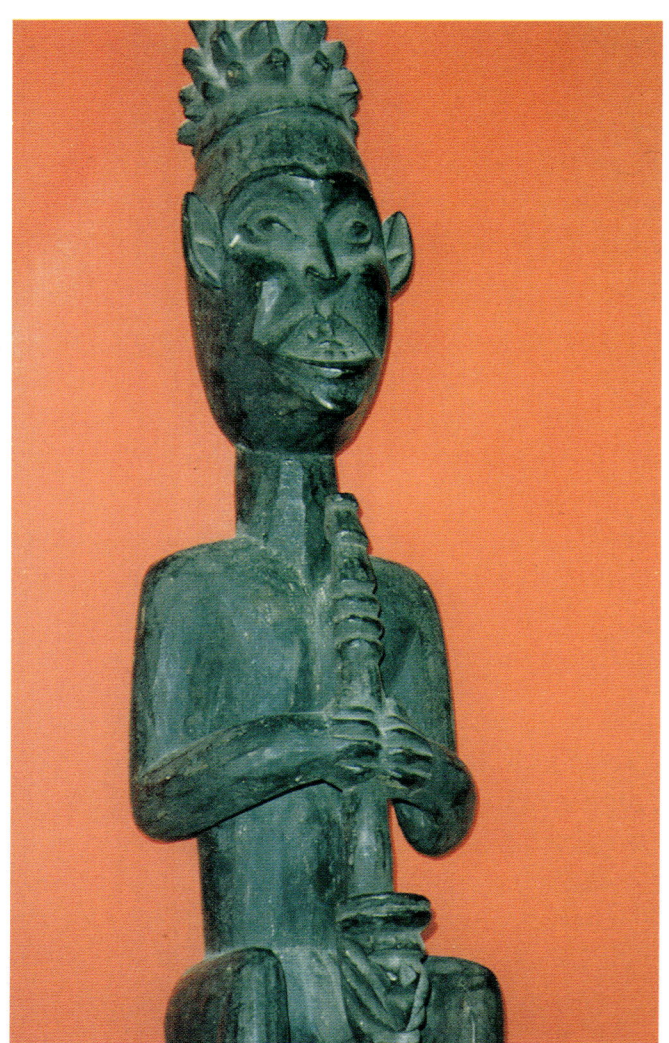

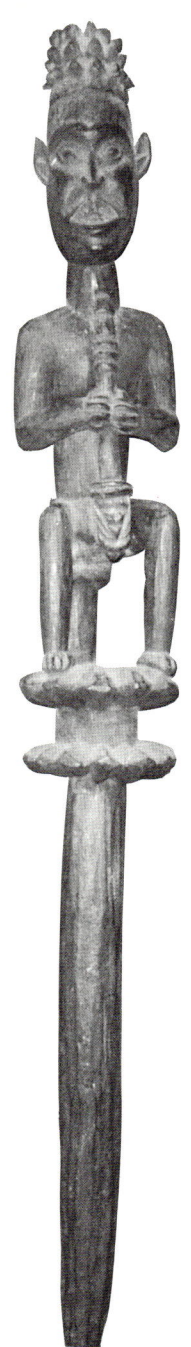

*Fig. 162
Staff, origin unknown,
wood, H. 51 ½ in.*

*Fig. 163
Detail of staff 162.*

to the business of pounding rice or millet. A cyclist in the top panel (figure 165) seems undisturbed by the fierceness of a warrior on horseback carved in relief just below (figure 167). The horseman presents a baffling puzzle. Fastened to his horse's reins and appearing to drift overhead is what at first glance seems to be a baby. Frank Willet, in *African Art,* clarifies this with a photograph of a similar incident carved on a door exhibited at the Nigerian Museum in Lagos. Willett explains that the figure is a prisoner tied to the reins of a warrior's mount but is represented floating over the horse's head.[78]

Doors of finely carved wood rank high among the objects upon which the Yoruba and other western sub-Saharan African people place value. Symbolically, a gate or door marks a threshold between the outside, where there may be threatening forces and the inside, where safety waits. A door is a protection against marauding animals, enemies, witches, and witchcraft. It is both a physical and a spiritual deterrent to bodily harm and psychic dangers. It is a protection against loss of property, but it is also a sign of status and identification indicating a lodge or a palace, or marking the village granaries. Sadly, the old doors are rapidly disappearing.

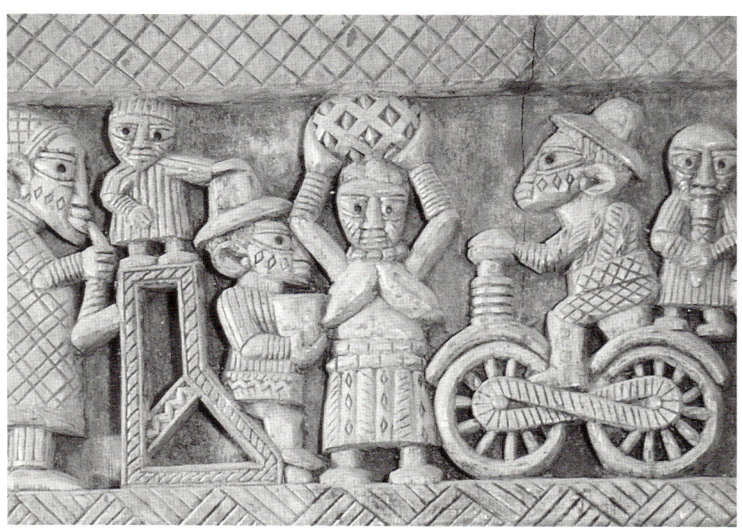

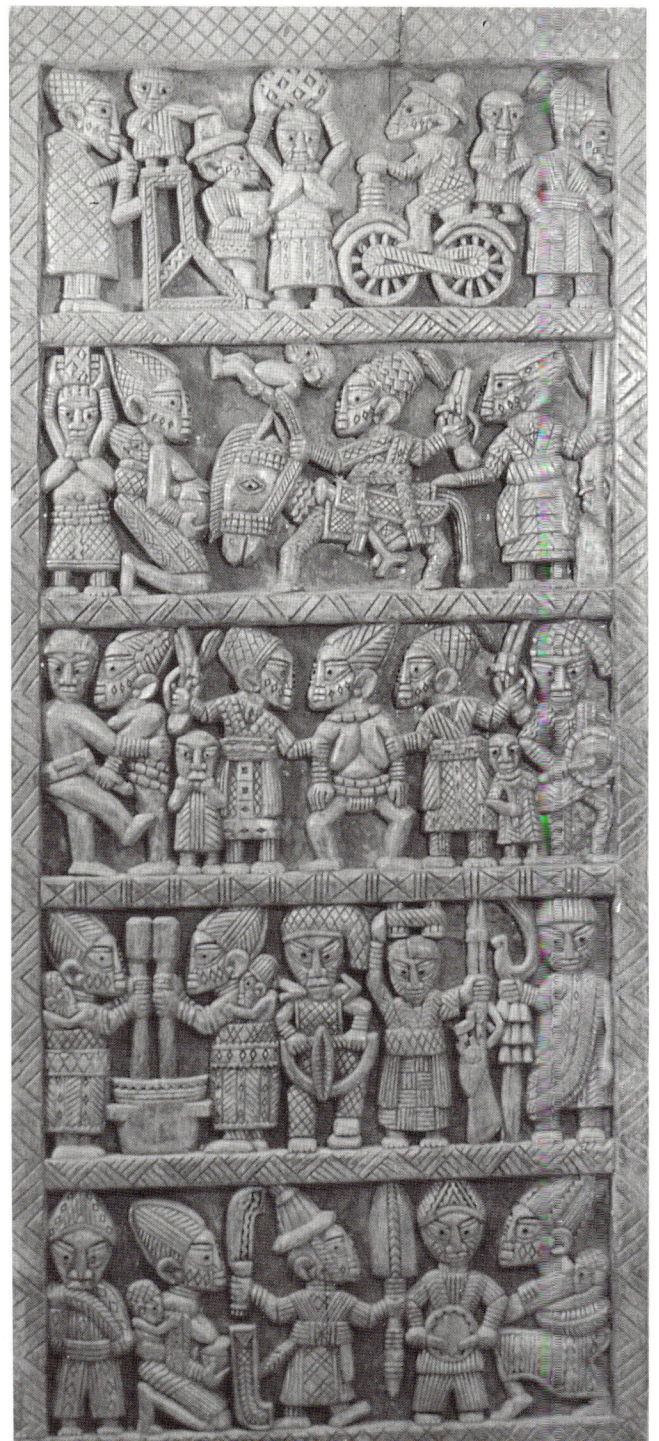

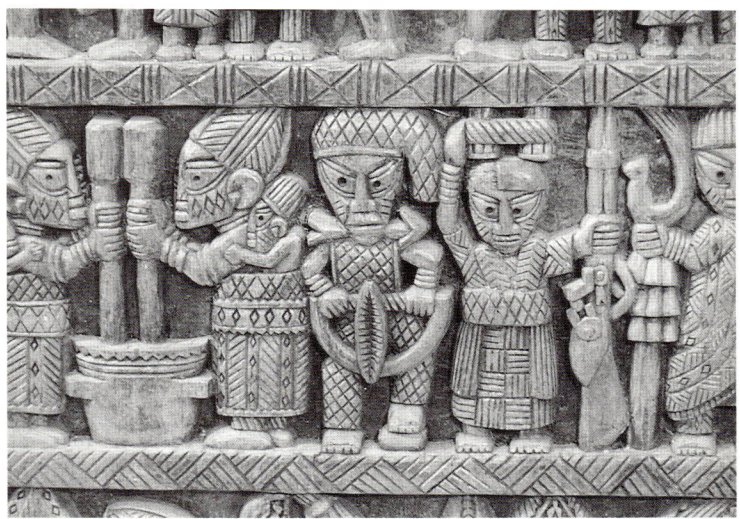

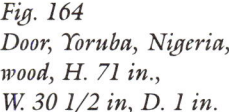

Fig. 164
Door, Yoruba, Nigeria,
wood, H. 71 in.,
W. 30 1/2 in, D. 1 in.

Fig. 165
Detail of door 164.

Fig. 166
Detail of door 164.

Fig. 167
Detail of door 164.

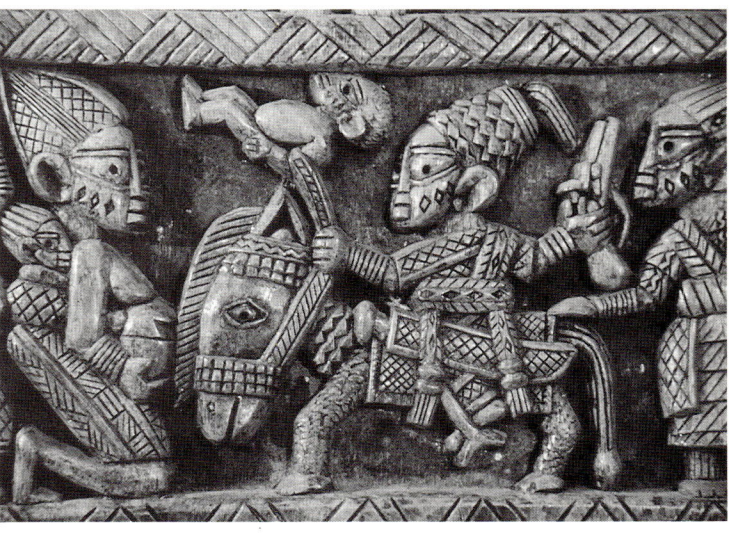

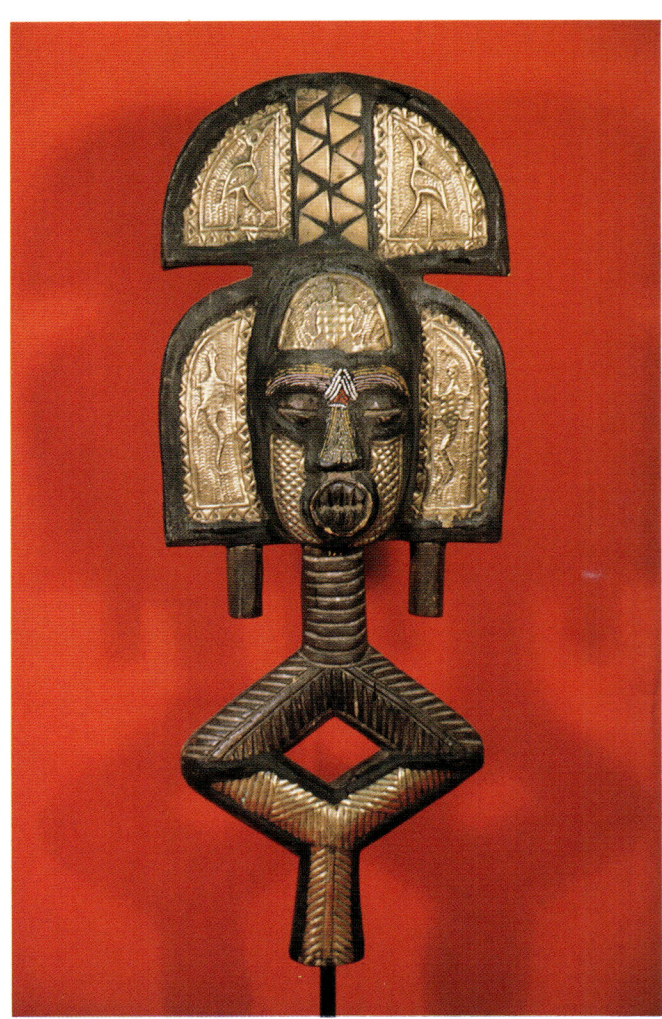

*Fig. 168
Reliquary-guardian
figure, Kota, Gabon,
wood, brass, glass beads,
H. 27 in.*

The carver, Olowe of Ise, mentioned earlier, was a dominant force among Yoruba artists of the first half of the twentieth century. One of his most famous works was a double door carved for the palace of the Ogoga of Ikere. In 1924, the English borrowed the doors for a British Empire Exhibition in London. Olowe's permission was first asked by the Ogoga. It was given by the artist, who gracefully refused the invitation to accompany the doors to London on the grounds that "he was a family man with many wives and children and thus did not wish to leave home."[79] The British Museum was eager to keep the doors permanently at the close of the exhibition. To this end they arranged an exchange, the doors for a throne for the Ogoga, made in England, in accord with His Majesty's specifications. William Fagg has observed that this "does not seem to me to have been a very good bargain . . . for the wooden throne is not a very distinguished piece of British craftsmanship, but I am happy to say that Olowe, being still alive, carved a fine new door to fill the gap left by ours."[80]

Another type of sculpture that has intrigued Europeans is made by the Kota of Gabon (figure 168). Flat, nearly two-dimensional oval heads are carved of wood and covered with brass or copper. Considered

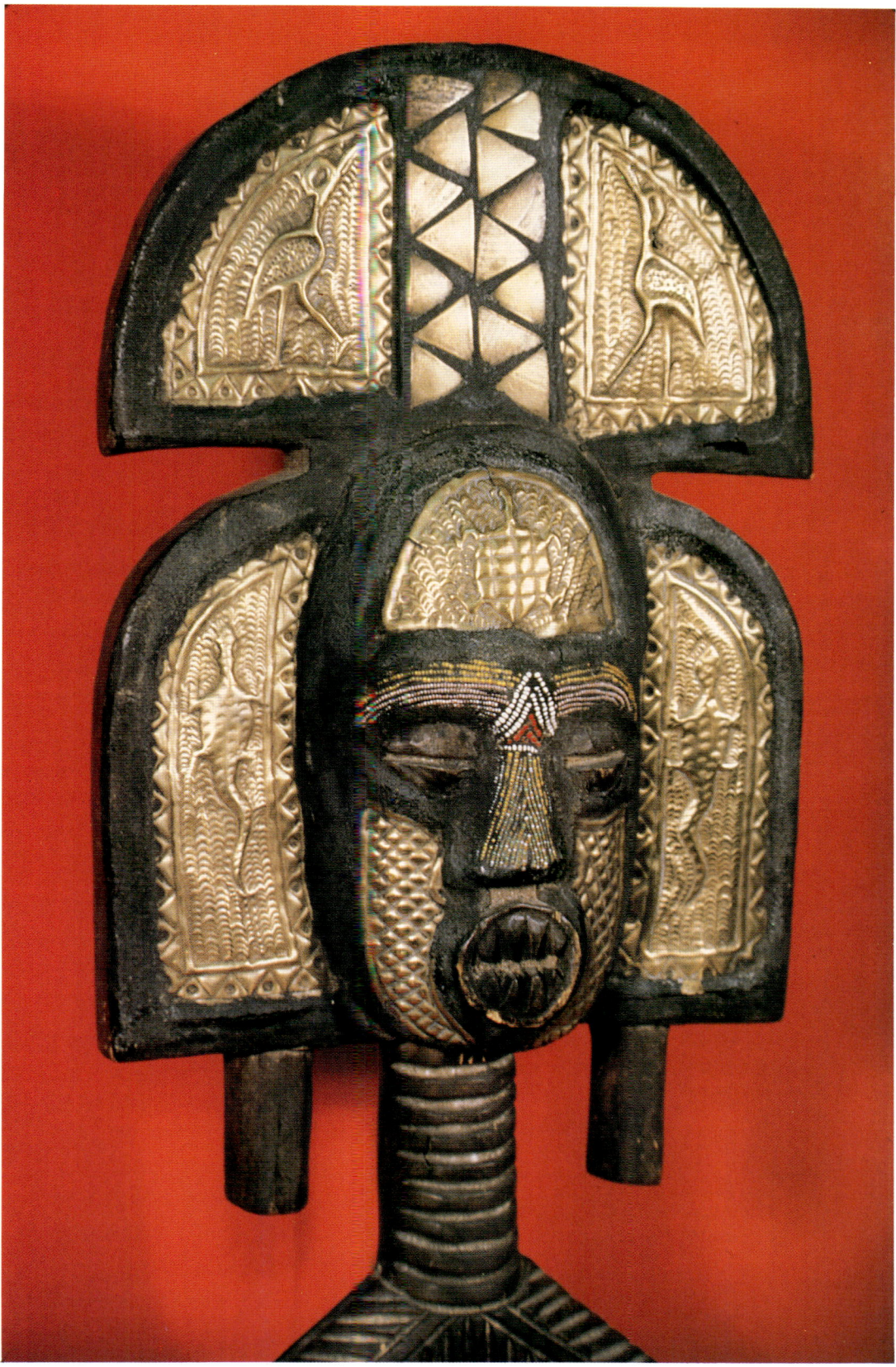

Fig. 169
Detail of reliquary-guardian figure 168.

caretakers of the dead, the heads are held on long wooden necks above reliquary baskets that contain the larger bones and the skulls of the deceased. Over the basket or barrel, the vertical support becomes a diamond shape, open at the center. Some maintain this rhomb corresponds to the arms, whereas the basket to which the sculpture is secured represents the body.[81] Whatever the meaning, the guardians are expected to protect the ancestors from witchcraft and to secure their goodwill on behalf of living descendants. Carried away from village houses, the bone bundles are kept in special sanctuaries or shrines.

It is the abstractness of the heads that caught the attention of early Cubists. In the 1920s, a Kota carving attracted the French painter Juan Gris, who is said to have made a similar one of cardboard for his Paris studio.[82] The copper (or brass) covering the faces is worked in repoussé, a technique in which a design is pressed with a blunt instrument onto the back of a piece of metal. When the metal is reversed, the pattern stands out in low relief. Another method of design/construction used by the Kota was wrapping a head entirely in thin strips of metal or wire. Not easily available, copper and brass were originally imported from Europe by Africans to use as a below the waterline hull covering of ships to protect the wood from teredo worms.[83]

The faces watching over the ancestral remains gleam in their metal casing. A crescent shape, possibly referring to the moon, surmounts a head in the collection of the Museum of Texas Tech University (figure 169). Two lateral curving projections, interpreted as plaited or elaborately dressed hair, frame the face. Some faces have large eyes but no mouths. The logic of this is explained by the observation that those who watch need eyes, but they neither eat nor speak. Figure 169, however, has a round mouth, open to reveal filed teeth that are considered a mark of beauty.

Figure 169 is a fascinating improvisation from a variety of sources. For example, the repoussé designs on the face represent symbols frequently found among the Yoruba-speaking Ijebu, who live close to the coast between the Osun River and the Ogun, at the mouth of which Lagos is located. The Ijebu were referred to in the early sixteenth century by Duarte Pacheci Pereira as "a prime brass-importing kingdom."[84] On the forehead of the Kota face there is a tortoise, a creature that plays a role in Ijebu art usually in the company of a python. At the beginning of the Agbo festival, a ritual sacrifice of a tortoise in preparation for the coming of the water spirits is symbolized visually by a coiled python catching a tortoise in its jaws.[85] On the crescent crowning the head of the sculpture, there is another water creature, a fishing eagle, or *ogolo*, who communicates messages from the water people to humans.

Two of the long-legged birds balance each other on opposite sides of the curving plane.[86]

In raised relief, on either cheek there is a chameleon/lizard, the national symbol of the Ijebu. Like most of the creatures represented, this recalls an Ifa story. It explains how the chameleon, challenged by his enemies, adopted a successful tactic. "Each time his foes tried a new approach, the chameleon imitated, neutralized, and then made the strategy his own. His powers of transformation defeated them all."[87] The terrifying hiss made by the chameleon when it is frightened is interpreted as a life-threatening curse. The chameleon is also a necessary ingredient in one of the most potent medicines. Like their national emblem, the Ijebu, who have not had strong military capabilities, developed a reputation for being adept at poisons, earth-shaking curses, and adaptive techniques that confused and subdued their enemies. A curious characteristic of the chameleon relates to its large eyes. They work independently, suggesting another virtue sought by canny people—the ability to see all and know all.[88]

The eyes of the Kota head at the Museum are treated in an unusual way, more often found among the Kuba. The almond shapes are framed by beadwork that extends along the nose. A red triangle outlined in white beads stands out between the eyebrows. This is probably no more than a pleasing design, but it is at least amusing to turn to Tabwa symbolism (Zaire and Zambia) described by Christopher Roy in his comments on a stunning bead-covered mask. Roy cites an identification that interprets triangular beaded motifs of red and white as "doors of possessing spirits that emanate from Kibawa's cavern" a place identified with "the rising of the new moon." The new moon is considered a symbol of "enlightenment, courage, and the dawning of hope after a period of 'obscurity.'"[89]

The last part of the twentieth century is ushering in a period of enlightenment and growing interest and enthusiasm for African art. After decades of "obscurity," except in large metropolitan centers, it is an unexpected pleasure to discover the art of Africa at home on the rangelands of West Texas. Appropriately, this is at a time when long overdue recognition is given the African-American cowboys. And where could a collection of western sub-Saharan African art be more appropriately placed than in the company of southwestern ethnic artists—American Indians, Spanish Americans, and African-Americans? An awakening appreciation of all ethnic arts leads to an awareness of deeply rooted values and art traditions, crossing over old boundaries to a world filled with unsuspected communications and perceptions to explore.

AFTERWORD

About the Elliot Howard Collection

Apart from the African artists that produced these incredibly stunning pieces illustrated in *The World of Spirits and Ancestors*, the Elliot Howard Collection on view at the Museum of Texas Tech University in Lubbock is due: (1) to a synchronicity of events; (2) to the noteworthy expertise of the University's staff, namely, Dr. Elizabeth Sasser, Professor Emeritus of Art and Architectural History, Dr. Collette Murray, at that time, Tech's Vice-President of Development, and Gary Edson, Director of the Museum of Texas Tech University, himself an artist, who selected the very finest pieces from the original collection; (3) to the generosity of the Helen Jones Foundation; and (4) to the faithful friends and patrons of the Museum of Texas Tech University who helped to fund the acquisitions. The collection is composed of pieces that were seen, experienced, appreciated, and collected by one man. The acquisitions were paid for by his best friend, a doctor. For over forty years, the doctor was the enthusiast and the underwriter of the artist who admired and put together the sculptures which are now on display in a new gallery designed for the collection of African art and funded by the Helen Jones Foundation. The artist was the late Elliot Howard. The doctor is Bayard Herr, now eighty-four at the time of this writing.

Elliot Howard came from a family of lawyers. Howard is the last name that Elliot legally assumed when his father disinherited him for not studying law. His sister and uncles were lawyers; his father was a prominent attorney and a representative for the state of New York.

Elliot studied art as a child in Manhattan constantly visiting the museums and galleries. His dream was to be part of the art world on the left bank in Paris. Instead, disinherited, he left his plush home in New York City to work in the Disney studios across the country in California as a cartoonist; he was only seventeen. Later, Elliot served in the Navy during the last two years of World War II.

After the war he did study in Paris for a short time, only to return to New York City when his funds ran out. He got a job teaching at the Art Student's League at night. During the day he worked as an apprentice at Sajette, a Dutch-Jewish antique shop in Manhattan that was one of the top stores of its kind in the city.

During this period of his life, Elliot started collecting African art. He had purchased a broken stone piece from someone who had brought it into the shop. As to what it was, he had no idea; but he liked something about it and he paid about forty-five dollars for it. While he was trying to glue it together, someone else came into the the shop, knew what it was, and offered Elliot eighteen hundred dollars. An art merchant was born.

Dr. Bayard Herr, or Dr. Bud as he is called by those who know him, is neither a big game hunter nor an African art enthusiast, he simply invested his faith, loyalty and trust in his best friend's instinctive choices. Although Dr. Bud had served in Africa during World War II, he had no interest in African art, but he was willing to finance any and all purchases that Elliot wanted.

Dr. Bud is a member of the seventeenth generation of a Pennsylvania Dutch family. He ranked third out of five hundred at the University of Pennsylvania and thirteenth in a class of three hundred at the Pennsylvania State Medical School. After having served in all of the theaters of war operations and the war was won, he was shipped to a M.A.S.H. unit in the Pacific. He served seven years in total. He became the head pathologist at the original Methodist Hospital in Brooklyn after he returned stateside, and was in charge there for twenty years.

Dr. Bud has always been interested in antiques because his own family has handed down some things through the years. His sister was a professional musician and he has always loved music. He was in an antique shop in Bucks County, Pennsylvania long before he moved to New York City. He saw a beautiful violin and asked the price. "Four" was the answer. After thinking for a while, he picked up the bow and knowing that the bow sometimes cost between two and three thousand dollars, he asked the cost of it also. The man said, "That's included in the four-dollar price." Dr. Bud decided then and there that collecting had many values!

Elliot and Dr. Bud opened their first shop on Fifty-ninth Street in Manhattan in 1968. Anything that Elliot chose, Dr. Bud paid for without question. Dr. Bud believed completely in Elliot's eye for beauty. It was the eye and the creative imagination of Elliot, the artist, who governed the selection of the African and Tibetan art objects in the years to come. Elliot had the gift for recognizing quality, and Dr. Bud believed explicitly in his artistic judgment

They moved to Houston in 1975. An antique dealer from Bucks County, Pennsylvania joined them in their move to Texas. Between them, it took eighteen eighteen-wheel trucks to move their combined collections.

Elliot was known to be generous to artists starting out in their careers. He would give thousand-dollar scholarships to gifted students yearly. In 1982, Elliot developed the Howard Group, a collection of professional craftsmen and artists who would meet to exchange ideas and to socially interact in Houston. It still meets. It was a member of the Howard Group that knew of Dr. Sasser's expertise and wonderful reputation that convinced Elliot to consider Texas Tech as a site for his collection.

Elliot would not sell the pieces that he really loved, for example, the Upper Volta butterfly mask that hung over his bed for ten years. He would put outrageous prices on some pieces so no one would buy them. He also adamantly refused to sell individual pieces that he considered to be sets, for example, a large [woodcarved] couple . . . . A gentleman from Mexico offered him sixty thousand dollars for the female figure and he refused saying, "They've been together [and] I'm not about to separate them now. '

Elliot had wanted the entire collection to be kept together and to live at one site. To this end, Dr Sasser directed the queries to Gary Edson, Director of the Museum of Texas Tech University. In a short while, Dr. Edson came to Houston to see the carvings and returned to Lubbock determined that the Tech museum, which specializes in art and artifacts from arid lands, should have the collection. Soon, Dr. Murray flew to Houston to interview Elliot and to see the collection at the Rice University shop and what was even more critical for Elliot, to be interviewed by him as a representative of the ideal recipient for his beloved collection.

They spent the morning together on his last day outside of the hospital. He explained his collection and she understood. They got along as old friends. Dr. Murray found Elliot as intriguing as the Dali Lama whom she had met a few years earlier. Elliot ultimately decided that Texas Tech Univerisity was the ideal location.

For the last time, Dr. Bud has seen that Elliot's decision was implemented.

M. Ethelene Bucy

NOTES

Introduction

1. Esther A. Dagan, *Tradition in Transition* (Montreal: Galerie Amrad African Arts, 1989), 11.

2. John C. Messenger, "The Carver in Anang Society" in *The Traditional Artist in African Societies,* ed. Warren L. d'Azevedo (Bloomington: Indiana University Press, 1989), 126-127.

3. Dagan, 15.

4. William Bascom, "A Yoruba Carver: Duga of Meko," in *The Traditional Artist in African Society,* ed. Warren L. d'Azevedo (Bloomington: Indiana University Press, 1989), 62.

5. Herbert M. Cole, *Icons* (Washington, D.C.: Smithsonian Institution Press, 1989), 138.

Chapter 1

1. Marcel Griaule, *Conversations with Ogotemmeli* (London: Oxford University Press, 1970), 97.

2. Jacques Kerchache, Jean-Louis Paudrat, and Lucien Stéphan, *Art of Africa,* trans. Marjolijn de Jageré (New York: Harry N. Abrams, 1993). Francoise Stoullig-Marin in "Principal Ethnic Groups of African Art," 504.

3. Ibid., 505.

4. Chinua Achebe, *Things Fall Apart* (New York: Fawcett Crest, 1991), 120. Achebe's novel is about the Igbo people of Nigeria; however, the description of the coming of the rains envisions a common western sub-Saharan experience.

5. Kerchache, Paudrat, and Stéphan. See Francoise Stoullig-Marin's "Principal Ethnic Groups of African Art," 509.

6. Ibid., 506-507.

7. Ibid., 506.

8. Ibid., 509.

9. Ibid., 521.

10. Ibid.

11. Ibid., 526.

12. Ibid. 529

13. Ibid.

14. Ibid., 531.

15. Peter Matthiessen, *African Silences* (New York: Vintage Books, 1991), 43.

16. Kerchache, Paudrat, and Stéphan, 543.

17. Ibid., 554.

18. Ibid.

19. Ibid., 555.

20. J. Desmond Clark, "African Beginnings" in *Horizon History of Africa,* Alvin M. Josephy, Jr., ed., (New York: American Heritage Publishing, 1971), 47.

21. Kerchache, Paudrat, and Stéphan, 560.

22. Ibid., 564.

23. Ibid., 580.

24. Ibid.

25. Ibid., 578.

26. Ibid., 576.

27. Ibid., 579.

28. Ibid.

Chapter 2

1. "A Statement by Louis Kahn," *Arts and Architecture* 77, no. 2 (February 1961): 29.

2. Marcel Griaule, *Conversations with Ogotemmeli* (Oxford: Oxford University Press, 1970), 11.

3. René Gardi, *Indigenous African Architecture* (New York: Van Nostrand Reinhold, 1973), 107.

4. Ibid., 108.

5. Griaule, 92.

6. Ibid., 92, 93.

7. Ibid., 180.

8. Frank Willet, *African Art* (London: Thames and Hudson, 1988), 120, 124.

9. Ibid., 120.

10. Griaule, 16.

11. Ibid.

12. Ibid., 17.

13. Ibid.

14. Ibid., 29.

15. Ibid.

16. Ibid., 38.

17. Ibid., 31.

18. Ibid.

19. Ibid.

20. Ibid., 39.

21. Ibid., 41,42.

22. Ibid., 44.

23. Ibid., 101, 102.

24. Ibid., 102.

25. Ibid., 103.

26. Ibid.

27. Elsy Leuzinger, *The Art of Africa* (New York: Greystone Press, 1967), 99.

28. Ladislas Segy, *Masks of Black Africa* (New York: Dover, 1976), plate 13 and description opposite.

29. Leuzinger, 99.

30. Ibid.

31. Gardi, 149, 151.

32. Anita J. Glaze, *Art and Death in a Senufo Village* (Bloomington: University of Indiana Press, 1981), 9.

33. Ibid.

34. Ibid., 7.

35. Ibid., 8.

36. Gardi, 53.

37. Glaze, 29.

38. Ibid.

39. Ibid., 39.

40. Ibid., 30, 31.

41. Ibid., 101, 102.

42. Ibid., 181.

43. Ibid., 93.

44. Ibid., 12.

45. Ibid., 13.

46. Ibid., 62.

47. Ibid., 214.

48. Ibid.

49. Ibid., 111, pl. 14.

50. Ibid., 115.

Chapter 3

1. William Bascom, "A Yoruba Master Carves: Duga of Meko," in *The Traditional Artist in African Societies,* ed. Warren L. d'Azevedo (Bloomington: Indiana University Press, 1989), 68.

2. Ibid.

3. Ibid. See also in the same volume John C. Messenger's "The Carver in Anang Society," 104.

4. Ibid., 110.

5. Elsy Leuzinger, *The Art of Africa* (New York: Greystone Press, 1967), 36.

6. Anita J. Glaze, *Art and Death in a Senufo Village* (Bloomington: Indiana University Press, 1981), 101.

7. Ibid., 102.

8. *The Traditional Artist in African Societies,* 112. See Chapter 3, note 1.

9. Patrick R. McNaughton, *The Mande Blacksmiths* (Bloomington: Indiana University Press, 1988.) 33.

10. Robert Farris Thompson, *Flash of the Spirit* (New York: Vintage Books, 1984), 87.

11. McNaughton, 122,

12. Ibid., 125.

13. Marie-Thérèse Brincard, ed., *The Art of Metal in Africa,* trans. by Evelyn Fischel (New York: The African-American Institute, 1982), 26.

14. Ibid.

15. Ibid., 23.

16. Ibid.

17. Ibid., 15.

18. Ibid., 13.

19. Denise Paulme, *African Sculpture,* trans. by Michael Ross (London: Elek Books, 1963.) 33, 34.

20. Ibid., 33.

21. Roy Sieber and Roslyn Adele Walker, *African Art in the Cycle of Life* (Washington, D.C., and London: Smithsonian Institution Press, 1988), 14.

22. Robert Farris Thompson, "Yoruba Artistic Criticism," in *The Traditional Artist in African Society,* ed. Warren L. d'Azevedo (Bloomington: Indiana University Press, 1989), 37.

23. Ibid., 38.

24. Ibid., 48.

25. Ibid., 53.

26. Ibid.

27. Ibid., 56.

28. Ibid., 43.

29. Glaze, 197.

Chapter 4

1. Susan Vogel and Francine N'Diaye, *African Masterpieces* (New York: Center for African Art and Harry N. Abrams, 1985), 230.

2. Ladislas Segy, *Masks in Black Africa* (New York: Dover, 1976), 36.

3. Ibid., 37

4. Jacques Kerchache, Jean-Louis Paudrat, and Lucien Stéphan, *Art of Africa* (New York: Harry N. Abrams, 1993), 555.

5. Ibid., 524.

6. Ibid., 521.

7. Frank Willett, *African Art* (London: Thames and Hudson, 1971), 180.

8. Ibid., 184.

9. Ibid.

10. Werner Schmalenbach, ed., *African Art from the Barbier-Mueller Collection, Geneva* (Munich: Prestel-Verlag, 1988), 110.

11. Kerchache, Paudrat, and Stéphan, 522.

12. William Bascom, *African Art in Cultural Perspective* (New York: W. W. Norton, 1973), 61.

13. Ladislas Segy, *African Sculpture Speaks* (New York: A. A. Wyn, Inc., 1952), 212.

14. Christopher Roy, *Art and Life in Africa* (Iowa City: University of Iowa Art Museum, 1992), 223.

15. Ibid.

16. Susan Lerer, *African Metalwork and Ivory* (Newport Beach, Calif.: Susan Lerer, 1993), 10.

17. Ibid.

18. Roy, 218.

19. Kerchache, Paudrat, and Stéphan, 543.

20. Ibid.

21. Vogel and N'Diaye, 146.

22. Ibid..

23. Kerchache, Paudrat, and Stéphan, 541, pl. 926.

24. Henry John Drewal and John Pemberton III, with Rowland Abiodun, *Yoruba: Nine Centuries of African Art and Thought* (New York: Center for African Art with Harry N. Abrams, 1989), 197.

25. Bascom, 90.

26. Schmalenbach, 253.

27. Bascom, 154.

28. Hans-Joachim Kolass, *Art of Central Africa* (New York: Metropolitan Museum and Harry N. Abrams, 1990), 46.

29. Ibid.

30. Ibid.

31. Mary H. Nooter, *Secrecy: African Art That Conceals and Reveals* (Munich: Prestel-Verlag, 1993), 168.

32. Koloss, 46.

33. Ibid., 34.

34. Kerchache, Paudrat, and Stéphan, 154.

35. Ibid., 524.

36. Schmalenbach, 68.

37. Vogel and N'Diaye, 120.

38. Ibid.

39. Segy, *Masks,* pl. 41.

40. Vogel and N'Diaye, 117.

41. Roy, 37.

42. Ibid.

43. Vogel and N'Diaye, 130.

44. Martha G. Anderson and Christine M. Kreamer, *Wild Spirits, Strong Medicine: African Art and the Wilderness,* ed. Enid Schildkrout (Seattle: University of Washington Press, 1989), 117.

45. Schmalenbach, 74.

46. Ibid., 107.

47. Bascom, 54.

48. Robert Farris Thompson, *Flash of the Spirit* (New York: Vintage Books, 1984), 85.

49. Segy, *Masks,* see pl. 107.

50. Willett, 206.

51. Kersache, Paudrat, and Stéphan, 594.

Chapter 5

1. Chinua Achebe, *Arrow of God* (New York: Doubleday Anchor, 1974), 203.

2. Anita J. Glaze, *Art and Death in a Senufo Village* (Bloomington:

University of Indiana Press, 1981), 87.

3. Herbert M. Cole, *Icons, Ideals, and Power in African-American Art* (Washington, D.C.: Smithsonian Institution Press, 1989), 32.

4. Roy Sieber and Roslyn Adele Walker, *African Art in the Cycle of Life* (Washington, D.C.: Smithsonian Institution Press, 1992), 36.

5. Chinua Achebe, *Things Fall Apart* (New York: Fawcett Crest, 1991), 19.

6. Ibid., 17, 18.

7. Elsy Leuzinger, *The Art of Africa* (New York: Greystone Press, 1967), 189

8. Werner Schmalenbach, ed., *African Art from the Barbier-Mueller Collection, Geneva* (Munich: Prestel-Verlag, 1988), 276.

9. Ibid., 229.

10. Pierre Meauze, *African Art* (New York: Arch Cape Press, 1968), 62-63.

11. Susan Vogel, ed., *For Spirits and Kings: African Art from the Paul and Ruth Tishman Collection* (New York: Metropolitan Museum and Harry N. Abrams, 1981), 92.

12. Robert Farris Thompson, "Yoruba Artistic Criticism," in *The Traditional Artist in African Societies*, ed. Warren L. d'Azevedo (Bloomington: Indiana University Press, 1989), 35, 36.

13. Esther Dagan, *Tradition in Transition* (Montreal: Galerie Amrad African Arts, 1989), 43.

14. Vogel, 73.

15. Ibid., 48.

16. Ibid.

17. Geoffrey Parrinden, *African Mythology* (New York: Peter Bedrick Books, 1982), 18.

18. William Bascom, *African Art in Cultural Perspective* (New York: W. W. Norton, 1973), 33.

19. Glaze, 14.

20. Ibid., 197.

21. Ibid., 53.

22. Ibid., 66.

23. Sieber and Walker, 29.

24. Alvin M. Josephy, Jr., ed., *The Horizon History of Africa* (New York: American Heritage Publishing Co., Inc., 1971), 206.

25. Cole, 85.

26. Vogel, 125.

27. Ibid., 13.

28. Leuzinger, 178.

29. Sieber and Walker, 144.

30. Christopher D. Roy, "Mossi Dolls," *African Arts Magazine* UCLA, Vol. XIV, (1981):47-48.

31. Ibid., 50.

32. Ibid., 47.

33. Ibid., 48.

34. Peter Sarpong, *The Sacred Stools of the Akan* (Rottenburg, Germany, 1971), 65.

35. Kate Ezra, *Royal Art of Benin* (New York: Harry N. Abrams, 1992), 228.

36. Thompson, "Yoruba Artistic Criticism," 37.

37. Ibid., 55.

38. Henry John Drewel and John Pemberton III, with Rowland Abiodun, *Yoruba: Nine Centuries of African Art and Thought*, ed. Allen Wardwell (New York: Harry N. Abrams and Associates, 1989), 156, 162.

39. Ibid., 170.

40. Ibid.

41. Cole, 87. Cole quotes Judith Timyan as his source for the folk saying.

42. Elys Leutzinger, 151.

43. Drewel and Pemberton, 221-222.

44. Cole, 103.

45. Ibid., 120.

46. Ibid.

47. Louis Desplagnes, *Le plateau central Nigerien: Une mission archeologique et ethnographique au Sudan francais* (Paris: Larose, 1907), 233.

48. Sieber and Walker, 133.

49. Schmalenbach, 63.

50. Cole, 128.

51. Drewel and Pemberton, 26.

52. Ibid.

53. Ibid.

54. Ibid., 32.

55. Ibid.

56. Glaze, 70.

57. Ibid.

58. Ibid.

59. Ibid., 64.

60. Amos Tutuola, *The Palm Wine Drinkard* (New York: Grove Press, 1980), 41.

61. Ibid., 42.

62. Schmalenbach, 239.

63. Ibid.

64. Ibid.

65. Ladislav Segy, *African Sculpture Speaks* (New York: A. A. Wyn, 1952), 77.

66. Martha G. Anderson and Christine Mullen Kreamer, *Wild Spirits, Strong Medicine: African Art and the Wilderness*, ed. Enid Schildkrout (New York: Center for African Art, 1989), 60.

67. Schmalenbach, 239.

68. Harold Courlander, *A Treasury of African Folklore* (New York: Crown Publishers, n.d.), 78.

69. Frank Willett, *African Art* (London: Thames and Hudson, 1971), 200.

70. Ibid., 205-206.

71. Sieber and Walker, 105.

72. Ibid.

73. Robert Farris Thompson, *Flash of the Spirit* (New York: Vintage Books, 1984), 13

74. Ibid.

75. Ibid.

76. Hans-Joachim Kolass, *Art of Central Africa* (New York: Harry N. Abrams, 1990), 64.

77. Ibid.

78. Frank Willett, 229 (see pl. 227).

79. Drewel and Pemberton, 210.

80. Ibid.

81. Willett, 189.

82. Pierre Meauze, 110.

83. Leutzinger, 137.

84. Ibid.

85. Drewel and Pemberton, 117.

86. Ibid., 144-145.

87. Ibid., 120.

88. Ibid.

89. Christopher Roy, *Art and Life in Africa* (Iowa City: University of Iowa Art Museum, 1992), 243.

SELECTED BIBLIOGRAPHY

Achebe, Chinua. *Things Fall Apart.* New York: Ballantine Books, 1991.

Anderson, Martha G., and Christine Mullen Kreamer. *Wild Spirits, Strong Medicine: African Art and the Wilderness.* Edited by Enid Schildkrout. Seattle: University of Washington Press, 1989.

Art et Mythologie. Paris: Fondation Dapper, 1988.

Atmore, Anthony, and Gillian Stacey. *Black Kingdoms, Black Peoples.* London: Orbis, 1985.

Azevedo, Warren L. d', ed. *The Traditional Artist in African Societies.* Bloomington: Indiana University Press, 1989.

Bambara Sculpture from the Western Sudan from the Museum of Primitive Art, New York. New York: University Publishers, 1960.

Bascom, William. *African Art in Cultural Perspective.* New York: W. W. Norton, 1973.

Black Art, Ancestral Legacy: The African Impulse in African-American Art. New York: Harry N. Abrams, 1989.

Borgatti, Jean M., and Richard Brilliant. *Likeness and Beyond: Portraits from Africa and the World.* New York: The Center for African Art, 1990.

Brincard, Marie-Thérèse, ed. *The Art of Metal in Africa.* New York: The African-American Institute, 1982.

Cole, Herbert M. *Icons, Ideals and Power in the Art of Africa.* Washington, D.C.: Smithsonian Institution Press, 1989.

Courlander, Harold. *A Treasury of African Folklore.* New York: Crown Publishers, n.d.

Cultural Atlas of Africa. Edited by Joycelyn Murray. New York: Facts on File, 1989.

Dagan, Esther A. *Tradition in/en Transition.* Montreal: Kaylon Graphiques, 1989.

Davidson, Basil. *The African Genius.* Boston: Little, Brown, 1969.

Drewel, Henry John, and John Pemberton III, with Rowland Abiodun. *Yoruba: Nine Centuries of African Art and Thought.* Edited by Allen Wardwell. New York: Harry N. Abrams, 1989.

Duerden, Dennis. *African Art.* London: Hamlyn, 1986.

Ezra, Kate. *Royal Art of Benin.* New York: Harry N. Abrams, 1992.

Fagg, William. *Yoruba: Sculpture of West Africa.* New York: Alfred A. Knopf, 1982.

Fisher, Angela. *Africa Adorned.* New York: Harry N. Abrams, 1984.

Gardi, René. *Indigenous African Architecture.* Translated by Sigrid MacRae. New York: Van Nostrand Reinhold, 1973.

Glaze, Anita J. *Art and Death in a Senufo Village.* Bloomington: Indiana University Press, 1981.

Goss, Linda, and Marian E. Barnes. *Talk That Talk: An Anthology of African-American Storytelling.* New York: Simon & Schuster, 1989.

Graule, Marcel. *Conversations with Ogotemmeli: An Introduction to Dogon Religious Ideas.* London: Oxford University Press, 1970.

Holy, Ladislav. *Masks and Figures from Eastern and Southern Africa.* London: Paul Hamlyn, 1967.

Josephy, Alvin M., Jr., ed. *Horizon History of Africa.* New York: American Heritage Publishing Company, 1971.

Jablow, Alta. *Yes and No: The Intimate Folklore of Africa.* New York: Horizon Press, 1961.

Kerchache, Jacques, Jean-Louis Paudrat, and Lucien Stéphan. *Art of Africa.* New York: Harry N. Abrams, 1993.

Kolass, Hans-Joachim. *Art of Central Africa.* New York: Harry N. Abrams, 1990.

Kreamer, Christine Mullen. *Art of Sub-Saharan Africa: The Fred and Rita Richman Collection.* Wisbech, England: Balding + Mansell, 1986.

Lem, F. H. *Sculptures Soudanaises.* Paris: Arts et Metiers Graphiques, 1948.

Lerer, Susan. *African Metalwork and Ivory.* Newport Beach, California: Susan Lerer, 1993.

Leuzinger, Elsy. *The Art of Africa.* New York: Greystone Press, 1967.

Loth, Heinrich. *Woman in Ancient Africa.* Translated by Sheila Marnie. Westport, Conn.: Lawrence Hill and Co., 1987.

Mack, John. *Émil Torday and the Art of the Congo, 1900-1909.* Seattle: University of Washington Press, n.d.

McNaughton, Patrick. *The Mande Blacksmiths.* Bloomington: Indiana University Press, 1988.

Meauze, Pierre. *African Art: Sculpture.* New York: Arch Cape Press, 1968.

Meyer, Laure. *Black Africa: Masks, Sculpture, Jewelry.* Paris: Editions Pierre Terrail, 1992.

Murray, Jocelyn, ed. *Cultural Atlas of Africa.* New York: Facts on File, 1989.

Nooter, Mary H. *Secrecy: African Art That Conceals and Reveals.* Munich: Prestel-Verlag; New York: The Museum for African Art, 1993.

Ogbaa, Kalu. *Gods, Oracles and Divination: Folkways in Chinua Achebe's Novels.* Trenton, N.J.: Africa World Press, 1992.

Oliver, Paul, ed. *Shelter in Africa.* New York: Praeger Publishers, 1971.

Ousmane, Sembene. *God's Bits of Wood.* Translated by Francis Price. Oxford: Heinnemann Educational Books, 1986.

Parrinder, Geoffrey. *African Mythology.* New York: Peter Bedrick Books, 1991.

Paulme, Denise. *Les Sculpture de l'Afrique Noire.* Paris: Presses Universitaires de France, 1956.

Pelton, Robert D. *The Trickster in West Africa.* Berkeley: University of California Press, 1989.

Perrois, Louis. *Ancestral Art of Gabon.* Edited by Jean Paul Barbier. Geneva: Roto-Sadag, 1985.

Perspectives: Angles on African Art. Interviews by Michael John Weber. New York: Harry N. Abrams, 1987.

Rubin, William, ed. *"Primitivism" in Twentieth-Century Art.* Vol. 2. New York: The Museum of Modern Art, 1984.

Radin, Paul, ed. *African Folktales.* New York: Schocken Books, 1981.

Robbins, Warren M. *African Art in American Collections.* New York: Frederick A. Praeger, 1966.

Roy, Christopher D. *African Art from Iowa Private Collections.* Iowa City: University of Iowa Press, 1982.

——. *Art and Life in Africa (from the Stanley Collection).* Iowa City: University of Iowa Museum of Art, 1992.

Sarpong, Peter. *The Sacred Stools of the Akan.* Tema, Ghana: Ghana Publishing Corporation, 1971.

Schmalenbach, Werner, ed. *African Art from the Barbier-Mueller Collection.* Munich: Prestel-Verlag, 1988.

Sculpture of Western Nigeria. Ibadan, Western Nigeria: Ministry of Information, 1966.

Segy, Ladislas. *African Sculpture Speaks.* New York: A. A. Wyn, 1952.

——. *Masks of Black Africa.* New York: Dover Publications, 1976.

Sieber, Roy, and Roslyn Adele Walker. *African Art in the Cycle of Life.* Washington D.C.: Smithsonian Institution Press. 1989.

Stanley, Janet L. *African Art: A Bibliographic Guide.* New York: Africana Publishers, 1985.

Thompson, Robert Farris. *Flash of the Spirit.* New York: Random House, 1984.

Trowell, Margaret. *Classical African Sculpture.* New York: Praeger Publishers, 1970.

Tutuola, Amos. *Feather Woman of the Jungle.* London: Faber & Faber, 1962.

——. *My Life in the Bush of Ghosts.* London: Faber & Faber, n.d.

——. *Simbi and the Satyr of the Dark Jungle.* London: Faber & Faber, n.d.

——. *The Palm-Wine Drinkard.* New York: Grove Press, 1980.

——. *The Village Witch Doctor and Other Stories.* London: Faber & Faber, 1990.

Vogel, Susan, and Francine N'Diaye. *African Masterpieces from the Musée de l'Homme.* New York: Harry N. Abrams, 1985.

Vogel, Susan, ed. *For Spirits and Kings: African Art from the Paul and Ruth Tishman Collection.* New York: Harry N. Abrams, 1981.

Wardwell, Allen. *African Sculpture from the University Museum, University of Pennsylvania.* New Haven: Eastern Press, 1986.

Wassing, René S. *African Art.* Translated by Diana Imber. London: Alpine Fine Art Collection, 1968.

Willett, Frank. *African Art.* London: Thames and Hudson, 1988.

——. *Ife in the History of West African Sculpture.* New York: McGraw-Hill, 1967.

Zahan, Dominique. *The Religion, Spirituality, and Thought of Traditional Africa.* Translated by Kate Ezra and Lawrence M. Martin. Chicago: University of Chicago Press, 1979.

INDEX

Printed in Hong Kong

The World of Spirits and Ancestors
in the Art of Western Sub-Saharan Africa
was supported generously
by the Helen Jones Foundation.